T0401324

Straight nation

Manchester University Press

Straight nation

Heteronormativity and other exigencies of postcolonial nationalism

Pavan Mano

MANCHESTER UNIVERSITY PRESS

Published by Manchester University Press
Oxford Road, Manchester, M13 9PL

www.manchesteruniversitypress.co.uk

British Library Cataloguing-in-Publication Data
A catalogue record for this book is available from the British
Library

ISBN 978 1 5261 7678 3 hardback

First published 2025

EU authorised representative for GPSR:
Easy Access System Europe, Mustamäe tee 50, 10621
Tallinn, Estonia gpsr.requests@easproject.com

Typeset by Newgen Publishing UK

Contents

Acknowledgements

Shortly after we had both graduated from the National University of Singapore, Jasper Quek and I struck up a routine of meeting for a round of tennis before chatting, late into the night, about an array of topics – something he took to calling 'amateur philosophizing'. For better or for worse, I have turned that into some semblance of a career. It seems utterly obvious to me, but given we live in a world that is entrenched in neoliberal logics and firmly in the thrall of the individual genius, it bears stating that I simply could not have done this on my own – many people offered me support and guidance throughout this project, and you would not be holding this book in your hands if not for them.

I'm grateful to the Sarah Parker Remond Centre (SPRC) at University College London for supporting this project through a research fellowship that gave me that precious commodity – undisturbed time – to write this book. Thanks as well to King's College London for funding this project in its earlier stages through a doctoral scholarship that allowed me to commit my energies to reading and writing on a full-time basis. Further small grants from the Faculty of Arts & Humanities and the Department of English supported conference attendance and research trips.

Paul Gilroy, Sita Balani, and Michelle Lazar held long discussions with me and provided detailed commentary on chapters and earlier drafts of this project. I am extremely grateful for their time, patience, and – most of all – incredible generosity.

Clare Birchall generously helped me with some specific theoretical questions I had in the early stages of the project. Selvaraj Velayutham provided me with a copy of his book chapter that was out of print and provided further reading recommendations. Tariq Jazeel kindly invited me to give a talk at the SPRC Colloquium Series that drew on many aspects of what has become Chapter 4. Adi Mittal invited me to give a TED talk at Oxford Town Hall that drew on some of my work on nationalism. I'm also very grateful to have had the opportunity to present my work at various conferences and workshops over the years, and my thanks go to everyone who has been in attendance at my presentations for their comments and questions – including those questions that were, in fact, more of a comment. Editing a special issue of the *Journal of Language and Sexuality* together with Adi S. Bharat and Robert Phillips precipitated the reward of talking ideas with two wonderful thinkers who are keenly attuned to the Singaporean context. Some of the notions we discussed have found their way into this book – unquestionably to its overall benefit.

A number of people read drafts and earlier versions of this manuscript: Paul Gilroy, Sita Balani, Michelle Lazar, Clare Birchall, Seb Franklin, Josefina Venegas Meza, Ya'ara Notea, Javiera Lorenzini Raty, Katie Arthur, Seng Jun Yuan, Rosalind Harvey, Alice Albinia, Sivamohan Valluvan, and Rahul Rao. I'm deeply appreciative of all the time and energy they spent on it and the helpful suggestions they offered, as well as the multiple typos and spelling errors they caught.

Blessed are those who maintain little corners of intellectual refuge amidst the general detritus of higher education today. One such corner is the Liberal Arts Department at King's College London, where my considerably unearned good fortune has deposited me. I'm grateful for the regular 'Write Now' sessions, which were instrumental in allowing me to complete this book. I'm even more grateful to my colleagues in my current department as well as my former colleagues at the SPRC for their warmth and conviviality.

It has been a real pleasure to work with Shannon Kneis at Manchester University Press, who has been a wonderfully supportive editor and a valuable steward in patiently guiding me through the entire publication process from beginning to end. Laura Swift and Gail Welsh helped coordinate the production phase of the book. Tanya Izzard mercifully took the task of putting together the book's index off my hands. Robert Whitelock copy-edited this book exquisitely carefully and very graciously indulged my proclivity for the split infinitive. My appreciation as well to the anonymous reviewers for reading the full manuscript and their very generous and helpful comments.

I owe plenty of debts of gratitude to friends for supplying the amity that makes life worth living: Seng Jun Yuan for many years of housemateship and including me in debates as to whether a second caramel macchiato is indeed one too many. Vinod Ashvin Ravi for his splendid Spotify playlists of A. R. Rahman, Hariharan, and Unnikrishnan from the 1990s, as well as his reading and podcast recommendations. Sarah Lim and Tricia Low for their strong record as convenors of dinner and dessert – I hope we get to wander the Botanic Gardens again. Joseph Chan for all the memes, solid football chat, and also explaining to me how a bill becomes law. In spite of our increasingly weak ankles, I look forward to resuming our goal-scoring battles on the pitch at some point. Whenever I happen to be in Singapore, Wong

Joo Fei and Su Myat Htun are always solid bets for hangouts over pandan waffles amongst other bits of delectable confectionery. This always makes my heart as full as my stomach. If the coalescence of kindness, humour, and quirkiness could be embodied, I reckon it would look very much like Jasper Quek. I'm grateful for our gentle friendship.

My brother Aravind and sister-in-law Tiffany are guaranteed sources of warmth and laughter. I look forward to the day that we can all sit down together and watch Manchester United triumph once more. Amongst many other things, Amma and Appa have been responsible for sorting me out with the values of fairness and integrity for which I will always be grateful.

Josefina Venegas Meza has patiently read all I've written, listened to me rehearse talks and presentations, and provided incisive comments about things I would otherwise have overlooked. She was my first friend at King's and – as further evidence of my frankly unreasonable luck – is my partner, whom I get to think, cook, and dance with, often all at the same time. If my life were written up as a script, it would be rejected for being too soporific in this respect – unless it were a script for a telenovela, in which case it would probably be a regular episode. I'm only too happy to repeat this story whenever I can. *Te amo*.

Finally, when all is said and done, there is only one name on the cover of this book – responsibility for all errors and shortcomings therefore lies with me alone.

Abbreviations

CMIO	Chinese-Malay-Indian-Others
CPF	Central Provident Fund
EIP	Ethnic Integration Policy
HDB	Housing & Development Board
ISA	Internal Security Act
JSS	Joint Singles Scheme
LGBT	Lesbian, Gay, Bisexual, and Transgender
LGBTQ	Lesbian, Gay, Bisexual, Transgender, Queer
MND	Ministry of National Development
MP	Member of Parliament
MSF	Ministry for Social and Family Development
NIC	National Integration Council
NPTD	National Population and Talent Division
NRIC	National Registration Identity Card
NS	National Service
PAP	People's Action Party
SIT	Singapore Improvement Trust
UPR	Universal Periodic Review
USA	United States of America
WHO	World Health Organization

Introduction: producing a straight nation

Straightness, a foundational logic

Time can behave in strange ways, stretching and compressing around differ- ent moments and memories. It is sometimes referred to as time telescoping. Which is why for many people it can feel as though 11 March 2020 belongs to an entirely different era altogether. That was when the World Health Organization (WHO) declared that COVID-19 could be 'characterized as a pandemic'.[1] In the immediate aftermath of the WHO Director-General's comments, complete 'lockdowns' became the emergency measure-of-choice for many governments as they sought to curb widespread virus transmission in their countries.

In Singapore, all physical interactions between members of different households were forbidden for two months from April to June, with resi- dents instructed to stay home except for essential purposes. When the eight weeks ended, the government acknowledged that the extended period of iso- lation had taken a toll on the population's mental health and general sense of wellbeing. Plenty of people needed to socialize again – and to do so in the physical company of others instead of on screen. The government weighed this need to socialize against the risk of uncontrolled viral transmission and so, in the first phase of emergency measures being eased, only certain in- person social interactions were permitted. Which were they? Minister for Health Gan Kim Yong had a pithy answer: 'We will allow children to visit their parents or grandparents.'[2] This would 'allow families to spend time and provide support to one another' after eight difficult weeks of isolation.[3] The minister did not mention what people who did not have these family members were meant to do – who they could spend time with or get support from. Neither did any journalist care to ask. As it turned out, they were not permitted to socialize with anyone – until social restrictions were next eased 17 days later, visiting one's parents or grandparents was generally the only form of in-person social interaction permitted and all others continued to be banned.

Some people might be tempted to say that 17 days was not a particularly long time. The Venn diagram of those who espouse this view and those who were lucky enough to have loving kin they could physically spend time with after eight weeks of isolation is, in all likelihood, a circle. It is akin to telling someone wet and shivering in the depths of winter that it is, in fact, not particularly cold – whilst ensconced in a thick, warm coat and hugging a hot water bottle. The particular configuration of kinship, care, and subjectivity in Singapore – the imagination of care as travelling exclusively through heterosexual kinship relations – can mean that heteronormativity provides a kind of comfort whilst queerness can leave one out in the cold, so to speak. Or to put it another way, comfort in Singapore can often be contingent on living according to a certain heteronormative logic. Instead of litigating the precise difficulty quotient of this moment, therefore, I find it far more valuable – both as far as this book is concerned and also more generally – to note how, particularly within the discursive space the state generates, 'the rationalisation and naturalisation of social ties within the heteronormative matrix as eligible for physical interaction points to a hierarchisation of social relations guided by an extant logic of heteronormativity'.[4] It is one snapshot of how straightness, as a 'deeply foundational heteronormative logic', can organize life in Singapore.[5]

The remarkable thing about the government's decision – and Gan's comment, which vibrates with assumptions of heteronormative familial primacy – is that there was actually nothing particularly remarkable about it. It was merely an example of how the Singaporean state reflexively prioritizes the heterosexual nuclear family and anoints it the most privileged set of social relations available to anyone.[6] Laws and policies are regularly justified and legitimized on the basis that the nuclear family is an inherently important social institution that ought to be protected.[7] Equally significantly, few people vocally contest or challenge this rhetoric. Youyenn Teo rightly makes the point that '[t]he dominance of "the Singaporean family" – heterosexual, formed through marriage, two-parent, with a younger, working generation ultimately responsible for an ageing generation – renders alternative ways of doing "family" unthinkable'.[8] It is taken to be common sense that one's life revolves around one's nuclear family; and, as was made clear in the aftermath of the circuit-breaker, the nuclear family has the capacity to suffuse all other possibilities of social relation in the Singaporean political imagination.

I begin with this episodic manifestation of heteronormativity to give an indication of how heteronormativity often functions as common sense in the formal discourses of the state and how it narrates the nation. By common sense, I am referring to the way it functions as 'a form of "everyday thinking" which offers us frameworks of meaning with which to make sense of the world'.[9] Heteronormativity in its various iterations and manifestations appears the natural way to govern, the most fair way of distributing resources, the most rational and logical mode of thinking, the most normal way of organizing life, and is always punctuated by an 'Of course!' that insists it is simply common sense.

Antonio Gramsci makes the point that common sense is a 'strangely composite' tapestry of 'stratified deposits' that produces a set of notions and contradictions capable of holding together and feeling coherent even though it is replete with internal contradictions.[10] I am interested in examining these moments of contradiction in state discourse and rhetoric and asking what they might tell us about how heteronormativity functions in conjunction with nationalism in postcolonial independent Singapore. Heteronormativity is not realized as an internally coherent project – and the partiality of its articulations reveals its interactions and co-constitution with other social forces such as 'race', gender, and class. For instance, the expectations of heterosexual coupling and reproduction that apply to Singaporeans and predominantly white Euro-American 'expats' simultaneously do not apply to brown South Asian or Southeast Asian migrant workers who are categorized as undesirable and expressly forbidden from participating in these circuits of heterosexuality. These contradictions and proscriptions are neither arbitrary nor random. They reflect particular arrangements of state power – racialized, gendered, classed, and more – that enunciate themselves in the name of the putative nation and can often find discursive expression through heteronormativity. By situating these contradictions within the terrain produced by state discourse, reading them in light of nationalism and demonstrating how they are both made, and have been made, to make sense, we can see how heteronormativity is central to the operation of postcolonial nationalism in Singapore. That is the elemental focus of this book.

Invisibilizing the historical process of subject formation invests common sense with its tremendous power; it is able to demand obedience precisely because it is able to refuse a provenance. For Gramsci, this is where critical work begins. As he puts it, 'The starting-point of critical elaboration is the consciousness of what one really is and is "knowing thyself" as a product of the historical process to date which has deposited in you an infinity of traces, without leaving an inventory.'[11] In a similar spirit, this book takes the formal discourse of the state as its object of analysis to excavate heteronormativity's inventory in the Singaporean nation. In postcolonial independent Singapore, the state draws the contours of the nation according to a logic of heteronormativity and 'heteronormative familism' that centralizes and reifies a very specific lifeworld.[12] Making that logic visible shows how the connection between heteronormativity and nationalism generates a whole host of minoritized subject positions. Reading against the 'Of course!' that – sometimes silently, sometimes terribly vocally – guides and rationalizes postcolonial Singaporean nationalism through the multifarious sites of heteronormativity provides the analytical impulse for this project. Ultimately, it shows that the sedimentation of heteronormativity, and its co-constitution with 'race', gender, and class within the postcolonial nation, is the product of a predominantly state-led historical process and seeks to unearth its traces that are continually being deposited into subjects.

Throughout colonialism, in the colonial imagination, the colonies were regarded as repositories of sexual impropriety, debasement, and savagery that not only reflected the colonized's apparent unmodernized state but posed a danger to colonial officials themselves. Philip Holden makes the point that:

> Colonial governmentality, and its incitement of the colonized to a modern, self-regulating subjectivity ... is paralleled by the colonial official's own self-discipline, his harnessing the desires, wants and fears of his nominally primitive body which is reinvigorated by the regressive delights of the colonial environment.[13]

British government guidance warned colonial officials against staying too long in the colonies because of the danger of 'individual and racial degeneration' as well as 'cultural contamination and neglect of the conventions of supremacy and agreement about what they were'.[14] Anxieties over sexual relations between white British colonial officials and colonized subjects combined homophobic logics with racial logics and motivated the eventual establishment of Section 377A of the Straits Settlement Penal Code, which criminalized sex between men.[15] The roots of this law can thus be found in not just a project of sexual normativity but also a project of racial normativity that was animated by fears of racial mixing and punctured purity.[16] As Rahul Rao reminds us:

> The criminalisation of sodomy was one element in a broader biopolitical apparatus of colonial regulation animated by a range of concerns including the sexual relations of prostitution and concubinage, the control of venereal disease, the proper rearing of children and management of the household, and the 'improvement' of the population through the use, among other things, of eugenicist practices of selective sterilisation.[17]

The British might have eventually left Singapore, but Section 377A was one of the many artefacts of colonial detritus left behind – and in its postcolonial afterlife, Section 377A became an increasingly important vehicle that produced non-heterosexuality as deviance. In a way that is not dissimilar to other postcolonial contexts, the People's Action Party (PAP)[18] government maintained the statute and, with a strong dose of postcolonial irony, legitimized pejorative representations of non-normative sexualities 'based on a discourse of Western moral degeneracy'.[19] The government justified retaining Section 377A in Singapore's Penal Code by insisting that it was invaluable in protecting the nation from a Western 'sexual libertine ethos'.[20] As George Radics put it, whereas 'the European [had] implemented Section 377A to protect himself from the over-sexualized Asian, now the Singaporean uses it to protect himself from the "wild wild West"'.[21]

The heterosexual nuclear family was placed at the centre of the nation and loaded with the responsibility of 'passing on traditional Asian values and Singaporean culture, which the PAP government continually emphasizes as markers of national identity that need to be vigilantly defended from the corrosive forces of globalization'.[22] Non-normative sexuality is thus constructed as a 'Western' import into Singapore that the government has little choice but to expose itself to because the country must engage with the West for its own economic growth. Here, discourses of vulnerability and duress collide with notions of queerness as a cost that can only be mitigated but nonetheless must be incurred in the pursuit of capital accumulation and material prosperity. Domesticity, then, becomes synonymous with heteronormativity, traditionality, and the opposite-sex dual-parent family, whilst queerness is affiliated with individuality, the foreign (the 'West'), and regarded as an unfortunate side effect of prosperity.[23]

Like it does to varying degrees in so many other places, heteronormativity structures subjectivity in Singapore. As Monique Wittig puts it, 'to live in society is to live in heterosexuality … Heterosexuality is always already there within all mental categories. It has sneaked into dialectical thought (or thought of differences) as its main category.'[24] It asserts itself 'as the elemental form of human association, as the very model of intergender relations, as the indivisible basis of all community, and as the means of reproduction without which society wouldn't exist'.[25] Allied with nationalism, heteronormativity renders many people both queer and foreign in Singapore – thus displacing them from the putative nation.

Whilst confronting and analysing the heteronormative present by historicizing sexuality and explaining it in terms of the current nationalist moment, it became increasingly necessary to work 'between disciplines', stretching across them, moving from one to another in what might be considered a transdisciplinary manner.[26] I drew plenty of inspiration here from the intellectual style of thinkers such as Sara Ahmed, bell hooks, and Stuart Hall. Hall suggests that:

> many of the existing paradigms established and developed within traditional intellectual disciplines either no longer in themselves adequately correspond to the problems that we have to resolve, or require supplementing from other disciplines with which they have not historically been directly connected.[27]

Resolving the problems of the present, then, could be said to require a mode of enquiry that encourages reading against the grain, sometimes to the point of creative failure, holding open the possibility that 'the failure to return texts to their histories will do something'.[28] My approach to writing this book and its analytical style lies in consonance with this general sentiment as well as its concomitant mode of intellectual engagement.

Vocabulary matters: on *LGBT* and *queer*

The terms *queer* and *LGBT* are taken from the distinctly Global North, Anglo-American lexicon of sexual identity that the majority of activists and sexual minorities in Singapore use to index their minoritization by heteronormativity as well as to express their own identities. *LGBT* is the term that most sexual minorities in Singapore have generally used, as have scholars working on Singapore queer studies, and the state.[29] A more recent development has been the growing usage of *queer*, particularly in its identarian sense amongst minoritized sexualities, but it generally does not feature in state discourse.[30] Pink Dot, the largest LGBT social movement in the country, has consistently used *LGBT* to index non-normative sexualities in its messaging since its inception in 2009, with the terms *LGBTQ* and *queer* appearing more recently.[31]

It is important to provincialize these terms in their contexts – neither *LGBT* nor *queer* is a perfect signifier for what they claim to describe. In the same vein, we should pay attention to how these terms have travelled, and the roles that they play in the sense of the cachet that *LGBT* and *queer* have in Singapore. In part, their emergence in Singapore is a function of a significant and growing digitally connected, English-educated population that is plugged in to Anglo-American popular culture (largely coming out of the USA) popular culture, as well as LGBT/queer activist and social justice discourses.[32] The emergence of these terms thus speaks to a certain transnational current in the flow of ideas challenging heteronormativity – even if it is only very occasionally outwardly embraced by local activists for a range of tactical reasons that I detail more in Chapter 5.[33] But at the same time, the terms are neither used nor mobilized in the same way as they are in Anglo-American contexts – instead, they are translated and mediated by their entanglements with other specificities of the Singaporean context.[34] For instance, whilst the term *LGBT* has nestled quite comfortably into local parlance to refer to sexual minorities, its associated discourses of 'coming out' are often supplanted, particularly amongst the Chinese majority, by discourses of 'coming home' and integrating into familial structures when it comes to disclosing or explaining one's sexual identity.[35] More generally, the notion of visibility that accompanies being 'out' of the closet can often be less salient in Singaporean communities.[36] Instead, many sexual minorities often opt to communicate their non-normative sexualities implicitly – particularly to their families.[37] I therefore want to dwell for a moment on how these terms are parsed in Singapore and think about what they are taken to mean and what they do, especially in the context of how they are marshalled in state discourse.

Even though in its full form the acronym is for lesbian, gay, bisexual, and transgender people, in Singapore *LGBT* is often used as shorthand for minoritized sexualities; transgender people have been included comparatively late in mainstream LGBT activism, as well as the larger conversation around battling sexual bigotry and resisting heteronormativity. Whilst this has started to change in recent years, *LGBT* in Singapore has functioned much more prominently as a signifier that operates mainly on the axis of sexuality. In *Mobilizing Gay Singapore* – one of two book-length projects on the gay movement in the country – Lynette Chua identifies this tendency both in her own work as well as in Singaporean LGBT activism more generally. Chua writes that:

> Though the movement is sometimes referred to colloquially as *LGBT*, I excluded transsexual and transgender individuals from my study. They deal with different laws and issues in Singapore, and gay activists also do not address their concerns or do so more as an afterthought.[38]

Chua's reflexive point draws attention to the way activist efforts resisting heteronormativity in Singapore have, for the most part, focused on sexuality, and the *LGBT/queer* signifiers have functioned in a largely identarian sense pertaining to sexuality.

It is also worth registering that whilst non-normative sexualities are delegitimized (and, in the case of sexual relations between men, were explicitly criminalized until Section 377A's repeal at the beginning of 2023) as a function of heteronormativity, non-normative gender is also pathologized. The state regards transgender persons as presenting a biological problem that could be mitigated, if not 'corrected', through medical intervention which technically remains available as treatment through the public healthcare system. Actually accessing the medical care they need, however, is often less than straightforward for transgender people. The volunteer collective TransgenderSG notes, for instance, that 'there are currently no healthcare providers in Singapore who publicly offer [gender-affirming] surgeries specific to transgender individuals'.[39] And it is precisely this pathologization of gender coupled with an avowed commitment to gender binarism that forecloses all other form of gender diversity. Audrey Yue sums up this logic as such: 'it encourages those who experience gender dysphoria to "correct the wrong body type"; on the other hand, it discourages those who simply wish to embody gender variance as part of a gender diverse identity'.[40]

The state's stance here is reflective of a much broader investment in biology and genetics as the legitimate determiner of identity; and biology is not only invoked to justify the state's attitude towards gender – it also underscores its approach to governing sexuality and non-normative relations of desire. In 2007, Lee Kuan Yew, postcolonial independent Singapore's first prime minister, expressed his conviction that homosexuality ought not to be criminalized because it was a biological fact, saying 'If in fact it is true, and I have asked doctors this, that you are genetically born a homosexual – because that's the nature of the genetic random transmission of genes – you can't help it. So why should we criminalize it?'.[41] Later that same year, prime minister Lee Hsien Loong made a similar argument in Parliament, saying that 'there is growing scientific evidence that sexual orientation is something which is substantially inborn'.[42] This was not enough for either Lee to actually do anything substantive about the criminalization of sex between men at the time but it was used as justification for not harassing sexual minorities.[43] It was a mix between a Clintonian 'don't ask, don't tell' and a 'live and let live' message that LGBT people should be left alone as long as they did not 'impose' their values on the rest of society, whose tone, according to Lee, 'remains conventional, it remains straight'.[44]

This turn and return to biology and genetics also structures the state's management of 'race' and migration. As I show in Chapter 4, for instance, its logics structure the way in which undesirable non-citizens are expressly prevented from biologically reproducing the nation. The discourse of biology-as-fact has propped up the gender-as-biology conviction – and its grip is vice-like. The sense in which gender presents as a biological problem that ostensibly makes itself available for a medicalized resolution into an established normative gender framework lies in contrast to sexuality and sexual desire. By no means is this meant to imply that the state does what it can to support trans people instead of minoritized sexualities or that it treats them preferentially in comparison to sexual minorities. Particularly against the background of the current political moment where the trans figure can be and *is* often pitted against women and sexual minorities to disrupt historical community formations and to fracture solidarity amongst all queered people, I want to emphasize this point. Indeed, it is clear and it has been documented that trans people in Singapore encounter a range of challenges in their day-to-day lives.[45] They also face plenty of difficulties as the direct consequence of extant social policies – types of duress that Dean Spade urges us to think of as 'administrative violence'.[46]

Having said that, articulating specifically how the intersection of heteronormativity and nationalism presses down on the minoritized communities is beyond this book's remit – mainly because I am aiming to intervene in the discursive space produced by the state rather than lived experiences and social realities of minoritized individuals. By and large, rather than thinking about identity categories and how they are lived, I am concerned with the logics of heteronormativity across the state's discursive and rhetorical terrain, its intersections with nationalism to produce particular subject positions, and the broader implications of these political currents. The state's treatment of transgender people – pathologizing them, viewing them through the lens of biology, and seeking to gender-stabilize them into the category of male or female – taken together with its insistence on the biological origins of homosexuality reflects an acute investment in a much broader bio-essentialist and eugenicist approach that exceeds the management of gender and sexuality per se to encompass population control and the management of the nation, and this is relevant to understanding nationalism.

I do not claim to have resolved any of the local complexities and contradictions around vocabulary but, for the most part, when I use *LGBT* it is echoing Singaporean activists, scholars, and minoritized sexualities who often use it as shorthand for non-heterosexuals. Used in this way, *LGBT* functions as a signifier of non-normative sexuality rather than in its Anglo-American sense of an acronym of sexual and transgender identities. *Queer* is a theoretical pillar of this project. Whilst queer theory took it up very much as a pointed critique of identity categories themselves, in its contemporary iterations *queer* has accrued a loose identarian function that enables it to signify any number of non-normative sexual or gender identity categories.[47] Even though it is 'not a term commonly used in the community', when *queer* is invoked in Singapore it is typically used in this identarian sense, and is sometimes used interchangeably with *LGBT*.[48] In general, *queer* has evolved to sit quite comfortably within a single-issue-styled queer politics that asks for minoritized sexualities to be included into dominant systems and formations of the nation instead of a more radical transformation.[49]

But this identarian understanding of *queer* can hem in the radical potential of queer politics, and I want to distance the project from this sense. Cathy Cohen's warning resounds here, reminding us that:

> in many instances, instead of destabilizing the assumed categories and binaries of sexual identity, queer politics has served to reinforce simple dichotomies between heterosexual and everything 'queer'. An understanding of the ways in which power informs and constitutes privileged and marginalized subjects on both sides of this dichotomy has been left unexamined.[50]

Queer as heuristic gestures towards this notion. Instead of using it to denote LGBT people, non-normative genders, and sexualities, or indeed to index groups of people occupying any number of identity categories, at least in this book I prefer to use *queer* as a critical tool to unsettle the circulation of heteronormativity. As Michael Warner puts it, *queer* 'also suggests the difficulty in defining the population whose interests are at stake in queer politics'.[51] A queer heuristic thus nudges the book's analytic focus away from specific identity categories and towards the operation of heteronormativity as well as its co-constitution with other social forces such as 'race', gender, and class. hooks' notion of queerness, or 'queer-past-gay' as she memorably puts it, is an inspiration here.[52] hooks urges us to think of queer in an expansive sense, saying '[consider] queer as not being about who you're having sex with – that can be a dimension of it – but queer as being about the self that is at odds with everything around it and has to invent and create and find a place to speak and to thrive and to live'.[53] At the same time, I do not want to valorize a kind of blanket anti-normativity that romanticizes deviance. Theorists in queer studies caution against a summary dismissal of all norms and normativities by opening the question of whether they should be viewed exclusively as manifestations of duress.[54] This is an important point. To put it plainly, norms are necessary for day-to-day life. We need norms for the simple act of living in a state (both in a personal *and* political sense) that is not perpetually unsettling. What is helpful, however, is to bear in mind that '[some] norms and conventions ... permit people to breathe, to desire, to love, and to live, [whilst others] restrict or eviscerate the conditions of life itself'.[55]

An expansive, ambitious, and daring version of *queer* helps draw attention to the 'variety of ways in which norms are lived and inhabited, aspired to, reached for, and consummated' whilst thinking about the work they do in defining and circumscribing liveable lives.[56] It opens a way of interrogating how particular norms place particular forms of duress on particular people. The value it offers, particularly in this leftist/progressive queer-of-colour tradition, is in its extension of an invitation to entertain the notion 'that sexuality isn't always or only about sexuality, that it is not an autonomous dimension of experience'.[57] It offers an understanding that the governance of sexuality is bound up with gender, 'race', class, and that the interaction of these social forces can produce substantively different heteronormativities. And as Eve Kosofsky Sedgwick reminds us, in this sense, it 'spins the term outward along dimensions that can't be subsumed under gender and sexuality at all: the ways that race, ethnicity, postcolonial nationality criss-cross with these and other identity-constituting, identity-fracturing discourses'.[58]

This goes some way towards explaining why, despite its origins in the Global North, within the Anglo-American context, many scholars working in Singapore and other parts of the Global South in Asia have readily taken up *queer* as a critical tool in rethinking and questioning extant understandings of sexuality.[59] It has a certain theoretical use and explanatory capacity. A queer heuristic helps understand that even though not everyone who is rendered queer is necessarily queer in an identarian sense, or marginalized and disenfranchised in the same way, or to the same degree, heteronormativity's disciplinary force bears down upon multiple others in addition to sexual minorities thereby queering them too. Natalie Oswin articulates what is at stake here:

> When 'queer' is understood to stand in only for GLBT (gay, lesbian, bisexual, transgendered), the ways in which not all heterosexuals have access to heterosexual privilege are overlooked. Heteronormativity is not simply an expression of the valorisation of heterosexuality over homosexuality. Rather, it is a set of norms that makes not just heterosexuality, but particular expressions of heterosexuality seem right.[60]

Queering the state and its policies thus does not entail simply sifting it through a heterosexual/non-heterosexual binary. Lest we forget, ' "nonnormative" procreation patterns and family structures of people who are labelled heterosexual have also been used to regulate and exclude *them*'.[61] Queering the state entails challenging heteronormativity where heteronormativity is understood as 'both those localized practices and those centralized institutions which legitimize and privilege heterosexuality and heterosexual relationships as fundamental and "natural" within society';[62] and it entails interrogating a political system built on presuppositions that 'have posited and naturalized a heterosexual society' that consequently structures its subjects into particular ways of being, living, and behaving.[63]

This is why the spirit of queer enquiry must question the very notion of inclusion itself and has to 'entail radical (re)thinkings, (re)drawings, (re)conceptualisations, (re)mappings that could (re)make bodies, spaces and geographies'.[64] This is also why manifestations of homophobia, of which Section 377A is a glaring example, do not figure very prominently throughout this book. For homophobia is merely one of the most visible symptoms of a system plagued by heteronormativity. As Urvashi Vaid reminds us, 'homophobia arises from the nature and construction of the political, legal, economic, sexual, racial and family systems within which we live'.[65] This project's critical thrust takes aim squarely at these systems. What I am interested in analysing is how heteronormativity is a constitutive logic of the subjectivity that is produced as a function of the government of social life in Singapore, and how various groups of people are rendered queer as a result.

It should be clear by now that I use *queer* less in its identarian sense, and more as a verb in its processual sense of queering someone or rendering them queer. *Queer* is more than a synonym for LGBT people – the queered category refers to the entire category of persons minoritized and marginalized by the smooth operation of heteronormativity. Beyond sexual minorities, it can include, at various moments, unmarried heterosexuals, non-citizens, single parents, migrant workers, and more. To be clear, I am not suggesting that everybody queered in this sense experiences it in the same way or faces the same kinds of difficulties. Rather, I am suggesting that 'we ought to pay critical attention to the fact that many more than LGBT persons are "queered" in the sense that they are put on a different trajectory of life and death than those cast as licit and proper through the maintenance of narrow familial and domestic norms'.[66]

Methodological choices

My analytical vantage point in this book is strongly informed by Michael Warner and Laurent Berlant's foundational insistence that '[h]eteronormativity is more than ideology, or prejudice, or phobia against gays and lesbians; it is produced in almost every aspect of the forms and arrangements of social life'.[67] In a similar vein, Ahmed argues that:

> To become straight means that we not only have to turn toward the objects that are given to us by heterosexual culture, but also that we must 'turn away' from objects that take us off this line. The queer subject within straight culture hence deviates and is made socially present as a deviant.[68]

In this sense, what heteronormativity demands is a particular expression of life and living that is delivered according to a script of straightness. Equally importantly, it can also require a disavowal and rejection of things that lie outside this script in addition to the demonstration of affiliation, affection, and affinity for the things that are on it.[69] The operation of heteronormativity therefore does not correspond to the boundaries of putative identity categories; and it is not reserved solely for non-heterosexual subjects. Instead, it applies a pressure on both non-heterosexual and heterosexual subjects not just to be straight but to actively express their straightness in a particular acceptable way. In this way, the state's maintenance of a regime of 'compulsory heterosexuality' reflects not so much an identarian investment in straightness as it does a political investment that in turn requires reading heterosexuality as a 'political institution'.[70]

Heteronormativity's power is therefore not just that it can result in homosexual exclusion or even that it can ascribe different sets of duties to men and women as 'natural' – an important point that Nira Yuval-Davis' work makes in insisting on paying attention to how 'gendered relations [can contribute to] several major dimensions of nationalist projects'.[71] Heteronormativity structures subjectivity in Singapore, what it means to be Singaporean, through its grip on political and social life in Singapore. It is insufficient to simply be heterosexual; one must actively demonstrate one's heterosexuality correctly and in an appropriate manner in relation to the nation. Whilst the imperative for individuals to couple is inflected by logics of heterosexual desire, the expression of heterosexuality that is elevated as the right one also brings with it a gendered division of duties within the heterosexual couple. For instance, as we will see in Chapter 2, men are charged with protecting the nation whilst women are expected to reproduce the nation and take responsibility for caregiving duties. Queerness, then, lies in the inability or refusal to demonstrate a sufficient fidelity to this script of straightness – which can range from an imperfect recital to completely disobeying it and going 'off-script' – that invites a range of consequences.[72] Because life is organized around a certain permissible expression of heterosexuality, 'the effects of such a disturbance are uneven, precisely given that the world is already organized around certain forms of living – certain times, spaces, and directions'.[73]

A number of scholars working on Singapore have already examined topics related to heteronormativity, homophobia, and minoritized sexualities. Copious ink – or perhaps toner, as tends to be the case these days – has been spilt across plenty of pages examining various sites of homosexual exclusion from the law and especially Section 377A,[74] the configuration of social and economic policy,[75] the workplace,[76] and the obsessive maintenance of the heterosexual nuclear family in Singapore.[77] Significant critical attention has also been paid to the ways in which LGBT people resist this minoritization in their day-to-day lives,[78] whilst also organizing for better outcomes.[79] However, whilst most of this work recognizes that sexuality functions as a marker of exclusion, the focus remains on the exclusions that LGBT people face; it does not quite recognize the production of a heteronormative space (much less a nation) that shapes the lives of people in ways that exceed identity categories.[80]

The edited collection *Queer Singapore* was the first to critically examine the politics of sexuality and its governance in Singapore.[81] Its title could be read as an invitation, a call, to consider how queerness is not quite part of Singapore, and we can mine something useful from this sentiment. *Queer* can function as a modifier that challenges and changes *Singapore* as it is conventionally constituted. It stands apart, separate, as a non-constituent characteristic of how the nation is understood. In this reading, queerness is external to Singapore and displaced from the national formation. This displacement, the specific political motivations that enable and sustain it, is a central concern in this book. I am interested in the range of implications that arise from the alliance between nationalism and heteronormativity. If heteronormativity is a key condition upon which admission into the putative Singaporean nation hinges, what are the consequences for people who are queered?

It is crucial to recognize the ways in which a particular expression of heterosexuality is elevated at the expense of other forms of living, and tightly tethered to admission into the Singaporean nation. As a consequence, those who are unable or unwilling to recite from the script of straightness are not only queered, they are also xenologized – rendered foreign (*xenos*) through the operation of a certain set of heteronormative logics (*logos*) that are co-constituted with a host of racialized, gendered and classed logics.

The overbearing, paternalistic, highly interventionist nature of the Singaporean state lends itself very well to a functionalist analysis. Conventional approaches in political economy tend to read the state (particularly the developmental state in East and Southeast Asia) this way, relying on a theoretical conception of power as a vertex bearing directly down upon citizens who are effectively treated as objects in this formulation.[82] From this vantage point, one could comfortably read social outcomes as issuing immediately from the actions, policies, and interventions of a strong state. But this neatness does not exist as it is imagined. The Singaporean state certainly looms large in people's lives; and it certainly subjectivizes people in particular ways. At the same time, however, people navigate and often do get around the constraints placed upon them in myriad ways, whether in housing policy,[83] state welfare policies,[84] dissent and protest,[85] and so on. Even though it is an enticing analytical position, adopting a functionalist posture can contribute 'to the very imaginary and myth of an all-knowing state, reifying its timelessness and contributing to its dominance in the public imagination'.[86] In other words, to grant the Singaporean state a functionalist reading would be too generous because it conjures up an image of a state that is far more coherent than it actually is.

In contrast to this set-up, the sociologist Chua Beng Huat has theorized governance in Singapore through a model of what he calls 'illiberal pragmatism'.[87] Chua gets significant mileage out of a Gramscian approach and suggests that what the government reflexively labels pragmatism 'embodies a vigorous economic development orientation that emphasises science and technology and centralised rational public administration as the fundamental basis for industrialisation within a capitalist system, financed largely by multinational capital'.[88] In quotidian language, which is also how the government popularly represents this mode of governance, 'it translates simply into "being practical" in the sense of earning a living'.[89] The Singaporean state's brand of pragmatism, Chua argues, should thus be understood as an '*ad hoc* contextual rationality that seeks to achieve specific gains at particular points in time and pays scant attention to systematicity and coherence as necessary rational criteria for action'.[90]

This conceptual framework for understanding and making sense of the state has become exceedingly difficult to budge – or even hegemonic, depending on one's fondness for wry humour – in Singapore studies. It has been anointed the 'singular prerequisite for continuous self-renewal to manage change and continuity' in Singaporean governance.[91] Even in critical scholarship, theorizing the state through this lens of 'pragmatism' remains pervasive, and much of the recent work on sexuality in Singapore uses Chua's theorization as a starting point. In work on Singapore queer studies alone it has been used to theorize 'pragmatic resistance' in activism and social movements.[92] It has been extended to make sense of the state's ambivalence towards LGBT people in Singapore – particularly the post-2000s attitude of 'we'll leave you alone so long as homosexuality is not encouraged and is no more than a marketplace commodity'.[93] And it has been used to develop a reading of homonationalism in Singapore as a form of activist resistance.[94]

The pragmatism model offers a way in to understanding how a state where 'the formal features of democratic electoral politics remain in place and intact' but is 'thoroughly sceptical regarding the rationality of the ordinary citizen and unapologetically anti-liberal' manages to retain political legitimacy – and Chua's work is at its strongest here.[95] But it seems to me that the banner of pragmatism at times offers a suspiciously convenient space where all contradictions, ambivalence, and untidiness can be parked. Any kind of analysis that takes seriously the need to contextualize resisting heteronormativity very quickly runs into the challenge that, like other identity categories, sexuality does not exist in isolation – it is one in relation to other positions. This is Hall's point in suggesting that the various 'antagonisms [of multiple identity categories] refuse to be neatly aligned; they are simply not reducible to one another; they refuse to coalesce around a single axis of differentiation'.[96]

Pragmatism can function as a kind of theoretical *deus ex machina* that resolves these differences instead of compelling us to grapple with their complexities seriously. Analytically, we can do more and do better by paying attention to the delimitation of pragmatism itself – how does something become pragmatic and what are the conditions under which pragmatism is eschewed, for example, in relation to heteronormativity? Being practical does not sufficiently explain why, in some contexts, LGBT people can be accommodated whilst in others they become threats; but without understanding this conditional acceptance it is difficult to make sense of how, when, and why queerness is partially tolerated. Earning a living alone does not properly explain the paranoia around ensuring female foreign domestic workers do not become pregnant in Singapore; but it is crucial to make sense of this prohibition in order to understand how heteronormativity functions with racialized and gendered and classed dimensions.

Instead of investing explanatory capacity in the conceptual framework of pragmatism, then, I prefer an approach that focuses on the processual

production of Singaporean subjectivity as a historical consequence of heteronormativity's sedimentation as common sense. In other words, mine is a
Foucauldian approach. Michel Foucault's point in *The History of Sexuality*
is that 'a normalizing society is the historical outcome of a technology of
power centred on life'.[97] Out goes the functionalist top-down conception
of power.[98] Instead, he suggests that 'what defines a relationship of power
is that it is a mode of action which does not act directly and immediately
on others. Instead it acts upon their actions: an action upon an action, on
existing actions or on those which may arise in the present or the future.'[99]
It is the 'conduct of conduct'.[100] Here, power is conceptualized as 'the taking charge of life' with the capacity to shape and mould the field of what
is thought and imagined to be possible such that the 'action of the norm'
becomes overwhelmingly important.[101] It produces a particular subject position that is distinctly marked out as normal. Deviance is thus obtained from
producing normativity.[102] From this point of view, the focus shifts away
from the actor to the process such that it is the regulation and regularization
of the normal subject, the circumscription of the bounds of normality itself,
that lies at the heart of the Foucauldian diagnostic.

This sensibility runs through the entire book, attempting to piece
together the various elements that place pressure on life in Singapore,
shaping what it means to be a 'normal' Singaporean. Working out how
heteronormativity structures subjectivity in Singapore entails thinking
about how queerness is produced and manifests in various forms of exclusion. But, as an indication of its theoretical and political commitments,
searching for inclusion is not the aim of this book. It might be helpful at
this point to remember that regardless of whether one is looking to include
(*inclaudere*) or to exclude (*exclaudere*), both gestures bring with them a
sense of closing (*claudere*), to shut, to trap, restrict, and confine. The question of inclusion/exclusion can thus be read as a question of whether one is
shut in or shut out.[103] Here, even as the associations of exile, outcast, and
rejection accompany the notion of shutting out, one might also glimpse
the rough edges of prison walls, the trappings of a cell, the darkness of
a dungeon, in the notion of being shut in.[104] It is precisely in the smooth
functioning of *both* inclusion and exclusion that one is subjectivized. The
point of the analysis presented in this book is not to examine processes of
exclusion and then work out how to mitigate that with inclusion. Rather
it is to understand how the inclusion/exclusion operation itself is run. The
objective is not to simply focus on the people who are shut in or shut out.
Instead, I want to work out along what lines and under what conditions
one is shut in or out. For, only once the workings of heteronormativity's
operation are properly sussed out can the work to tear it down properly begin.

Methodologically, therefore, I approach the project seeking to provide a historicization. Through a set of close readings, dwelling on what is often taken as common sense, and making visible the range of contradictions and pressure points in received wisdom, the book advances an argument about the present nationalist conjuncture that Singapore finds itself in and tries to understand what led up to it – so as to say something about what to do about it. This is an approach that steadfastly refuses 'to explain history by reference to origins, causes, and inner truths; rather, genealogy traces the inherently political process by which some institutional and discursive effects get constituted as original, causative truths'.[105] This is not a book where I am writing an originary account of nationalism in Singapore; neither does it seek to trace the creation of the heteronormative present. Rather, the book provides an account of the ways in which a certain version of heteronormative futurity has come to be naturalized as fundamental to the nation. It asks for an understanding that the present we live in did not materialize out of nothing – even though it may be made to feel as if it has – but is instead an emergent and inherited present.[106] As Hubert Dreyfus and Paul Rabinow remark, '[t]his approach explicitly and self-consciously begins with a diagnosis of the current situation'.[107] The genealogical approach allows us to pay attention to the process of inheritance itself to understand how its contingencies have contributed to the formation of the present.[108]

I began this project trawling the National Archives of Singapore for documents relating to the anti-sodomy law, homophobia, and the normalization of heterosexuality through family policies. Tugging at the thread of one manifestation of heteronormativity led to others and, not unexpectedly, spun out in multiple directions. The National University of Singapore's Singapore/Malaysia collection was another site of information, as were the records of the Colonial Office and Foreign and Commonwealth Offices in The National Archives, Kew, in London. Across these historical repositories, I drew on reports pertaining to the family and its functions, migrant workers and migrant policies, LGBT rights and related social movements, media reports, the parliamentary Hansard, legal records from the Singapore Penal Code as well as other laws and statutes such as the Women's Charter, records of state agencies such as the Housing & Development Board (HDB) and Ministry for Social and Family Development (MSF), political speeches, oral interviews, doctoral theses as well as policy documents, and reports such as the MSF's State of the Family report. The British Library in London and King's College London's Maughan Library were sources of secondary literature as well as doctoral theses used for reference.

Singapore's postcolonial story cannot be told without accounting for the role of the PAP government that has governed Singapore with an overwhelming parliamentary majority since independence. The PAP has dominated the electoral and political landscape and exerted a huge influence on the postcolonial nation through instruments of the state.[109] Biographical literature and interviews with the country's influential early leaders such as Goh Keng Swee; S. Rajaratnam; Goh Chok Tong; and, of course, independent Singapore's first prime minister, Lee Kuan Yew, were essential to understanding the manufacturing of political rationality.

There is some risk in making this methodological choice of turning to, and thereby inadvertently assembling, an archive. Particularly with respect to postcolonial queer studies, there is often the temptation to put a historiography of heteronormativity to work by insisting it illustrates that homophobia is non-indigenous ('Western') and therefore illegitimate. In a strictly instrumental sense, and as an activist tactic, this is understandable. But as Chandan Reddy cautions, 'the archive is not a passive domain in which differences ... can be found, extracted, and restored to their fullness'.[110] Anjali Arondekar is similarly cautious of loading history and archives with recuperative potential and the hope that if one were to reach back far enough, historicize sufficiently, and identify the moment of its creation, the spell of heteronormativity might suddenly be broken.[111] Far better instead that we 'question the dependence on a recovered history to sanction our surviving present'.[112] For, as Rao argues:

> postcolonial claims and counterclaims about the spatiotemporal provenance of 'homosexuality' seem to have bought into a common nativism, whereby forms of desire and prohibition that cannot be shown to have existed within the boundaries of the nation are *ipso facto* illegitimate.[113]

These cautionary words should give us reason to pause but they are not signals to abandon this mode of enquiry altogether. Instead, they are useful as a stimulus to remember that in putting together a historiographical postcolonial account of the governance of sexuality, one must negotiate the temptation of redemption that history can often offer. This is a form of postcolonialism that uses the colonial past to disavow a present that can sometimes be even more colonial.[114] The postcolonial state may well have inherited the vestiges of a heteronormative and homophobic colonial state; but if colonial vestiges have rich postcolonial afterlives, it is often because the postcolonial state has actively entrenched and enriched them.[115] Working with postcolonial studies and postcolonial enquiry necessarily means engaging, grappling, wrestling with these complexities instead of expunging them through recourse to 'history'.

Ultimately, I want to suggest that history is an advantage instead of a contaminant – a means of engaging and grappling with the present. Historicizing the present, building a 'history of the present', is vital not only to understanding the consequences of paths taken and not taken but also to helping us see ways of shifting onto different paths than those that appear given.[116] It 'commits us to thinking of [the present's] anterior conditions of existence'.[117] The waters of the present are, after all, drawn from the wells of the past. To echo Foucault, the challenge is that whilst 'important and even invaluable political effects can be produced by historical analyses ... the problem is to let knowledge of the past work on the experience of the present'.[118] And in so doing, it sets the stage for us to theorize a future that is different from the heteronormative present that lies before us today.

It bears mentioning at this point that in studying heteronormativity and the elevation of heterosexuality, I want to excavate nationalism as a force. One reason for titling the book *Straight Nation* is to call attention to the way the nation can be contingent on straightness. *Straight* functions as a way of unsettling its immanence within the nation. In analysing nationalism as a force, what happens if we tug at the thread of straightness? How might the edifice of the nation, or the national-state, unravel when straightness is disturbed or extracted? What possibilities present themselves if straightness is expelled, and made to stand outside the nation? But there are also gestures towards disciplinary and corrective registers buried in *straight*. Let us think about the myriad ways in which, by making a particular way of living seem 'right', nationalism can function like a straitjacket, trying to set one straight, compelling one to straighten up and remain on the straight and narrow, delimiting a strait way of life that is also a straight way of life. It not only acts to queer and xenologize various communities – even though that is a major part of it – it also claims to write an 'acceptable' script for the model subject to follow, making a myriad set of exigencies on them.[119] My basic contention is simply that this script is written in the language of heteronormativity.

This book theorizes nationalism in postcolonial Singapore and its transmission through circuits of heteronormativity. Specifically, it investigates how different forms, functions, and expressions of sexuality are not only regulated along the lines of permissibility but placed in a hierarchy. This process of hierarchization, I argue, both powers and is powered by nationalism in Singapore. Tracing sexuality's history, articulating *a* history of sexuality (*pace* Foucault) in Singapore, opens a way of analysing nationalism and its demands through sexuality and its governance.

Reading heteronormativity as nationalism's propellant also gives us an opportunity to say something about nationalism. It is not only that nationalism functions on an affirmation of an enemy figure, or contingencies of exclusion where certain people are xenologized in certain contexts, but that nationalism as a force propagates the myth of a coherent nation.[120] It is a seductive whisper promising that if only the elements of impurity can be expunged from the nation then it will be whole again. It is

a force that continually seeks to shed whatever is constructed as a pollut-
ant in pursuit of some kind of imagined purity. It is a teleological project
that can never be completed because it can only explain its inadequacies by
replicating itself – the only way it addresses its continual failure is to double
down and further subdivide its internal constituencies.[121] But because those
excluded people who form what I call the counter-nation are simultaneously
constitutive of the nation, they cannot ever really be expelled – instead they
will reappear, demanding to be accounted for.

Radical queer critique is unsympathetic towards mainstream LGBT politics that seeks inclusion into the status quo.[122] Much of it is positioned
against queer liberal politics, arguing that queered individuals should
instead lift their eyes and push more ambitiously for the transformation
of the social sphere itself.[123] Its larger preoccupation, as Jasbir Puar puts
it, is dealing with the question of 'what happens after certain liberal rights
are bestowed, certain thresholds or parameters of success are claimed to
have been reached: What happens when "we" get what "we" want?'.[124]
Despite the fact that the geography of this argument is quite evidently an
Anglo-American one, I am generally inclined to agree with this position – in
particular, with the question that Puar poses. If nothing else, this branch
of literature forces us to consider how the putative 'we' is constituted and
how the threads that bind this 'we' might fray with differentiated triumphs.
Bracketing for a moment the argument that participating in what can be
extremely conservative and heteronormative institutions is often experienced as a substantively difficult move – a position that I retain sympathy
for – difficulty alone is not a bellwether of emancipation.[125] Envisioning a
future that is simply integration into a heteronormative present is either a
failure of imagination or an inability to imagine boldly enough – and neither
will quite lead to effectively repudiating heteronormativity.

Again, it bears repeating that I am not particularly interested in litigating
the precise difficulty quotient of integration because it is more politically
useful to examine exactly why imaginations are circumscribed in this way.
In that sense, I am more interested in analysing the forces – social, political,
cultural – that exert a pressure on the imagination so as to make thinking
about a transformative future difficult. As I make clear in the book's final
chapter, Pink Dot's overarching demand for integration and its inability (or
refusal?) to imagine a different kind of future is telling. At the same time,
when the nation purports to offer so much via its heteronormative present,
it is unsurprising that some queered people might want nothing more than
to be included in the nationalist project. It is also entirely possible that some
of those who manage to successfully carve a niche for themselves within
the current nationalist conjuncture will not only be satisfied with their lot,
but will also participate in actively propagating nationalist logics further in

different contexts.[126] I am therefore less interested in the position of wanting to integrate than I am in the cultural and political forces that shape the process through which resisting heteronormativity is conceptualized in such limited terms.

Puar persuasively theorizes this bind through the conceptual frame of 'homonationalism' where the failure to recognize LGBT rights is framed as characteristic of an uncivilized and barbaric state.[127] Chandra Mohanty's important feminist critique that articulates how the discourse of a lack of women's rights in non-western sites can function as a useful foil for the West to reassert itself as the bastion of civilization is relevant here as well.[128] However, as a function of its postcolonial status and the anti-imperialist/anti-West sentiment that can easily be generated in postcolonial societies, the soft, foreboding *mission civilisatrice* tunes that play in homonationalism's background are far less able to take hold and rise to a roar in Singapore like they can in the USA.

Rao's theoretical frame of 'homocapitalism' here offers a useful remedy particularly in relation to postcolonial nationalism.[129] Its basic tenet is that the marginalization of non-normative sexual identities is an impediment to capital accumulation. Whereas homonationalism wields the figure of the brute as a consequence of sexual marginalization – something that postcolonial nations are, frankly, quite used to facing and these days quite adept at deflecting – homocapitalism wields the promise of prosperity – whose allure is far harder to resist. Put differently, homonationalism suggests that if LGBT integration is denied, one is a savage; homocapitalism intimates that one will be left poorer. Taken together, these two frames of understanding offer a powerful theoretical way of understanding how, and under what conditions, minoritized sexualities in Singapore look for inclusion into the nation. It is also a way to understand how nationalism can operate internally as well, subdividing putatively othered constituencies and offering conditional forms of acceptance in some racialized and classed contexts to mediate nationalism's xenology.

The vast majority of critical work on nationalism has focused on its exclusionary capacities and the ways in which it renders different people other.[130] But there is also something to be said about the rewards it offers. Nationalism has the capacity to marginalize but it also has the capacity to reward its idealized subjects. Heteronormativity is the elevation of a particular performance of heterosexuality above other ways of living and being – which, as I argue, results in multiple communities being queered; but it can also result in some people – including some queered people – seeking the reward of being elevated themselves in the national formation, perhaps even at the expense of others. I have little interest in advancing an apologist argument defending such a tactic; but I think it is important to understand why some might decide to make these choices so as to properly understand the siren call of nationalism before hoping to be in any position to undo it.

There are a few fundamental questions I am asking in this book. How can the nation be theorized through the governance of sexuality, desire, and other social relations? What are some major sites of heteronormativity; what kinds of work are they made to do in sustaining the nation; and amidst all this, how is queerness produced, sedimented, and militated against? What can extant forms of resistance tell us about the limits of an identarian understanding of queerness, and what implications does this hold for undoing heteronormativity and imagining a different kind of futurity?

The chapters in the rest of this book follow as responses to these three broad questions. All of them attempt to articulate a historicized present because this project is built on a conception of the present heteronormative nationalist moment as one that has been actively made and shaped and produced. Their order reflects an argumentative arc that aims to foreground nationalism as an organizing political force as well as the nation's investment in heteronormativity to understand the political possibilities and futurities that might lie ahead for those queered in and by Singapore.

Chapter 1 considers what it means to understand Singapore as a straight nation where heteronormativity – the expression of a particular, prescribed form of heterosexuality – is the condition upon which subjectivity and admission into the nation rests. In contrast to liberal orthodox theories of the nation that view it as functioning on logics of inclusion, this chapter draws attention to nationalism's investment in producing figures of otherness. Across the formal discourses of the state – the way the state narrates the nation – ethnicity and 'race' are less vivid markers of difference, in part because of the specifics of Singapore's postcolonial condition. I want to suggest that across this discursive terrain, the otherness that nationalism requires finds its expression more perspicuously in the governance of sexuality and desire. Heteronormativity thus becomes a key modality through which nationalism is transmitted in Singapore and forms a dividing line that outlines what I call the counter-nation – the collection of the various groups of people that nationalism renders other in order to replicate and reproduce itself.

Chapter 2 identifies three major sites of heteronormativity in Singapore – housing, family, and the military. It explores their interaction and commingling in the postcolonial nation-building project and how they produce a subject position between each other. Singapore's independence was marked by currents of strife, vulnerability, and crisis. The military and compulsory conscription play a key psychic role in assuaging the affects of vulnerability and relies on citizens' willingness to potentially lay their lives on the line defending Singapore. Rather than relying on the abstract concept of the nation, however, persuasion here rests on a more material logic that uses home ownership as an affect that turns one's home into a scalar substitute for the nation such that citizens have something material to protect; defend; and, if necessary, kill for. Access to public housing, however, is premised on heterosexual marriage and family formation where women are charged with the expectations of reproducing the nation, whereas men are designated the duty of protecting the nation via compulsory conscription. In this way, the triad of defence, domesticity, and the heterosexual nuclear family rests on a set of heteronormative and gendered logics that animate the nation. Queerness poses a problem because it becomes mutually exclusive to these logics.

Chapter 3 interrogates the work that kinship is made to do in service of the nation. Historicizing the heterosexual nuclear family shows how the abstract concept of family is narrowly defined by the ontological relations given to us by the language of kinship. Gendered relations of care and support are transformed into obligations, aided and abetted by gestures towards 'Asian' values. Kinship, together with its attendant obligations, is thus given pride of place in the hierarchy of social relations. Whilst treating kinship in this way typically privileges the heterosexual nuclear family unit, the chapter examines the historic 2018 judgment in *UKM* v. *Attorney-General* as an instance where logics of kinship were placed in direct contestation with the logics of heterosexual coupling. Whilst non-normative forms of kinship and parenting are far from entrenched, I read the outcome of *UKM* v. *Attorney-General* as reflecting the salience of heteronormative familism in organizing social relations in Singapore.

Chapter 4 investigates the relation between heteronormativity, citizenship, and membership of the nation. If the nation saddles its members with the expectations of heteronormativity, queerness can be read as conceptually stranded in the space of the non-domestic. Where does this leave non-citizens? And what is to be said about people who are prohibited from participating in this heteronormative spectacle? Without resorting to a simple local–foreigner or citizen–denizen binary, I suggest that some non-citizens – those who are classified as irredeemably foreign – have their incompatibility with the nation confirmed by being rendered queer. There is a racialized dimension to this classification. Non-citizens classified as 'foreign talent' – typically white, Euro-Americans – are invited into the nation, granted citizenship, and encouraged to help reproduce the nation. On the other hand, those classified as 'foreign workers' – typically South and Southeast Asians – are expressly denied any possibility of becoming part of the nation, much less reproducing it. A raft of laws work together to exclude them from membership of the nation whilst also excluding them from the possibility of marriage (and, in the case of women, child-bearing), thus ensuring that the paradigmatic figure of the foreign is rendered such by also being rendered queer.

Chapter 5 thinks through Pink Dot – the largest and most well-known LGBT movement in Singapore. It locates the social movement as the product of a long process of anti-politicization that has delegitimized overt displays of dissent and point-blank refusal of state narratives in favour of an assimilationist approach that emphasizes consensus between civil society and state actors. This, together with the reification of kinship in Singapore, helps explain why Pink Dot's demands have generally been limited to little more than integration into the heteronormative present. Whilst remaining cognizant of the real constraints on civil society and movement organizers, I read Pink Dot as exemplifying a tactic that seeks to domesticize Singaporean sexual minorities by creating a subject position compatible with the nation. I would like to suggest this reflects the limits of imbricating queerness with nationalism in Singapore.

The epilogue briefly summarizes the book and its arguments. This section also offers a brief discussion on the limits of instrumentalizing nationalism and the pitfalls of a narrow identarian understanding of sexuality. I suggest that the tactic of assimilationist, third-way activism that Pink Dot has historically adopted has reached an inflection point. I draw attention to the Singaporean ambassador's comments at the 3rd Universal Periodic Review in 2021 at the United Nations Human Rights Council when Pink Dot was invoked to strengthen the hand of the state. The ambassador's claim that Pink Dot's annual events show that LGBT people in Singapore do not face discrimination should be read as part of a state strategy to co-opt resistance to fortify itself. It is in this sense I argue that flirting with nationalism like this risks backfiring, and if nothing else, is unlikely to lay the foundations for a larger emancipatory project. A reading of the repeal of Section 377A in 2022 helps show how, rather than treating sexual rights as an identity-based single-issue topic, it is only when a broader assault on heteronormativity is launched that the state will make concessions and there are substantive gains to be had. The closing pages thus suggest that undoing heteronormativity requires recognizing the potential for solidarity amongst the various queered people who form the counter-nation and entails rejecting the heteronormativity–nation nexus.

Finally, a word on style. I have tried to give an aerial view of what I am aiming to do in the book in this introduction, as well as the broad intellectual and theoretical commitments that guide me; but it must be said that this book does not sit comfortably 'within' a discipline. Disciplines have certain conventions and perspectival limitations that I have ended up traversing – inadvertently or otherwise.[131] To a certain extent, this is a serendipitous consequence of my own intellectual formation, but it is also the result of a commitment to a transdisciplinary approach that relies on a kind of bricolage of intellectual traditions. Working with different disciplines like this can place one on multiple sites of shifting theoretical terrain; I am influenced by a number of thinkers and traditions, and I have written this book in a somewhat essayistic fashion that lets me situate the texts I am working with, drawing on, and responding to within my own arguments. It also gives me affordance to dispense with some of the parochialisms of traditional academic writing. Above all, I hope writing like this opens the door to a way of reading that is generative, meditative, and – with some luck – maybe even transformative.

Notes

1 World Health Organization, 'WHO Director-General's Opening Remarks at the Media Briefing on COVID-19 – 11 March 2020', www.who.int/director-general/speeches/detail/who-director-general-s-opening-remarks-at-the-media-briefing-on-covid-19---11-march-2020#:~:text=Good%20afternoon.,for%20their%20lives%20in%20hospitals (accessed 12 September 2024).

2 'Covid-19: Children May Visit Their Parents and Grandparents after June 1 with Restrictions', *TODAYonline*, 19 May 2020, <www.youtube.com/watch?v=2albEsrHuQg (accessed 20 September 2024).

3 Ibid.

4 Pavan Mano, 'Rethinking the Heteronormative Foundations of Kinship: The Reification of the Heterosexual Nuclear Family Unit in Singapore's COVID-19 Circuit-Breaker Restrictions', *Culture, Theory and Critique*, 62.1–2 (2021), 142–53 (p. 144).

5 Natalie Oswin, *Global City Futures: Desire and Development in Singapore* (Athens: University of Georgia Press, 2019), pp. 17–18.

6 Regarding the example above about the easing of emergency measures, one could point out – probably not without reason – that the grandparent–grandchild relation does not sit within the nuclear familial structure. Making sense of the state's position here requires reading grandparents as part of a multigenerational nuclear family structure (i.e. grandparent–parent–child) and a more general logic that privileges biological kin relations over others. After all, a child's parents are also the children of the child's grandparents. This reading carries more explanatory potential and is central to Chapter 3, which theorizes how the relations inscribed within the multigenerational nuclear family structure contain both parental and filial care obligations central to the functioning of heteronormative familism that is crucial to the workings of heteronormativity in Singapore.

7 This is, of course, a contradiction in terms. If the heterosexual nuclear family really were inherently important, it would not require special protection; and if it does require special protection, then it cannot be inherently important.

8   Youyenn Teo, *Neoliberal Morality in Singapore: How Family Policies Make State and Society* (New York: Routledge, 2011), p. 102.

9   Stuart Hall and Alan O'Shea, 'Common-Sense Neoliberalism', *Soundings: A Journal of Politics and Culture*, 55.17 (2013), 9–25 (p. 8).

10 Antonio Gramsci, *Selections from the Prison Notebooks of Antonio Gramsci*, trans. Quintin Hoare and Geoffrey Smith (New York: International Publishers, 1971), p. 324; see also Stuart Hall, 'The Narrative Construction of Reality: An Interview with Stuart Hall', *Southern Review*, 17 (1984), 3–17.

11 Gramsci, *Selections from the Prison Notebooks*, p. 324.

12 John (Song Pae) Cho, '"Deferred Futures": The Diverse Imaginaries of Gay Retirement in Post-IMF South Korea', *Culture, Theory and Critique*, 58.2 (2017), 243–59 (p. 245).

13 Philip Holden, *Modern Subjects/Colonial Texts: Hugh Clifford & the Discipline of English Literature in the Straits Settlements & Malaya 1895–1907* (Greensboro: ELT Press, 2000), p. 48.

14 Ann Laura Stoler, 'Making Empire Respectable: The Politics of Race and Sexual Morality in 20th-Century Colonial Cultures', *American Ethnologist*, 16.4 (1989), 634–60 (p. 646).

15 'Discipline under Colonial Regulations CO850/170/1', The National Archives, UK; 'Straits Settlements Government Gazette CO276/148', 1938, The National Archives, UK.

16 Ann Laura Stoler, *Race and the Education of Desire: Foucault's History of Sexuality and the Colonial Order of Things* (Durham: Duke University Press, 1995). See also Ronald Hyam, *Empire and Sexuality: The British Experience* (Manchester: Manchester University Press, 1998).

17 Rahul Rao, *Out of Time: The Queer Politics of Postcoloniality* (New York: Oxford University Press, 2020), p. 8.

18 The PAP has formed the government in Singapore with an overwhelming parliamentary majority at every election since independence in 1965. See Chapters 1 and 2 for more on the PAP's role in cultivating nationalism in Singapore.

19 Kenneth Paul Tan and Gary Lee, 'Imagining the Gay Community in Singapore', *Critical Asian Studies*, 39.2 (2007), 179–204 (p. 185).

20 'Parliamentary Debates: Official Report' (Singapore: Hansard, 2007).

21 George Baylon Radics, 'Decolonizing Singapore's Sex Laws: Tracing Section 377A of Singapore's Penal Code', *Columbia Human Rights Law Review*, 45.1 (2013), 57–99 (p. 77).

22 Tan and Lee, 'Imagining the Gay Community', p. 186.

23 Gilles Kleitz, 'Why Is Development Work So Straight?', Queering Development Seminar Series (Brighton: Institute for Development Studies, 2000).

24 Monique Wittig, *The Straight Mind and Other Essays* (Boston: Beacon Press, 1992), pp. 40–43.

25 Michael Warner, 'Introduction', in *Fear of a Queer Planet: Queer Politics and Social Theory*, ed. Michael Warner (Minneapolis: University of Minnesota Press, 1993), pp. vii–xxxi (p. xxi).

26 Sara Ahmed, *Queer Phenomenology: Orientations, Objects, Others* (Durham: Duke University Press, 2006), p. 22.

27 Stuart Hall, 'Through the Prism of an Intellectual Life', in Stuart Hall, *Essential Essays*, Vol. II, *Identity and Diaspora*, ed. David Morley (Durham: Duke University Press, 2018), pp. 303–23 (p. 276).

28 Ahmed, *Queer Phenomenology*, p. 22.

29 Lynette J. Chua, *Mobilizing Gay Singapore: Rights and Resistance in an Authoritarian State* (Pennsylvania: Temple University Press, 2014); Audrey Yue and Jun Zubillaga-Pow, eds, *Queer Singapore: Illiberal Citizenship and Mediated Cultures* (Hong Kong: Hong Kong University Press, 2012); Robert Phillips, *Virtual Activism: Sexuality, the Internet, and a Social Movement in Singapore* (Toronto: University of Toronto Press, 2020).

30 Ng Yi-Sheng, *SQ21: Singapore Queers in the 21st Century* (Singapore: Oogachaga, 2006); Audrey Yue, 'Creative Queer Singapore: The Illiberal Pragmatics of Cultural Production', *Gay and Lesbian Issues and Psychology Review*, 3.3 (2007), 149–60; Chua, *Mobilizing Gay Singapore*.

31 Pink Dot SG, 'About', 2019, https://pinkdot.sg/about-pink-dot-sg/ (accessed 22 October 2019).

32 Dennis Altman, *Global Sex* (Chicago: University of Chicago Press, 2001).

33 Chua, *Mobilizing Gay Singapore*, p. 131.

34 Sally E. Merry, *Human Rights and Gender Violence: Translating International Law into Local Justice* (Chicago: University of Chicago Press, 2006); Michelle M. Lazar, 'Linguistic (Homo)Nationalism, Legitimacies, and Authenticities in Singapore's Pink Dot Discourse', *World Englishes* (2020), DOI: 10.1111/weng.12497; Pavan Mano, Adi Saleem Bharat, and Robert Phillips, eds, 'Pink Dot: Discursive Formations, Constructions, and Contestations', *Journal of Language and Sexuality*, 10.2 (2021), 97–215.

35 Shawna Tang, *Postcolonial Lesbian Identities in Singapore: Re-Thinking Global Sexualities* (London: Routledge, 2017); Phillips, *Virtual Activism*, pp. 10–12.

36 Eve Kosofsky Sedgwick, *Epistemology of the Closet* (Berkeley: University of California Press, 2005).

37 For more on how sexual minorities negotiate expressions of sexual identity differently, see Robert Phillips, ' "We Aren't Really That Different": Globe-Hopping Discourse and Queer Rights in Singapore', *Journal of Language and Sexuality*, 2.1 (2013), 122–44; Vincent Pak, 'Coming out "Softly": Metapragmatic Reflections of Gay Men in Illiberal Pragmatic Singapore', *Gender and Language*, 15.3 (2021), 301–23; and Pamela Mary Devan, 'Longing and Belonging in Queer Singapore: Navigating Outness through Pragmatic Acceptance', PhD thesis (Boston University, 2021); and Tang, *Postcolonial Lesbian Identities*.

38 Chua, *Mobilizing Gay Singapore*, p. 170.

39 TransgenderSG, 'Surgeries', https://transgendersg.com/surgeries/ (accessed 25 March 2024). It is also worth noting that gender affirming surgery can sometimes lead to permanent sterility. See, for example, Kristen Gelineau, 'Dubbed Torture, ID Policies Leave Transgender People Sterile', AP News, 2022, https://apnews.com/article/transgender-sterilization-e2cd525389eb17bf5201fa0fc babdbf3 (accessed 12 September 2024).

40 Audrey Yue, 'Trans-Singapore: Some Notes towards Queer Asia as Method', *Inter-Asia Cultural Studies*, 18.1 (2017), 10–24 (p. 14). Yue theorizes the state's stance as 'illiberal pragmatics' (p. 14) – I have a different reading and I will discuss it further along.

41 Reuters, 'Singapore's Lee Kuan Yew Questions Homosexuality Ban', 9 August 2007, www.reuters.com/article/world/singapores-lee-kuan-yew-questions-homo sexuality-ban-idUSSIN333510/ (accessed 12 September 2024).

42 'Speech to Parliament on Reading of Penal Code (Amendment) Bill' (Singapore: Hansard, 2007).

43 Relatedly, LGBT people and activists too (in Singapore and further afield) have leveraged the 'born this way' notion, using it to insist that because sexuality is biologically determined they should not be discriminated against. Whilst perhaps useful in an instrumental sense, it is also worth considering the stakes of hinging a case for equality on biology and genetics. See Janet E. Halley, 'Sexual Orientation and the Politics of Biology: A Critique of the Argument from Immutability', *Stanford Law Review*, 46.3 (1994), 67.

44 'Speech to Parliament on Reading of Penal Code (Amendment) Bill'.

45 See, for example, Tessa Oh, 'Living with Gender Dysphoria: Transgender Youths Face Stigma and Inadequate Institutional Support', *TODAY*, 21 March 2021, www.todayonline.com/singapore/living-gender-dysphoria-tran sgender-youths-face-stigma-and-inadequate-institutional-support (accessed 12 September 2024); and Beh Lih Yi, ' "Invisible yet Visible": Singapore's Transgender People Live in the Shadows', Reuters, 31 March 2019, www. reuters.com/article/world/invisible-yet-visible-singapores-transgender-people-live-in-the-shadows-idUSKCN1RC0B5/ (accessed 12 September 2024).

46 Dean Spade, *Normal Life: Administrative Violence, Critical Trans Politics, and the Limits of Law* (Durham: Duke University Press, 2015). I owe a debt of gratitude to Clara Bradbury-Rance for a conversation that helped me mine this seam.

47 For a history of the term, see Annamarie Jagose, *Queer Theory: An Introduction* (New York: New York University Press, 1996).

48 Audrey Yue, 'Queer Singapore: A Critical Introduction', in Yue and Zubillaga-Pow, *Queer Singapore*, pp. 1–29 (p. 4); Ng, *SQ21: Singapore Queers in the 21st Century*.

49 Lisa Duggan, *The Twilight of Equality? Neoliberalism, Cultural Politics, and the Attack on Democracy* (Boston: Beacon Press, 2003).

50 Cathy Cohen, 'Punks, Bulldaggers, and Welfare Queens: The Radical Potential of Queer Politics?', *GLQ: A Journal of Lesbian and Gay Studies*, 3 (1997), 437–65 (p. 438).

51 Michael Warner, ed., *Fear of a Queer Planet: Queer Politics and Social Theory* (Minneapolis: University of Minnesota Press, 1993), p. xxvi.

52 The New School, 'bell hooks: Are You Still a Slave? Liberating the Black Female Body', YouTube, 2014, www.youtube.com/watch?v=rJk0hNROvzs (accessed 12 September 2014).

53 Ibid.

54 Robyn Wiegman and Elizabeth A. Wilson, 'Introduction: Antinormativity's Queer Conventions', *Differences: A Journal of Feminist Cultural Studies*, 26.1 (2015), 1–25.

55 Judith Butler, *Undoing Gender* (New York: Routledge, 2004), p. 8.

56 Saba Mahmood, *Politics of Piety: The Islamic Revival and the Feminist Subject* (Princeton: Princeton University Press, 2005), p. 23.

57 Michael Warner, 'Something Queer about the Nation-State', in *After Political Correctness: The Humanities and Society in the 1990s*, ed. Christopher Newfield and Ronald Strickland (Boulder: Westview Press, 1995), pp. 361–71 (p. 368).

58 Eve Kosofsky Sedgwick, *Tendencies* (Durham: Duke University Press, 1993), p. 8.

59 Yue, 'Trans-Singapore'; Howard Chiang and Alvin K. Wong, 'Asia Is Burning: Queer Asia as Critique', *Culture, Theory and Critique*, 58.2 (2017), 121–26.

60 Natalie Oswin, 'The Modern Model Family at Home in Singapore: A Queer Geography', *Transactions of the Institute of British Geographers*, 35.2 (2010), 256–68 (p. 260).

61 Cohen, 'Punks, Bulldaggers, and Welfare Queens, p. 447 (emphasis in original).

62 Ibid., p. 440.

63 Warner, 'Introduction', p. vii.

64 Kath Browne, 'Challenging Queer Geographies', *Antipode*, 38.5 (2006), 885–93 (p. 888).

65 Urvashi Vaid, *Virtual Equality: The Mainstreaming of Gay and Lesbian Liberation* (New York: Anchor Books, 1995), p. 183.

66 Oswin, *Global City Futures*, p. 107.

67 Lauren Berlant and Michael Warner, 'Sex in Public', *Critical Inquiry*, 24.2 (1998), 547–66 (p. 553); See also Warner, *Fear of a Queer Planet*.

68 Ahmed, *Queer Phenomenology*, p. 21.

69 Sedgwick, *Tendencies*, pp. 6–7.

70 Adrienne Rich, 'Compulsory Heterosexuality and Lesbian Existence', *Signs: Journal of Women in Culture and Society*, 5.4 (1980), 631–60 (p. 637).

71 Nira Yuval-Davis, *Gender & Nation* (London: Sage Publications, 1997), p. 3.

72 There is an interesting distinction that the anthropologist Johannes Fabian makes between being denied a place in the normative and refusing to take up a place in the normative: whereas the former suggests marginalization, the latter opens the possibility of liberation. See Johannes Fabian, *Time and the Other: How Anthropology Makes Its Object* (New York: Columbia University Press, 2014), p. 154.

73 Ahmed, *Queer Phenomenology*, p. 161.

74 Radics, 'Decolonizing Singapore's Sex Laws'.

75 Meredith Weiss, 'Who Sets Social Policy in Metropolis? Economic Positioning and Social Reform in Singapore', *New Political Science*, 27.3 (2005), 267–89; Shawna Tang and Sharon Ee Ling Quah, 'Heteronormativity and Sexuality Politics in Singapore: The Female-Headed Households of Divorced and Lesbian Mothers', *Journal of Sociology*, 54.4 (2018), 647–64.

76 Chris K. K. Tan, ' "But They Are like You and Me": Gay Civil Servants and Citizenship in a Cosmopolitanizing Singapore', *City & Society*, 21.1 (2009), 133–54.

77 Kamalini Ramdas, 'Contesting Landscapes of Familyhood: Singlehood, the AWARE Saga and the Pink Dot Celebrations', in *Changing Landscapes of Singapore: Old Tensions, New Discoveries*, ed. Elaine Lynn-Ee Ho, Chih Yuan Woon, and Kamalini Ramdas (Singapore: NUS Press, 2013), pp. 109–25; Oswin, 'The Modern Model Family at Home in Singapore'.

78 Tang, *Postcolonial Lesbian Identities*; Kamalini Ramdas, 'Is Blood Thicker than Water? Single Indian Singaporean Women and the Geographies of "Being" Family', *Gender, Place & Culture*, 22.2 (2015), 255–70.

79 Kamalini Ramdas, 'Negotiating LGBTQ Rights in Singapore: The Margin as a Place of Refusal', *Urban Studies*, 58.7 (2020), 1–15; Michelle M. Lazar, 'Ideological Manoeuvres in and around Pink Dot: A Geopolitics of Gender/ Sexuality in Asia', *Journal of Language and Sexuality*, 10.2 (2021), 203–11.

80 Oswin, *Global City Futures*, p. 55.

81 Yue and Zubillaga-Pow, *Queer Singapore*.

82 See, for example, Meredith Woo-Cummings, ed., *The Developmental State* (Ithaca: Cornell University Press, 1999); and Robert Wade, *Governing the Market: Economic Theory and the Role of Government in East Asian Industrialization*, 2nd edn (Princeton: Princeton University Press, 2004).

83 Yue, 'Queer Singapore'.

84 Teo, *Neoliberal Morality in Singapore*; Ramdas, 'Is Blood Thicker than Water?'.

85 Pavan Mano, 'Disarming as a Tactic of Resistance in Pink Dot', *Journal of Language and Sexuality*, 10.2 (2021), 129–56; Michelle M. Lazar, 'Homonationalist Discourse as a Politics of Pragmatic Resistance in Singapore's Pink Dot Movement: Towards a Southern Praxis', *Journal of Sociolinguistics*, 21.3 (2017), 420–41.

86 Teo, *Neoliberal Morality in Singapore*, p. 11.

87 Chua Beng Huat, *Communitarian Ideology and Democracy in Singapore* (London: Routledge, 1995); Chua Beng Huat, *Political Legitimacy and Housing: Stakeholding in Singapore* (London: Routledge, 1997); Chua Beng Huat, *Life Is Not Complete without Shopping: Consumption Culture in Singapore* (Singapore: NUS Press, 2003); Yue, 'Queer Singapore'.

88 Chua, *Communitarian Ideology*, p. 59.

89 Chua, *Political Legitimacy and Housing*, p. 131.

90 Chua, *Communitarian Ideology*, p. 58.

91 Linda Low, 'The Singapore Developmental State in the New Economy and Polity', *The Pacific Review*, 14.3 (2001), 411–41 (p. 437); Chan Heng Chee and Sharon Siddique, with Irna Nurlina Masron and Dominic Cooray, *Singapore's Multiculturalism: Evolving Diversity* (London: Routledge, 2019).

92 Chua, *Mobilizing Gay Singapore*.

93 Eng-Beng Lim, 'The Mardi Gras Boys of Singapore's English-Language Theatre', *Asian Theatre Journal*, 22.2 (2005), 293–309 (p. 298). Also see Audrey Yue, 'Creative Queer Singapore: The Illiberal Pragmatics of Cultural Production', *Gay and Lesbian Issues and Psychology Review*, 3.3 (2007), 149–60.

94 Lazar, 'Homonationalist Discourse'; Lazar, 'Ideological Manoeuvres in and around Pink Dot'.

95 Chua, *Communitarian Ideology*, p. 185.

96 Hall, *Essential Essays*, Vol. II, p. 92.

97 Michel Foucault, *The History of Sexuality*, trans. Robert Hurley (New York: Pantheon Books, 1978), p. 144.

98 Michel Foucault, 'Afterword: The Subject and Power', in *Michel Foucault: Beyond Structuralism and Hermeneutics*, ed. Hubert L. Dreyfus, Paul Rabinow, and Michel Foucault, 2nd edn (Chicago: University of Chicago Press, 1983), pp. 208–26.

99 Ibid., p. 220.

100 Colin Gordon, 'Governmental Rationality: An Introduction', in *The Foucault Effect: Studies in Governmentality. With Two Lectures by and an Interview with Michel Foucault*, ed. Graham Burchell, Colin Gordon, and Peter Miller (Chicago: University of Chicago Press, 1991), pp. 1–52 (p. 48).

101 Foucault, *The History of Sexuality*, pp. 143–44.

102 Nikolas S. Rose, *Powers of Freedom: Reframing Political Thought* (Cambridge: Cambridge University Press, 2010), pp. 8–9.

103 Michel Foucault, *Discipline and Punish: The Birth of the Prison* (New York: Vintage, 1975).

104 There is also the compendium question that is arguably at least equally if not more important: exactly what is one being shut in with?

105 Julian Carter, 'Introduction. Theory, Methods, Praxis: The History of Sexuality and the Question of Evidence', *Journal of the History of Sexuality*, 14.1 (2005), 1–9 (p. 8).

106 Michel Foucault, *The Foucault Reader: An Introduction to Foucault's Thought*, ed. Paul Rabinow (London: Penguin Books, 1991), p. 80.

107 Hubert L. Dreyfus and Paul Rabinow, eds, *Michel Foucault: Beyond Structuralism and Hermeneutics* (Chicago: University of Chicago Press, 1982), p. 119.

108 David Garland, 'What Is a "History of the Present"? On Foucault's Genealogies and Their Critical Preconditions', *Punishment & Society*, 16.4 (2014), 365–84.

109 Kenneth Paul Tan, 'Meritocracy and Elitism in a Global City: Ideological Shifts in Singapore', *International Political Science Review*, 29.1 (2008), 7–27.

110 Chandan Reddy, 'Asian Diasporas, Neoliberalism, and Family', *Social Text*, 23.3–4 (2005), 101–19 (p. 115).

111 Anjali Arondekar, *For the Record: On Sexuality and the Colonial Archive in India* (Durham: Duke University Press, 2009).

112 Anjali Arondekar, 'Without a Trace: Sexuality and the Colonial Archive', *Journal of the History of Sexuality*, 14.1 (2005), 10–27 (p. 16).

113 Rao, *Out of Time*, p. 19.

114 Philip Holden, 'Coda', in *Imperial Desire: Dissident Sexualities and Colonial Literature*, ed. Philip Holden and Richard J. Ruppel (Minneapolis: University of Minnesota Press, 2003), pp. 295–322.

115 Nisha Eswaran, 'The Nation-State Is Not Our Friend: On Celebrating the Repeal of Section 377', *Jamhoor*, 2018, www.jamhoor.org/read/2018/11/6/the-nation-state-is-not-our-friend-on-celebrating-the-repeal-of-section-377-in-the-indian-diaspora (accessed 12 September 2024).

116 Foucault, *Discipline and Punish*, p. 31.

117 Hall, 'Through the Prism of an Intellectual Life', p. 279.

118 Michel Foucault, *The Birth of Biopolitics: Lectures at the Collège de France, 1978–1979* (New York: Palgrave, 2008), p. 130.

119 Teo, *Neoliberal Morality in Singapore*, p. 41.

120 Carl Schmitt, *The Concept of the Political*, trans. George Schwab (Chicago: University of Chicago Press, 2007).

121 Nadine El-Enany *(B)Ordering Britain: Law, Race and Empire* (Manchester: Manchester University Press, 2020).

122 Duggan, *The Twilight of Equality?*; Elizabeth Freeman, *Time Binds: Queer Temporalities, Queer Histories* (Durham: Duke University Press, 2010).

123 David L. Eng, *The Feeling of Kinship: Queer Liberalism and the Racialization of Intimacy* (Durham: Duke University Press, 2010); Jasbir K. Puar, *Terrorist Assemblages: Homonationalism in Queer Times* (Durham: Duke University Press, 2007).

124 Jasbir K. Puar, *The Right to Maim: Debility, Capacity, Disability* (Durham: Duke University Press, 2017), p. xviii.

125 Mignon Moore, 'Reflections on Marriage Equality as a Vehicle for LGBT Transformation', in *Queer Families and Relationships after Marriage Equality*, ed. Michael W. Yarbrough, Angela Jones, and Joseph Nicholas DeFilippis (London: Routledge, 2019), pp. 73–79.

126 Sivamohan Valluvan, *The Clamour of Nationalism: Race and Nation in Twenty-First Century Britain* (Manchester: Manchester University Press, 2019).

127 Puar, *Terrorist Assemblages*.

128 Chandra Talpade Mohanty, *Feminism without Borders: Decolonizing Theory, Practicing Solidarity* (Durham: Duke University Press, 2003).

129 Rahul Rao, 'Global Homocapitalism', *Radical Philosophy*, 194 (2015), 38–49.

130 Anna Triandafyllidou, 'National Identity and the "Other"', *Ethnic and Racial Studies*, 21.4 (1998), 593–612.

131 Ahmed, *Queer Phenomenology*, p. 22.

1

'Qu'est-ce qu'une nation?': nationalism, the illusion of nation, and the counter-nation

So long as an illusion is not recognized as an error, it has a value precisely equivalent to reality. But once the illusion has been recognized as such, it is no longer an illusion. It is, therefore, the very concept of illusion, and that concept alone, which is an illusion.[1]

The alliance between heteronormativity and the postcolonial nation

In 1882, Ernest Renan famously posed the question 'What is a nation?'.[2] He then answered his own question by suggesting 'the essence of a nation is that all individuals have many things in common, and also that they have forgotten many things'.[3] Renan was foregrounding the nation as a constructed political unit and his point was 'to deny any naturalistic determinism of the boundaries of nations', emphasizing that 'these are not dictated by language, geography, race, religion, or anything else'.[4] He went on to suggest what tied French people together was that 'every French citizen has to have forgotten the Saint Bartholomew's Day massacre, the massacres in the South in the 13th century'.[5] But there is an obligatory, almost disciplinary, register in Renan's turn of phrase – 'has to have' ('doit avoir oublié') – that betrays the fact that he is gesturing towards something more than mere forgetting. It is deliberately ignoring something – perhaps even an institutionalized efface-ment. We might think of this as a disavowal, something that must be excised from the national imaginary as well as an excision one must agree to in order to be considered a member of the nation. Reading Renan's argument on these terms – that to be French is to essentially agree on certain exclu-sions – it becomes clear that the nation is only able to generate its affects of membership, inclusion, and belonging through the vector of exclusion.

Heteronormative logics structure subjectivity in postcolonial independ-ent Singapore by producing a shared script whose performance determines one's substantive membership of the Singaporean nation. As the outcome of

a state-driven national project, a certain version of straightness is inextricably entwined with subjectivity in Singapore – which invites us to read it as
a straight nation. As the conceptual unit that legitimizes and gives meaning
to Singaporean subjectivity organized around heteronormativity, the nation
thus simultaneously places queerness outside its limits. It trades on the production and subsequent exclusion of various queered persons – and what we
need to explain are the mechanics of this process. In other words, what is
heteronormativity's role in Singaporean nationalism, and how does it work
to xenologize queered people?

The term *Singaporean subjectivity* denotes how subjectivity in Singapore
is produced through the interaction of various institutions and systems that
are animated by logics of heteronormativity. In addition to understanding
Singaporean subjectivity as subjectivity in Singapore, it also invites one to
consider how subjectivity is produced and legitimized through the conceptual frame of the nation. Before moving on to anything else, therefore,
I want to theorize the formation of the nation and locate heteronormativity's role within it. Further along in the book, I will focus on the production of subjectivity and the culpability of heteronormativity in this process,
but before that I want to give emphasis to the adjective *Singaporean* and
how it is marshalled in relation to subjectivity. This chapter therefore theorizes nationalism by examining the collusion between nationalism and the
governance of sexuality – I am interested in how heteronormativity can be
enlisted in service of nationalism. Reading heteronormativity as a national
project in postcolonial independent Singapore shows how queered subjectivity can be rendered non-Singaporean, or what I term counter-national, by
being placed outside the national imaginary under certain conditions.

It might be useful to bear in mind that the forces of nationalism do not
automatically terminate at the frontiers of the nation-state – they extend
into it, moving within the putative nation, cleaving it 'not just along the
lines suggested by the old debate about civic or ethnic forms, but also
according to race, gender, religion, and class'.[6] This book adds the governance of sexuality to the list because of the postcolonial state's obsession with
perpetuating a specific heteronormative vision of the nation built upon the
heterosexual nuclear family. Reading the Singapore story can show us how
admission into the Singaporean nation is contingent on a certain expression of straightness. And here, by Singapore story, I mean both the narration of Singapore's history as an independent postcolonial nation and *The
Singapore Story* – Lee Kuan Yew's memoirs – both of which stand in a relationship that 'is simultaneously one of synecdoche and metonym'.[7]

In and of itself, the induction of heteronormativity into processes of
subjectivization is not a new story – what we now recognize as queer studies emerged in response to the reification, reproduction, and privileging of

heteronormativity. Having been reclaimed and reappropriated by activists and academics in the late 1980s and early 1990s, *queer* at its best and most radical 'embraced literally anyone who refused to play by the rules of heteropatriarchy'.[8] On some level, this seductive radical inclusivity was too good to be true, and even in its initial iterations, *queer* carried its own sets of divisions, orthodoxies, and hierarchies.[9] Nonetheless, the intellectual significance of queer studies was that it brought about an approach to theorizing sexuality as more than just an identity category that opened new ways of interrogating the politics of sexuality. Fran Martin puts it this way: 'As 1990s feminist theory did with "women" and postcolonial theory did with "race" and "culture," queer theory was concerned to disrupt the assumed universality and internal coherence of previous categories of identification in "gay and lesbian identity".'[10] Queer critique thus allows us to move beyond an identarian-based analytic because it 'challenges the presumed fixity of sexual and gender identities and critiques the ways in which sexual and gender norms are deployed as part of broad structures of governance'.[11] Working along this intellectual trajectory, particularly through queer-of-colour critiques, plenty of scholars have explored 'the ways in which discourses of sexuality are inextricable from prior and continuing histories of colonialism, nationalism, racism, and migration'.[12] Queer studies thus often forwards a subject-less critique that allows us to focus on the force of heteronormativity and the concomitant process in which people are queered.[13] Operating in this style where nationalism is concerned, the ways in which queerness has been beckoned into the nationalist fold has also been studied.[14] Even if it has not (yet) been unravelled, then, the way the governance of sexuality is stitched into the tapestry of nationalism has been recognized.

Singapore presents an extraordinarily intense instantiation of this condition because heteronormativity is placed in an almost unchallenged alliance with the nation. It extends full membership of the nation only under very specific circumstances that are tied to the expression of a particular form of heterosexuality, and it is this alliance with heteronormativity that beckons us to read it as a straight nation. To restate a point I made in the introduction, heteronormativity is more than simply the privileging of heterosexuality or the policing of homosexuality. Heteronormativity propagates an 'institutionalized, normative heterosexuality [that] regulates those kept within its boundaries as well as marginalizing and sanctioning those outside them' as a form of 'double-sided social regulation'.[15] In Singapore, it has precipitated a 'state valorisation and entrenchment of the narrow heteronormative ideal [and] has shaped the official positions of institutions and their agents'.[16] Through a range of mechanisms that we will see in the sections and chapters to follow, the state has an outsize capacity to make this heteronormative vision congruent with the nation – particularly through the elevation and regulation of the Singaporean family 'defined in the narrow and specific terms of a legally married [heterosexual] couple and their children, with the husband as head of the household'.[17] It is in this precise sense that I mean the alliance between heteronormativity and the Singaporean nation is quite extraordinary.

In his *History of Sexuality*, Foucault argues that 'a normalizing society is the historical outcome of a technology of power centred on life'.[18] Despite appearing to theorize virtually everything, however, Foucault had comparatively little to say about nations or nationalism. So whilst the Foucauldian approach certainly serves us well in showing the power of heteronormativity in rationalizing, organizing, and hierarchizing social relations, this alone is insufficient to fully draw out what is at stake when this normalizing power is exercised in the name of the nation. Introducing the nation into the calculus has significant implications because not only can queered people be subjectivized differently and consequently displaced from the national imaginary, but queerness also plays a psychically central role within the nation as its spectral antithesis. Queerness and queered people can be configured as the backdrop of otherness against which the putative nation is imagined.

Heteronormativity in Singapore is a project of governmentality and the postcolonial state's nation-building project continually legitimizes it. Even though governmentality as a form of modern disciplinary power emerged from colonialism, colonial power was always incapable of properly fulfilling it. Its obsession with perpetuating colonizer/colonized, enlightened/brute, civilized/native distinctions meant that 'the colonial state was necessarily incapable of fulfilling the criterion of representativeness – the fundamental condition that makes modern power a matter of interiorized self-discipline rather than external coercion'.[19] The postcolonial nation, however, offered 'the possibility of fulfilling the project of governmentality of which colonialism dreamed, but which it could never realize'.[20] Heteronormativity was placed front and centre in this project, and its institution 'would be perfected not by the colonialists but by the new nations that emerged from colonialism' – as such, it fell upon the PAP government, the men in white, to do what the white men could not achieve in Singapore.[21]

Beyond imagined communities: the constitutive antipathies of nationalism

As an organizing principle 'which holds that the political and the national unit should be congruent',[22] nationalism has proven an extremely resilient mode through which people living in a certain bordered territory are taught to understand themselves and relate to each other as a group. The nation as a concept first emerged in the Romantic period as a response to the Enlightenment's veneration of the individual and cold reason. Led by the likes of Herder, Goethe, and Schiller, this cultivation of a collective national spirit spread across Western Europe in particular, and the nation has become the hegemonic conceptual frame through which the modern state has realized itself. This model is typically understood as the primordial/perennialist conception of the nation that claims it is an eternal representation of an ethnic, linguistic, or religious group of people.[23] Since the 1980s, however, this conception of the nation has largely been displaced by constructivist theories of the nation.[24] Chiefly responsible for this was Benedict Anderson's *Imagined Communities* – arguably the most influential publication in nations and nationalism scholarship – which established the idea of the nation as an abstraction – or, in his words, an 'imagined political community'.[25]

Anderson rejects the foundational assumption of an a-priori homogeneity in the Herderian nation, insisting that 'from the start the nation was conceived in language, not in blood'.[26] For him, language 'is not an instrument of exclusion: in principle, anyone can learn any language. On the contrary, it is fundamentally inclusive.'[27] Since membership of the nation was contingent on language, Anderson argues that 'one could be "invited into" the imagined community'.[28] *Imagined Communities* is an exceedingly optimistic account of nationalism – a romanticization that other liberal modernist theories of the nation shared.[29] When this theorization was challenged, it was typically on account of its apparent spontaneity. Ernest Gellner, for example, suggests that instead of an organic process, the nation emerged as a result of an active state-led curatorial process. It is 'homogeneity imposed by objective, inescapable imperative [that] eventually appears on the surface in the form of nationalism'.[30] The imperative that he speaks of is the economic imperative and he argues that 'industrial or industrializing society is profoundly allergic to counter-entropic institutions'.[31] Regardless of their disagreements over precisely how the nation emerged, however, the thread that binds liberal modernist theories of the nation is the conception of the nation as an internally homogeneous project – and this is precisely their limit. Despite disagreeing in their respective genealogical theorizations of the nation, they view the nation itself through the rose-tinted, or -tainted, lens of belonging whilst considering exclusion a benign by-product.

It can seem terribly trite to make this point that the nation operates with a register of exclusion. After all, anybody who does not happen to belong to a particular group is, by definition, excluded. The particular will always strike a note of exclusion in relation to the universal. So to say the nation excludes some people can appear to be stating a rather bland and boring

fact. But what this sleight of hand conceals is that the nation not only operates with a register of exclusion – exclusion is all it has. Belonging writes
itself by dipping into the inkwell of exclusion. As Anna Triandafyllidou
puts it, '[the] identity of a nation is defined and/or re-defined through the
influence of "significant others", namely other nations or ethnic groups that
are perceived to threaten the nation, its distinctiveness, authenticity and/or
independence'.[32] The nation is saturated with exclusions, rife with cleav-
ages, persistently conjuring up the figure of the *xenos* – a point that an entire
swath of nations and nationalism scholarship has contrived to look past.
It continually concocts the fiction that 'the population over which a state
rules is an organic community which precedes any attempt to manage it'.[33]
Anderson is correct in theorizing the nation as an entity that produces a community capable of imagining itself as a 'we'. But what he fails to account for
is the qualifier that the '"we" made of inclusion, acceptance and confirma-
tion is the realm of gratifying safety cut out (though never securely enough)
from the frightening wilderness of the outside populated by "them".'[34] It is
therefore better to understand nationalism as a fundamentally xenologizing
operation that works through division – setting up dangerous foreign figures (*xenos*) against which the nation can continually be rendered relevant
through particular rationalizing logics (*logos*). The illusion of the nation
and belonging is imagined against this production of exclusion, which does
not necessarily terminate at the state's formal frontiers. For, instead of an
internally homogeneous space, the nation is in fact a heterogeneous 'multi-
status' space – and where one is located in this space has important implications for the legitimacy of being there and continuing to remain there.[35] It
is no coincidence that the quintessential comments that mark an individual
out as someone who does not belong are 'Where are you *really* from?' and
'Go back to where you came from!'. What nationalism does is to produce a
series of 'internal borders' within the putative nation itself that operate on
various groups of people who are differentiated and hierarchized according
to particular logics that are made salient across different spaces and times.[36]
In this way, nationalism both creates and perpetuates an 'endemic nervousness in [the] nations it spawns',[37] maintaining the nation in a constant state
of heightened alert to otherness within it that needs to be expelled.

  Those working in the critical traditions of cultural studies and sociology
have articulated the internal divisions wrought by nationalism to give the
lie to the apparent internal homogeneity of the nation. In the same decade
that liberal theories of the nation were taking hold, Paul Gilroy demonstrated how the idea of the nation is contingent on racial exclusion, and how
nationalism can work through racism. In *There Ain't No Black in the Union
Jack*, Gilroy argues that 'the politics of "race" ... is fired by conceptions of
national belonging and homogeneity which not only blur the distinction

between "race" and nation but rely on that very ambiguity for their effect'.[38] It is worth bearing in mind, therefore, that the 'blurring of the vocabularies of nationality and race is a founding strategy of the modern (nation) state'.[39]

Liberal theories of the nation that read it as a receptacle of homogeneous belonging cannot analytically handle this point, primarily because it would require a fundamentally different reading of the nation itself. Sivamohan Valluvan summarizes this by saying 'The complacency about the nation stems from a simple misunderstanding [that] misreads the nation as a politics of belonging as opposed to a politics of enmity; a matter of strong collective feeling as opposed to a matter of strong aversion.'[40] The assumption of a nation's internal homogeneity is as misguided as it is false because it does not account for the fact that 'it is the generally pathologized identification of those who do not belong that acts as the container for the remaining entity of belonging'.[41] And despite some differences that I will articulate presently, I share the overarching sensibility that the conceptual architecture of the nation is scaffolded by otherness instead of belonging. The basin of belonging that nationalism offers often appears benign but remains contingent on expelling figures of the foreign. As Gargi Bhattacharyya argues, 'Citizenship takes its meaning from the implication that there is an outside, a space of non-citizenship where such rights and entitlements do not apply.'[42]

Whilst this body of nationalism scholarship I am holding hands with theorizes nationalism essentially as 'the making present of the iconic ethnic absence',[43] the argument I am making in this book operates on a slightly different register by taking the relationship between heteronormativity and nationalism as its starting point. To a degree, this is inflected by the postcolonial state's overt embrace of a putative multicultural racial politics. But I neither want to suggest we ignore the problematic of 'race' in the constitution of the nation nor that heteronormativity is to be substituted for racism. As I stated in the opening of the book, we know that heteronormativity does not operate purely along the axis of sexuality; it multiplies across axes of 'race', gender, class, and more, and incorporates them into its operations. It propagates a 'sense of rightness' about a particular performance of heterosexuality.[44] It is 'the geographically and historically specific coincidence of "race", class, gender, and sexual norms that reaches far beyond sexual and gender-identity struggles to shape familial and intimate relationships, domestic norms, migration flows, national identities, and more', and the coincidence of these differences can produce substantively different heteronormative expectations.[45]

Remember, for example, how the putative sexual puritanism that, until early 2023, lay manifest in Section 377A of the Penal Code and greatly facilitated a dimension of heteronormativity in postcolonial Singapore, in fact flows from an anterior racial puritanism operating as part of the machinery of colonialism.

The colonial project was certainly a racialized project but it was also a gendered and sexualized one.[46] Because of the postcolonial state's avowed commitment to a multicultural or multiracial politics, however, the relationship between 'race' and nationalism in Singapore can often be submerged in the official discourses of the state. In this context, heteronormativity can become a key modality for the expression of nationalism.

At the point of its independence in 1965, Singapore comprised a multiethnic population. Approximately 75 per cent of people were Chinese, 15 per cent were Malays, and 8 per cent were Indians, with the remaining 2 per cent made up of Eurasians and other ethnic groups. I will return to this (frankly, untenable) classificatory schema in a moment but for now I want to note that whilst the fact of Singapore's multiethnic population is not unusual in a postcolonial nation, its ethnic make-up in relation to the postcolonial nation is quite singular largely as a result of the British colonial project. Syed Hussein Alatas documents in *The Myth of the Lazy Native* how, in the colonial period, indigenous Malays in British Malaya refused to cooperate with the British by working in the colonial plantations – efforts that resulted in British colonial officials summarily designating them as 'lazy'.[47] The success of imperial wealth extraction therefore had to be hitched to the wagon of indentured and imported labour that primarily comprised Chinese and Indian migrants.[48] The consequent inflow of migrants through the colonial period reshaped Singapore's ethnic composition and created an overwhelming Chinese majority, which meant that when it eventually became independent in 1965:

> the largest ethnic group [the Chinese] had no proprietary claim to the land, and … the nominally indigenous group [the Malays] was a distinct demographic minority. This demographic distribution meant that no conventional unity of race, land and culture could be evoked as the 'organic' basis for a new nation.[49]

Beyond these specific local conditions, it is also probably worth keeping in the back of our minds the global historical moment in 1965. The first and second worlds, capitalism and communism, were wrestling for global hegemony; Francis Fukuyama had yet to trumpet the end of history; and three-quarters of Singapore ostensibly represented the diasporic extension of the largest communist state in Asia. By any rudimentary geopolitical calculus, there was a good chance that attempting to govern as a majoritarian Chinese nation-state would attract imperialistic attention – from the USA this time. Upon independence therefore, Singapore immediately 'declared itself a constitutionally multiracial state'.[50]

It is because of this historicity that I suggest we ought to pay a little more attention to how 'race' operates as a category of difference in Singaporean

nationalism.[51] Because of its historical contingency, the set of racializations that the postcolonial government inherited, and its subsequent constitutional commitment to a very specific form of multiracialism, 'race' and
ethnicity can appear to be defanged as carriers of xenology within formal
discourses of the state – how it narrates itself and the nation. To be clear,
I am not dismissing 'race' in the nationalist conjuring – it remains relevant
as a maker of difference within the nation and thus in the lived social realities of racially minoritized subjects. But across the discursive terrain produced through the state's official speech acts, 'race' can seem to operate as a
second-order category that is submerged – even if Singaporean nationalism
still produces racialized outcomes – and this is in no insignificant part due to
the postcolonial state's formal commitment to multiracialism.

The Constitution enshrines this commitment to multiracialism, recognizing the three largest ethnic groups (the Chinese, Malays, and Indians) in
Singapore, and commits to treating them equally.[52] At the same time, racial
difference is taken to be a powder keg that requires active state management. 'Race' is deemed too sensitive for non-state-affiliated actors and ordinary citizens to engage with; therefore 'race' and its associated discourses
are marked as dangerous topics that must not be broached by ordinary
citizens, especially in the public sphere. In addition to state rhetoric, the
transformation of 'race' into a discourse that must not be invoked is given
further weight through a number of legal instruments such as the Sedition
Act, the Maintenance of Religious Harmony Act, and the forthcoming
Maintenance of Racial Harmony Act,[53] which further accent 'race' and ethnicity as dangerous topics. This is also why, when the government relaxed
laws regulating public speech and demonstrations in the 2000s, it added the
explicit proviso that topics concerning 'race' were precluded. These matters
are to be handled exclusively by the state, which places itself 'structurally
above race, as the neutral umpire that oversees and maintains racial peace
and racial equality'.[54] This self-designated role as arbiter of race relations
and racial equality goes some way to explaining why, as we traverse the
state's discursive ground, 'race' can seem less visibly salient as a category of
difference even if this does not necessarily correspond to the lived realities
of racially minoritized subjects.

Producing otherness in postcolonial independent Singapore

At the opening of independent Singapore's first Parliament, prime minister
Lee Kuan Yew said:

> independence has given us a unique opportunity to order our way of life, and
> I would like to believe that the two years we spent in Malaysia are years which

will not be easily forgotten, years in which the people of migrant stock here who are a majority learnt of the terrors and the follies and the bitterness which is generated when one group tries to assert its dominance over the other on the basis of one race, one language, one religion. It is because of this that my colleagues and I were determined, as from the moment of separation, that this lesson will never be forgotten. So it is that into the Constitution of the Republic of Singapore will be built safeguards, in so far as the human mind can devise means whereby the conglomeration of numbers, of likeness, as a result of affinities of race or language or culture, shall never work to the detriment of those who, by the accident of history, find themselves in minority groups in Singapore.[55]

Singapore's assertion of independence on the back of separation from Malaysia happened after a period of conflict that had manifested quite fiercely in three days of riots in 1964.[56] Whilst some scholars and historians have questioned ascribing the cause of these riots to racial and religious differences, in official state discourse they have been narrated as conflicts where 'race' (and religion) were the significant causal factors.[57] Postcolonial Singapore's state of independence and sense of self are therefore intimately tied to a paranoia surrounding the volatility of 'race' left ungoverned. It is not for nothing that Singapore's National Pledge begins with 'We, the citizens of Singapore, pledge ourselves as one united people, *regardless of race, language or religion* …'.[58] 'Race', language, and religion were the primary fault lines that the postcolonial state was both anxious about and keen to smooth over.

A consequence of gaining independence in this crucible of apparent racial chaos was that '[a] negative impression of the volatility of race was formed and ingrained in the psyche of the founding fathers of the nation, which was passed down to later generations of leaders'.[59] For Lee Kuan Yew, his PAP government, and successive PAP governments through to the current one, 'race' and ethnicity are always simultaneously a potential 'terror' as well as a 'lesson'; and the peace and racial harmony achieved through multiracialism[60] are always emphasized as potentially fracturable things.[61] The government constantly reiterates the fragility of the country's multiracial society by invoking the historical spectre of racial conflict in the formation of the nation; it affirms the importance of multiracialism whilst suggesting at the same time that 'Singaporeans must remain constantly vigilant as potential racial conflict lies just beneath the thin veneer of harmony.'[62] In state discourse, 'race' is thus always dangerous, rendered something that people must avoid invoking because of the potential turmoil that might be unleashed again; and the state is the only agent with the capacity to manage this inflammable interaction of 'races'.

Since independence, then, the PAP government has nailed its colours to the mast of multiracialism with explicit assurances that the three main ethnic groups in Singapore could expect to be treated equally, whilst simultaneously recognizing the special position of the Malays as locally indigenous. Singapore's brand of multiracialism formally accords 'equal status to the cultures and ethnic identities of the various "races" that are regarded as comprising the population of a plural society'.[63] And if here, in the term *plural society*, one spies the ruts of colonialism, one would not be mistaken, for the mural of Singapore's multiracialism is painted with the limited palette provided by the colonial classificatory system: the Chinese-Malay-Indian-Others (CMIO) model. The CMIO model is yet another colonial inheritance from the British, who, whilst like any proper colonial power were quite concerned with perpetuating a racial hierarchy privileging whiteness, 'were also concerned with the management and regulation of heterogeneity outside of the "motherland" '.[64] In this sense, Singapore's brand of multiracialism is a residue of the old colonial conviction that in the absence of an 'organic social will' between different 'races' chaos would ensue.[65] The concomitant CMIO model provides a conceptual framework and racializing infrastructure through which the government aims to maintain racial order within the nation. As a consequence, '[e]ven after over 50 years of decolonization ... ethnic relations and national politics still revolve around the racial categories used by the British colonial state to enumerate the population in its census'.[66]

The CMIO model recognizes the Chinese, Malays, and Indians as the three largest ethnic groups in Singapore. Everyone else is classified, unironically, as Others. The CMIO model gives the state an infrastructural tool of racialization to divide people into neat essentialized containers through which it has institutionalized its bureaucratic approach to managing the population and the interaction of the various 'races'. For instance, it informs the Ethnic Integration Policy (EIP), which works as part of the state's massive public housing programme (Chapter 2). The EIP controls the ethnic composition of individual blocks of HDB flats by setting ethnic quotas that effectively mirror the ethnic make-up of the nation,[67] such that only fixed percentages of flats in any given block can be occupied by Chinese, Malays, and Indians respectively. In addition to individual blocks of flats, entire neighbourhoods are also managed (albeit with slightly looser ethnic quotas that can fluctuate within 3 per cent of the national ethnic make-up). Taken together, the EIP 'ensures that the ethnic mix in all public housing estates reflect[s] the ethnic mix of Singapore'.[68]

The policy is justified on the basis of promoting social interaction between 'races' and ethnic groups as well as preventing the formation of 'ethnic enclaves'.[69] The former deputy prime minister and current president, Tharman Shanmugaratnam, rationalized the EIP by saying:

> once people live together, they're not just walking their corridors together every day and taking the same elevators up and down; their kids go to the same kindergartens, the same primary schools. Because all over the world, young kids go to schools very near to where they live. And they grow up together.[70]

Tharman has emerged as a most enthusiastic flag-bearer for this 'policy of intrusive integration' as he calls it.[71] If he is given the opportunity at a suitable pulpit, the chances are good that he will preach the PAP government's approach to multiculturalism. And whilst one might agree with Tharman on the general virtue of different people living together, what he quite conveniently elides is that the EIP does not simply legislate diversity and social mixing; it regulates both the nature and extent of that diversity. It permits only certain forms of diversity; and it permits only certain levels of social mixing. Again, to echo a point I made at the outset, it is important to remember that if colonial bequests continue to enjoy a rich afterlife, it is often only because the postcolonial state has made an active choice to grant them that afterlife. In this case, the state has built on residual colonial architecture that racializes brown minorities as threats that need to be contained. For, lest it be forgotten, in mandating that the HDB block strictly reflect the ethnic make-up of the nation, almost to the exact percentage point, the so-called 'ethnic enclaves' that the state is ostensibly keen to avoid fostering are only conceivable as brown (Indian or Malay) enclaves; every single HDB block, precinct, and neighbourhood in Singapore is, by the state's own definition, actively maintained as a Chinese enclave because of 'the accident of history', as Lee Kuan Yew put it.[72]

On the occasions the EIP has been challenged, it has generally been critiqued through an appeal to free market logics.[73] Because they are generally only able to sell their HDB flats to people from the same ethnic group, there is certainly a sound economic argument that the EIP imposes real material costs on ethnic minorities by limiting their selling options in the housing market compared to the ethnic Chinese majority.[74] Framing the issue in these terms goes some way towards demonstrating the unfair outcomes that can issue from the EIP and probably helps garner some measure of sympathy from those who are less affected. But choosing not to engage with its foundational racialized logic also lets it off the hook for its role as a tool of racialization. To debate whether the EIP is a good way of managing racial difference, however, risks missing the forest for the trees. The larger point here is that only through the filter of the CMIO model is racial difference rendered governable in Singapore. And the question that Tharman and the cohort of cheerleaders who champion this policy as a uniquely Singaporean achievement need to answer – but are never asked – is why their self-styled version of social mixing should require the specific maintenance of a Chinese demographic majority.

This is the racialized logic that is taken for granted not just as necessary but as an inherent good in Singaporean nationalist discourse. The PAP government's obsession with maintaining the extant ethnic make-up of the nation and 'preserving [its] racial balance'[75] also informs its race-based immigration policy.[76] This is something the government has repeatedly affirmed openly both in Parliament and in other official speeches.[77] In 2012, for example, responding to a motion on population and immigration policy, Grace Fu, minister in the Prime Minister's Office, said: 'We recognise the need to maintain the racial balance in Singapore's population in order to preserve social stability. The pace and profile of our immigration intake have been calibrated to preserve this racial balance.'[78] Four days later, the prime minister confirmed and reiterated these sentiments.[79] Again, one should remain alert to the link drawn between the maintenance of racial proportions, the maintenance of social stability, and how it ultimately relies on a latent logic that regards brownness as a problem.[80]

Singapore's brand of multiracialism extends further into nominal racial categories given by the CMIO model with a set of racializations particular to each ethnic community.[81] Another major site of the operation of racialization is the governance of languages.[82] Whilst Malay is designated the national language to recognize Malay indigeneity in Singapore, the state also recognizes 'Mandarin, Malay, and Tamil as the official mother tongues of the major ethnic communities: Mandarin for the Chinese, Malay for the Malays, and Tamil for the Indians'.[83] A fourth official language, the language of education, and the working language in Singapore, is English. It is 'the language of public administration, commerce, and industry because it was deemed to be the language that would enable the most direct and efficient path towards acquiring the technological and scientific knowledge necessary for a modern industrial economy'.[84]

Filtered through the CMIO model of racialization, English acquires a particular neutrality through its apparent equidistant separation from all the recognized ethnic communities. Because it does not 'belong' to any of the ethnic communities, it becomes equally 'foreign' to all of them.[85] For it to function as the county's lingua franca is rationalized as fair because it purportedly does not privilege any individual ethnic community. This neat ethnolinguistic set-up conveniently leaves out that English was the language of colonial administration, and it was effectively already the working language for the colonizer-adjacent class of people who worked as part of the colonial bureaucracy, thereby privileging them and their children. To paraphrase

Hall, this set-up also had the effect of turning language into a modality through which class was (and continues to be) realized.[86]

The neutralization and deracialization of English also simultaneously racializes Mandarin, Malay, and Tamil. To deploy these languages – particularly in official, formal, and institutional settings – is to confer an ethnic specificity to the message. It is a long-standing tradition, for instance, that whilst the prime minister delivers the National Day Rally speech in English, the English speech is in fact preceded by short segments in Chinese and Malay; these segments are essentially directed towards that particular ethnic community and they tend to revolve around topics that are loosely linked to a specific racialized concern.[87] This is also why the LGBT movement Pink Dot ensures its messaging is almost entirely delivered in English; and in the instances when the other official languages are used, such as in its video captions, all three non-English official languages are represented to avoid imputing any ethnic specificity to their message – and to avoid being accused of invoking 'race'.[88]

English was framed as necessary, both to provide a common language for all Singaporeans to communicate with each other, and for Singapore to be able to plug in to global trade networks. But at the same time, the state fretted that solely communicating in English would result in Singaporeans losing their 'traditional cultures and values' and individual ethnic specificities.[89] English is, in this way, regarded as 'Western' and foreign to Singapore – something that is materially necessary but potentially culturally damaging (a logic that foreshadows the Asian values master discourse that we will encounter later in Chapter 4). The various ethnic communities' respective mother tongues were thus constructed as vital to 'preserving for each child that cultural ballast and appreciation of [their] origin and [their] background'.[90]

Religion, the third category named in the National Pledge as a site of difference, also plays a role in the enterprise of racialization – though in quite imprecise and often clumsy ways. In 1968, for example, the PAP government amended the Holidays Act to reduce the total number of public holidays in a year.[91] Public holidays were revised and reallocated according to a logic of ethnic parity using the CMIO model. As such, the first two days of Chinese New Year were retained as public holidays and meant to function as holidays for the Chinese community, Hari Raya Haji and Hari Raya Puasa (the two Muslim holy days of Eid) were recognized as holidays for the Malay community, Deepavali (a Hindu festival) and Vesak Day (a Buddhist festival) were recognized as holidays for the Indian community, and Christmas and Good Friday (both Christian occasions) were designated holidays for the Eurasian community that is often lumped into the category of 'Others'.

The vast majority of Malays are also Muslims, so the racializing logic largely holds up, and intriguingly for the Chinese community an ethnic holiday precedes any religious one. It is where the Indian community is concerned, however, that it most clearly breaks down: first, because the Indian–Hindu nexus is not as strong as is made out to be in the state's matrix – first, there are a significant number of Indians who are Muslim or Christian; and second, because there are hardly any Indian Buddhists in Singapore – the vast majority of Buddhists in Singapore are ethnically Chinese. Vineeta Sinha and George Radics thus note that 'The decision to "count" Vesak Day as a holiday for the Indians has been controversial from the outset [because it] has been perceived by the Indian community as a day that has more significance for the Chinese Buddhist community in Singapore.'[92] Having said all that, I do not want to litigate much further the varied dissonances of the CMIO model; instead, I want to point out the limits of this brand of multiracialism, which hinges on the 'politics of recognition'.[93] Whilst the state's gaze can recognize and legitimize particular categories as available for inclusion in the nation, it can simultaneously fix and freeze particular ways of being that are unlikely to cohere adequately.[94] As Lois McNay argues, the valorization of recognition generally fails to account for the role and power of the 'agents who bestow recognition'.[95] This is what makes the CMIO model such an untenable system of categorization: it views the nation as eternally comprising three fixed, discrete, homogeneous ethnic groups that can be defined through particular racialized scripts.[96]

Nonetheless, despite its ponderous qualities, the state's commitment to the CMIO as an infrastructural tool means that the nation–ethnicity nexus operates with a legitimate, albeit limited pluri-ethnicity where the Chinese, Malay, and Indian communities are seen as coterminous with the nation. These racialized ethnic categories are, of course, further narrowed by linguistic and religious specificities that preclude, for example, a Telugu-speaking Indian or a Chinese Muslim from being a principal national subject.[97] But this is not to say that they are immediately xenologized and cast as foreign. After all, 'there is nothing solid or permanent' to 'race' – its meaning is made through 'the shifting relations of difference'.[98]

The inherited CMIO model that the state continues to swear by is a closed, insular and ultimately, hopeless, model that is unable to account for either the flows of racialized discourses or the flow of racialized populations of people. The multiple accumulated layers of meaning and assumptions that are imbricated in this model reflect the way racialized modes of belonging can be quite flexible. Plenty of Singaporeans confound the obdurate specificities of racialization in the country and fail to fit the portraits of the prototypical racialized subject but are ostensibly recognized as members of the nation nonetheless: 'No, you may not neatly fit into the CMIO model but *we* know you are one of *us*.'[99] 'Race' and ethnicity intersect with language intersects with religion to produce a set of prototypical racialized categories that are used to govern the Singaporean nation. Because of this complex Mobius strip of racialization, and the way it is parsed through the prism of equality, 'race' functions like a kaleidoscope in Singapore: it disseminates the subject into an array of positions and can be quite difficult to pin down. Despite the set of racializations that operate as part of nationalism in Singapore, what or who 'is' Singaporean can be messy and hard to define; what or who is *not* Singaporean, however, is much easier to point towards.

Whilst I do not disagree with the position that multiculturalism basically functions as an 'instrument of social control' in Singapore, we should pay attention to what it *does* accomplish – the perpetuation of a society divided along the lines of 'race' and ethnicity that requires active state management.[100] It rationalizes the state's move to turn 'race' into a kind of radioactive discourse – everyone can see it is there, knows too well that it is there, is told many times over that it is there but cannot actually go there and interact with it. 'Race' and ethnicity must be kept at a distance and can only be dealt with by nominated 'specialists' who are qualified to handle it – namely the state or state-affiliated actors. As a consequence, the production of otherness that nationalism requires is not always conducted explicitly through 'race' or ethnicity. This does not completely detach it from nationalism's operations – Singaporean nationalism is fully capable of conjuring up racialized others.

In 2014, for example, the Filipino/a community in Singapore attempted to organize their annual Independence Day celebration at Ngee Ann City Civic Plaza, a mall in Singapore's shopping district. Their announcement was met with a barrage of online abuse that eventually led to the organizers cancelling their plans – the first time in 20 years that they had had to do so.[101] Despite some claims that the pushback was to do with matters of sovereignty or people occupying an 'iconic' public space,[102] there was clearly a racialized dimension to this xenophobia – and here, one gets a glimpse of the set of racializations that operate under the sign of xenophobia in Singaporean nationalism. It was not a coincidence that the vitriol was directed at a group of brown Southeast Asians who, in the nationalist set-up, are classified as incompatible with the nation. In contrast, the American community in Singapore regularly organizes celebrations in public spaces commemorating the Fourth of July, with the 2023 iteration literally describing the Bay East Bridge venue as 'iconic and super cool'.[103] The Irish community too routinely celebrates St Patrick's Day by the Singapore River. None of these events attracts the kind of hostility directed towards Filipino/a organizers in 2014 – and neither should they. But the difference in hostility ought to be noted because it reflects how, whilst the predominantly white Irish and

American communities are certainly also recognized as foreign, unlike the Filipino/a community they are categorized as desirable non-citizens who are compatible with the nation.

At the same time, we cannot ignore how the device of Singaporean multi-racialism can appear to neutralize ethnicity as a channel of exclusion *within* the putative nation – and I do not think we have yet explained sufficiently multiracialism's purchase in submerging 'race' as a category of difference both in state discourse and in how it narrates the nation, as well as why that move works. Geopolitics and the institutional memory of racial riots may explain why the postcolonial PAP government elevated multiracialism as an organizing principle; but they do not sufficiently explain the widespread legitimacy that multiracialism continues to retain as an organizing principle of the Singaporean nation – even if only rhetorically. Put simply, the politicians may say they believe it, but why do the people believe it? To say that multiracialism is orthodoxy because Singapore was committed to multiracialism from its beginnings as an independent country is an unconvincing tautology. Instead, I want to suggest that multiracialism gains its cachet in Singaporean nationalism in contrast to Malaysia – the nation it severed itself from.

When Singapore separated from Malaysia, Lee Kuan Yew stressed it was because he had envisioned a ' "Malaysian Malaysia" not a Malay Malaysia'.[104] This rationalization of the two countries' separation turned the principle of majoritarian ethnic hegemony (nominally, at least) into a principle antonymic to Singapore. The cause for the geographical split was ostensibly this ideological rift. The principle of Malay hegemony was positioned as irreconcilable to the point where Singapore had to completely remove itself from Malaysia.[105] Singapore's establishment, therefore, is rhetorically tied to the rejection of majoritarian ethnic hegemony and the embrace of a politics of multiculturalism. The principle of a Malay Malaysia functioned as a bulwark for the principle of multiracialism in Singapore. What makes multiracialism so salient in relation to Singaporean nationalism is that it appears the logical opposite of Malaysia's system of governance. The Singaporean nation is putatively built on multiracialism because Malaysia is not; what makes us 'us' is that 'we' are multiracial whilst 'they' are not. Multiracialism in Singapore works in the backwash of the Malaysian idea of Malay primacy.

Singapore's foundational commitment to multiracialism can thus be read in relation to the Malaysian insistence on Malay primacy. Its legitimacy can be located as emerging in the wake of casting Malaysia as what 'we' are not. In addition to racializing members of the Singaporean nation, therefore, multiracialism gains its legitimacy by positioning itself in an antithetical relation with Malaysia. It gives valence to the principle of multiracialism within the Singaporean nation and, to a certain extent, insures against the overt production of certain ethnic absences within state discourse as a modality of nationalism because that is precisely not who 'we' are.

But, as a force, nationalism has proven extraordinarily flexible – primarily because it is always operating in the present. Appeals to the past – as Singaporean progressives are wont to do sometimes – recalling the country's own history of (Indian and Chinese) migration and migrancy are understandable but do not necessarily guarantee against future invocations of nationalism. The passage of time allows ideas such as good migrants/bad migrants to establish themselves, which produces fertile soil for the cultivation of nationalism in its more recognizable iterations. Indeed, there are already visible contours of precisely such an emergent future in the rhetoric surrounding migrants and naturalized citizens in Singapore – most notably 'PRC-Chinese' (citizens who have relatively recently migrated from the People's Republic of China) and 'India-Indians' (citizens who have relatively recently migrated from India).[106] Despite nominally occupying similar categories within the CMIO framework, newer co-ethnic migrants are regarded as 'less' Singaporean and xenologized for a range of reasons such as not being born in Singapore, speaking different languages, socio-economic status, or other essentialized cultural differences.[107] Migrants and naturalized citizens, too, can mobilize similar logics – typically by depicting themselves as superior, less removed, and therefore more 'authentic' representatives of their primordial ethnic communities compared to their Singaporean diasporic counterparts. In this way, as Elaine Ho and Lavanya Kathiravelu suggest:

> how the immigration hierarchy is perceived by the natal-born population can be reversed by migrants/immigrants, and vice-versa as each party invokes a range of identifiers, discourses and bodily enactments to devalue the other and seek higher [social] ranks for themselves.[108]

The intensification of these contradictory tensions within the various categories of the CMIO model means it is likely to crumble further as an organizing principle of multiracialism simply because it will reflect social realities even less accurately – even though this does not necessarily mean the state will abandon it as a bureaucratic classificatory system in its discursive space. What this emergent set of dynamics does show, however, is that Singaporean nationalism, like nationalisms elsewhere, will develop new and ever more absurd ways of articulating 'rightful' belonging that hinges on producing otherness.

Theorizing the counter-nation

Nationalism can be thought of as 'those particular moments when political discourse substantially centres the spectre of non-belonging when making sense of and reckoning with its various economic, cultural and security concerns, whether real or imagined'.[109] Filling the emptiness of who 'we' are is done by defining who 'we' are not – by building portraits of ostensibly dangerous and threatening others who can be caricatured as not 'us'.[110] 'We' are not a Malay Malaysia; 'we' are not the 'West'; 'we' are not individualists, and so on. These spectres of non-belonging do not terminate at the formal frontiers of the nation-state; they continue to make their inroads within the nation too, and those who fail to adequately disavow these spectres can have the validity of their membership of the nation questioned.

To conceive of the nation as 'an imagined political community' is therefore insufficient.[111] We know that the nation is not a narration of the self; it is the narration of the other against which the self can be defined. If we accept that nationalism rouses affects of belonging by summoning the spectre of non-belonging, then the nation cannot simply be a single imagined political community. Instead, it consists of multiple imagined communities that are hierarchized, often with the formidable institutional power and backing of the state. Affects of belonging are channelled by designating various imagined communities as foreign and casting them as suppositious Others against whose exclusion 'belonging' is understood.

The snake oil that nationalism sells is that once all manifestations of the *xenos* have been identified, banished, and if not banished then certainly named as such and made eligible for potential banishment, whatever remains will be the true constituent substance of the nation. The promised land can be achieved if only all the elements that do not belong are removed. This is where its allure lies and this is how it has been, admittedly, very successful. But the perpetual long division of nationalism is only capable of returning quotients in terms of the foreign. Its enduring magic trick lies in hiding the fact that there is, in fact, never any remainder. But magic tricks essentially traffic in illusions – and nationalism is no different. As long as it is 'not recognized as an error, it has a value precisely equivalent to reality', and the illusion of the nation can be kept alive.[112] Defining itself is a false project that the nation can never fulfil because the nation-building project is always destined to be a negative project. All it can do is offer a future deferred in perpetuity whilst marking the constituencies that allegedly run counter to it. It is fundamentally a construction project that is preoccupied with building walls. The nation therefore necessarily requires its constitutive outside, or what I call the counter-nation.

The counter-nation is not a continuous or homogeneous entity; neither is it a political unit or a space; it is not even necessarily a reflexive, self-conscious entity. It might contain multiple communities but it is itself not a community. It is not a kind of shadow-nation or revolutionary nation-in-waiting that seeks to subvert the nation or destabilize the power of the nation. The counter-nation is none of those things. What I call the counter-nation is a heterogeneous entity, a collection of disparate groups, a set of

multitudinous manifestations, that conjoins the various imagined communities that the nation xenologizes. It comprises the various subjectivities that
have been turned into spectres of non-belonging. The counter-nation is thus
always enchained to the nation because it exists in relation to the political project of the nation. Since the nation is built on a logic of belonging
that operates through a logic of exclusion – through the construction and
maintenance of a constitutive outside – it stands to reason that all nations
simultaneously instantiate counter-nations. It is an amorphous and flexible
construct that nationalism exploits in the sense that in different moments,
different formations in the counter-nation can be made more or less salient.
To use Valluvan's vocabulary, the counter-nation can be understood as 'the
container for the remaining entity of belonging'.[113]

Whilst various counter-national figures can be available for xenologization in service of nationalism, they do not have to be mobilized at the same
time. Different imaginaries can be pressed into service depending on the
specificity of the nationalist moment. So, in one particular moment, when
the heterosexual nuclear family as the 'building block' of society is in focus,
the queerness of LGBT 'lifestyles' can be foregrounded as a threat, and dis-
tinctively non-Singaporean.[114] But in another particular moment, when economic productivity is on the line, when notions of attracting 'talent' are
joined up with global competitiveness, when LGBT bodies can potentially
be mined for labour and capital accumulation, queerness' threat can be
discounted.[115]

This is why we need to do more than understand Singaporean subjectivity as balanced upon a homosexual/heterosexual binary. When one
appreciates the salience given to heteronormativity, the particular forms of
kinship it reifies, the instrumentalization of kinship as repositories of care,
and its function in the imagination of the nation, it is easier to appreciate
how heteronormativity sets the stage for manufacturing the otherness that
nationalism requires. Even though queerness is translated into otherness in
some configurations of nationalism, in other configurations, when there is
something of value to the nation to be extracted, it can be mitigated and
conditionally accommodated – with emphasis, of course, on *conditionally*.

This helps explain why Pink Dot in its rhetoric often seeks to frame
LGBT people's compatibility with the nation through heteronormative
familial logics – even though that very logic works to render other people – including some LGBT people – as foreign. After all, 'being minoritized, [and] not being read as the principal national subject does not of itself
entirely inure any such person from the nationalist rationale'.[116] It also does
not insure against minoritized subjects trying to place themselves adjacent
to the position of the principal national subject or even looking to occupy
it because there is much to be gained in such a move.[117] The possibility of

moving into that position can be very seductive. But the danger of trying tactically to appropriate nationalism to that end is that it vastly underestimates the cunning nationalism as a force. Put simply, Pink Dot's enthusiasm for the vocabulary of the nation runs the risk of perpetuating a straight nation but with a small number of minoritized sexualities welcomed – conditionally – into the nationalist fold. At the same time, it is important to acknowledge there are real obstructions to activism, civil society, and organizing in Singapore that place social movements such as Pink Dot under considerable duress and compel them to operate in conjunction with 'the politics of compromise'.[118] But I want to draw attention to how its approach is already inflected by an acute awareness that it could not invoke the sign of the nation without routing queerness through a mitigating logic such as heteronormative familism. Far from foreclosing possibilities of resisting how queerness is made other in Singapore, it suggests that it cannot be done sufficiently through an appeal to the nation.

Nationalism in Singapore relies on the xenologization of queerness – where queerness is understood as the failure to live up to a scripted, predefined performance of heterosexuality – which forms the constitutive outside of the nation: the counter-nation. The amorphous nature of the counter-nation – the fact that it can be bent, moulded, and pressed such that different features are rendered salient in different political circumstances – also helps us understand that the concept of the nation is an illusion, even if it is not recognized as such. This is not to diminish its power by any means – it is, after all, an illusion capable of persuading people to take a bullet to preserve its integrity. Rather, it is to put down the idea that the nation is built on some form of homogeneity even if only partial. It is precisely the illusory nature of homogeneity that allows nationalism to continue flourishing.

Whilst we have seen the role that 'race' and ethnicity play in configuring Singaporean nationalism, it is not the only organizing principle in how nationalism can xenologize various people – and often, in the state's discursive space, it is not the primary vector of xenology. Uniting these various rejections is the force of heteronormativity that compels us to read queerness as otherness. 'Race' and the racializations that endure as afterlives of colonialism are certainly a part of the operation of nationalism. The opprobrium directed towards the Filipino/a community that we saw earlier, for example, is propelled by neocolonial logics that can racialize brown Southeast Asian communities as undesirable. Equally, the passive indifference, if not active enthusiasm, directed towards similar celebrations of predominantly white American and Irish communities is fertilized by some of the sediment of old colonial racial hierarchies that elevated whiteness at the expense of brown and black people. However, the Singaporean state's avowed commitment to a constitutional multiracial politics also means that specific racialized differences located within the Singaporean nation can be made to seem less relevant as an instrument of differentiation in state discourse. Hence, I read subjectivity in Singapore as structured by heteronormativity, a force that governs relations of desire and kinship and is inflected by 'race', gender, and class amongst other things. Particularly in the context of formal state discourse, where racial difference is downplayed in the name of a formal equality, I suggest reading heteronormativity as an important modality through which nationalism is transmitted in postcolonial Singapore. In this context, the governance of sexuality can provide a more potent force that contributes to producing otherness, even as it is co-constituted by relations of 'race', gender, and class.

During the parliamentary debates over Section 377A in 2007, Lee Hsien Loong rationalized his government's decision to retain the law by saying it recognized that 'the [heterosexual nuclear] family is the basic building block of our society'.[119] Whether he was aware of it or not, he was channelling his father – it was a near-verbatim repetition of Lee Kuan Yew's conviction that 'the family unit … is the building brick of society'.[120] As an institution, the family is 'framed as necessary to Singapore's well-being and national survival, particularly to sustain a sense of local identity and moral standards as Singapore casts its lot as a global node'.[121] With the weight of this history behind him, the sociologist Mathew Mathews finds it easy to conclude that '[c]onservatives can count on the traditional concept of family persisting and informing public policy in Singapore'.[122] Heteronormativity is a cornerstone of nationalism because it offers to protect Singapore from elements of the foreign – whether it is the apparent decadence of liberal 'Western' individualism or the soulless capitalist nature of societies that supposedly fail to treasure their kin adequately. Kenneth Paul Tan and Gary Lee suggest that because of this, homosexuality has often been cast as 'an unhealthy threat to the traditional Asian family, which has been held up as the basic unit of Singaporean society'.[123] Tan and Lee are certainly not wrong. But it is not only homosexuality that is cast as a threat; it is queerness – the disruption of heteronormativity, of which homosexuality is a component – that is the threat. When the nation is constructed as necessarily straight, queerness runs counter, and, as such, it can be assembled as part of what is defined as foreign.

Singapore's history as an independent nation is typically narrated *in media res* with the image of Lee Kuan Yew tearing up during a press conference on 9 August 1965 as he explained Singapore's separation from Malaysia to become an independent country. How he describes that moment is instructive because it gives us a glimpse into the specific performance of heterosexuality and its associated racialized and gendered roles that have since multiplied into Singaporean subjectivity.

It was not a live telecast, as television transmissions then started only at 6 p.m. I asked P. S. Raman [director of Radio & Television Singapore] to cut the footage of my breakdown. He strongly advised against it. The press, he said, was bound to report it, and if he edited it out, their description of the scene would make it appear worse. I had found Raman, a Tamil Brahmin born in Madras and a loyal Singaporean, a shrewd and sound adviser. I took his advice. And so, many people in Singapore and abroad saw me lose control of my emotions. That evening, Radio & Television Malaysia in Kuala Lumpur telecast my press conference, including this episode. Among Chinese, it is unbecoming to exhibit such a lack of manliness. But I could not help myself.[124]

Associating shedding tears with disrupting masculinity is a classic hetero-/ gender-normative trope that we all recognize by now but here it is also racialized – for Lee, it is specifically 'among Chinese' that such a lack of manliness is unbecoming. In other words, it is not just the disruption of masculinity that bothers Lee – it is some version of a racialized gendered expectation that he is gesturing towards. In this account, the proper role of the Chinese man is head of the household and protector of the family.[125] What persuaded him not to have the footage cut was the possibility that people would imagine something even worse, even less manly, and thereby attribute to him an even greater 'lack of manliness'.[126] Caught between a rock and a hard place, he took the advice not to have the footage edited.[127]

In addition to the intense vulnerability of the moment, it should also be understood as a deeply heteronormative moment that, like the vulnerability associated with it, has since been inscribed into the Singaporean nation. It also demonstrates how heteronormativity is more than just sexual difference – it is co-constituted by racial, gender, and other differences that can produce substantively different heteronormative expectations.[128] It is worth bearing in mind that whilst Lee is fully aware 'many people in Singapore and abroad saw [him] lose control of his emotions',[129] his concern is specifically how his conduct would be viewed in the context of Chinese heteronormative expectations. The expectations of heteronormativity that become politically significant and salient, therefore, are also informed by gendered and racial logics, and these vectors can work on each other to produce substantively different kinds of heteronormativities. This moment set the stage for imagining the nation through the gendered roles engraved into the heterosexual nuclear family. It cast the Singaporean man as 'protector' of both family and nation, and the Singaporean woman as the complementary 'other half' responsible for the duties of care and reproducing that are integral to the reduplication of the family and nation.[130] As we will see in the chapters to come, this heteronormative vision of the ideal family multiplies into the nation through the HDB flat, through the military, and through the circumscriptions of care.

By now it should be clear that the idea the nation might function as an internally homogeneous container of broad-based comradeship deserves to be jettisoned. Theories of the nation that take for granted its homogeneity are found wanting in this regard. We know the nation is something that cannot be immediately accessed; it is imagined, narrated, discursive rather than something material and real – even though it has very real and material consequences in people's lives. Anderson's (perhaps all too influential) claim was that the nation exists in the minds of its members, formed in the 'image of their communion'.[131] But this does not necessarily imply that the nation itself *is* a communion – the nation can be formed in the image of a communion even without such a communion to speak of. If the nation is individually imagined and formed in the image of the communion of these imaginations, the question remains open if these are identical imaginations. Anderson and other liberal theorists would presumably say yes. But it is possible for the nation to be sustained by a communion built on a plurality of singular imaginations – and it is precisely because it is of the imagined order that this is possible. Members of a nation, therefore, can imagine the nation in a singular fashion whilst also imagining that it exists in communion with everyone else.

Rather than being formed in the image of their communion, then, the nation is formed at the interstices of a set of communal singularities, as the illusion of their communion. Consider this a communion that is multifarious in nature, even if it does not seem as such precisely because it resides in the imaginations of individuals. And these different imaginations are fundamentally held together collectively not by what the nation *is* but the various things it supposedly *is not*. Put another way, the nation crystallizes in the relief of the imagination of otherness. This is what unifies the diverse exclusionary forces of nationalism that so many critical scholars of nationalism have identified. It is the nation's constitutive outside that allows it to preserve its illusion of homogeneity even when it patently is not homogeneous. And if we understand that the counter-nation comprises multifarious manifestations of otherness, and different nationalist moments can bring to the fore different specificities of non-belonging, we can see that this process of crystallization does not produce a uniform set of crystals.

The nation therefore rests on an illusion of homogeneity arising from a set of individual singularities. It is a shapeshifting entity that reshapes itself according to what it is being defined against and what is being rendered salient in a particular political moment. This is why the nation remains an illusion – and it is only because it is an illusion that it can be rearranged so easily. The illusory nature of the nation allows it to exert such power over the arrangement of territorial lives, hierarchizing them, placing them on different life paths, and assigning to them different degrees of importance. In this sense, it is not that 'nationalism … engenders nations'.[132] Nationalism instead engenders the counter-nation. It produces queerness as otherness. It produces the decadent West, the neighbouring country that disavows multiracialism, the LGBT citizen who is a threat to family values, the obstinate graduate woman who refuses to have children, the citizen who refuses to get married and duplicate the nuclear family, the brown foreign worker whose dangerous sexuality must be curtailed, white foreign talent who must be invited to reproduce the nation, and so on. In different nationalist moments, different counter-national elements in this backdrop are brought to the fore; and it is against the general backdrop of the threat posed by queerness, amplified by the motifs of vulnerability and paranoia, calamity and doom, that the straight nation is imagined.

Notes

1 Jean Baudrillard, *The Perfect Crime* (London: Verso, 1996), p. 53.

2 Ernest Renan, 'Qu'est-ce qu'une nation?', in *Nation and Narration*, ed. Homi K. Bhabha, trans. Martin Thom (London: Routledge, 1990), pp. 8–23.

3 Ibid., p. 11.

4 Ernest Gellner, *Culture, Identity, and Politics* (Cambridge: Cambridge University Press, 1987), p. 8.

5 Renan, 'Qu'est-ce qu'une nation?', p. 11.

6 Anthony W. Marx, 'The Nation-State and Its Exclusions', *Political Science Quarterly*, 117.1 (2002), 103–26 (p. 107).

7 Lysa Hong, 'The Lee Kuan Yew Story as Singapore's History', *Journal of Southeast Asian Studies*, 33.3 (2002), 545–57 (p. 545).

8 David Bell and Gill Valentine, 'Introduction: Orientations', in *Mapping Desire: Geographies of Sexualities*, ed. David Bell and Gill Valentine (London: Routledge, 1995), pp. 1–27 (p. 19); also see Cohen, 'Punks, Bulldaggers, and Welfare Queens'.

9 See, for example, Cheryl Kader and Thomas Piontek, 'Introduction', *Discourse*, 15.1 (1992), 5–10; and Jo Eadie, 'We Should Be There Bi Now', *Rouge*, 12 (1993), 26–27.

10 Fran Martin, *Situating Sexualities: Queer Representation in Taiwanese Fiction, Film and Public Culture* (Hong Kong: Hong Kong University Press, 2003), p. 25.

11 Oswin, *Global City Futures*, p. 9.

12 Gayatri Gopinath, *Impossible Desires: Queer Diasporas and South Asian Public Cultures* (Durham: Duke University Press, 2005), p. 3; also see, for example, Eithne Luibhéid, *Pregnant on Arrival: Making the Illegal Immigrant* (Minneapolis: University of Minnesota Press, 2013); Jasbir K. Puar, *Terrorist Assemblages: Homonationalism in Queer Times* (Durham: Duke University Press, 2017); Roderick A. Ferguson, *Aberrations in Black: Toward*

a Queer of Color Critique (Minneapolis: University of Minnesota Press, 2004); and C. Riley Snorton, *Black on Both Sides: A Racial History of Trans Identity* (Minneapolis: University of Minnesota Press, 2017).

13 See, for example, Judith Butler, 'Against Proper Objects', *Differences: A Journal of Feminist Cultural Studies*, 6.2–3 (1994), 1–26.

14 Jyoti Puri, *Sexual States: Governance and the Struggle over the Antisodomy Law in India* (Durham: Duke University Press, 2016); Puar, *Terrorist Assemblages*; Rao, *Out of Time*.

15 Stevi Jackson, 'Gender, Sexuality and Heterosexuality: The Complexity (and Limits) of Heteronormativity', *Feminist Theory*, 7.1 (2006), 105–21 (p. 105); see also Steven Seidman, 'From Polluted Homosexual to the Normal Gay: Changing Patterns of Sexual Regulation in America', in *Thinking Straight: The Power, the Promise, and the Paradox of Heterosexuality*, ed. Chrys Ingraham (New York: Routledge, 2005), pp. 39–62.

16 Tang and Quah, 'Heteronormativity and Sexuality Politics', p. 661.

17 Ibid., pp. 649–50.

18 Foucault, *The History of Sexuality*, p. 144.

19 Partha Chatterjee, 'The Disciplines in Colonial Bengal', in *Texts of Power: Emerging Disciplines in Colonial Bengal*, ed. Partha Chatterjee (Minneapolis: University of Minnesota Press, 1995), pp. 1–29 (p. 8).

20 Holden, 'Coda', p. 313.

21 Ibid.

22 Ernest Gellner, *Nations and Nationalism* (Oxford: Basil Blackwell, 1983), p. 1.

23 See Anthony D. Smith, *The Ethnic Origins of Nations* (Oxford: Basil Blackwell, 1986); and Anthony D. Smith, *Ethno-Symbolism and Nationalism: A Cultural Approach* (London: Routledge, 2009).

24 The primordialist/perennialist conception of the nation has been so thoroughly debunked that few people expend much effort critiquing it any more. As Rogers Brubaker candidly remarks, '[n]o serious scholar today holds the view that is routinely attributed to primordialists in straw-man setups'; Rogers Brubaker, *Nationalism Reframed: Nationhood and the National Question in the New Europe* (Cambridge: Cambridge University Press, 1996), p. 15.

25 Benedict Anderson, *Imagined Communities: Reflections on the Origin and Spread of Nationalism*, 2nd edn (London: Verso, 2006), p. 6.

26 Ibid., p. 145.

27 Ibid., p. 134.

28 Ibid., p. 145.

29 See Gellner, *Nations and Nationalism*; Eric Hobsbawm and Terence Ranger, eds, *The Invention of Tradition* (Cambridge: Cambridge University Press, 1983); John Breuilly, *Nationalism and the State* (Chicago: University of Chicago Press, 1982); and Eric J. Hobsbawm, *Nations and Nationalism since 1780: Programme, Myth, Reality* (Cambridge: Cambridge University Press, 1990).

30 Gellner, *Nations and Nationalism*, p. 39.

31 Ibid., p. 82.

32 Triandafyllidou, 'National Identity and the "Other"', p. 594.

33 Sita Balani, *Deadly and Slick: Sexual Modernity and the Making of Race* (London: Verso, 2023), p. xiii.

34 Zygmunt Bauman, 'Soil, Blood and Identity', *The Sociological Review*, 40.4 (1992), 675–701 (p. 679).

35 Luke de Noronha, 'Deportation, Racism and Multi-Status Britain: Immigration Control and the Production of Race in the Present', *Ethnic and Racial Studies*, 42.14 (2019), 2413–30 (p. 2417).

36 El-Enany, *(B)Ordering Britain*, p. 3; also see Etienne Balibar, *We, the People of Europe? Reflections on Transnational Citizenship*, trans. James Swenson (Princeton: Princeton University Press, 2004), p. 104.

37 Bauman, 'Soil, Blood and Identity', p. 687.

38 Paul Gilroy, *There Ain't No Black in the Union Jack: The Cultural Politics of Race and Nation*, 2nd edn (London: Routledge, 2002), p. 44.

39 Radhika Viyas Mongia, 'Race, Nationality, Mobility: A History of the Passport', in *After the Imperial Turn: Thinking with and through the Nation*, ed. Antoinette M. Burton (Durham: Duke University Press, 2003), pp. 196–216.

40 Valluvan, *The Clamour of Nationalism*, p. 38.

41 Ibid., p. 34.

42 Gargi Bhattacharyya, *Crisis, Austerity and Everyday Life: Living in a Time of Diminishing Expectations* (Basingstoke: Palgrave Macmillan, 2015), p. 28.

43 Valluvan, *The Clamour of Nationalism*, p. 36.

44 Berlant and Warner, 'Sex in Public', p. 548.

45 Oswin, *Global City Futures*, p. 4.

46 See Stoler, *Race and the Education of Desire*.

47 Syed Hussein Alatas, *The Myth of the Lazy Native: A Study of the Image of the Malays, Filipinos and Javanese from the 16th to the 20th Century and Its Function in the Ideology of Colonial Capitalism* (London: Frank Cass, 1977); see also Shanon Shah, 'Lazy Bodies', *Critical Muslim*, 41.2 (2022).

48 Lenore Manderson, 'Colonial Desires: Sexuality, Race, and Gender in British Malaya', *Journal of the History of Sexuality*, 7.3 (1997), 372–88.

49 Chua Beng Huat, 'The Cultural Logic of a Capitalist Single-Party State, Singapore', *Postcolonial Studies*, 13.4 (2010), 335–50 (p. 337).

50 Chua Beng Huat, 'Multiculturalism in Singapore: An Instrument of Social Control', *Race & Class*, 44.3 (2003), 58–77 (p. 60).

51 Selvaraj Velayutham, 'Races without Racism? Everyday Race Relations in Singapore', *Identities*, 24.4 (2017), 455–73.

52 Geoffrey Benjamin, 'The Cultural Logic of Singapore's "Multiracialism"', in *Singapore: Society in Transition*, ed. Riaz Hassan (Kuala Lumpur: Oxford University Press, 1976), pp. 115–33.

53 In 2021, prime minister Lee Hsien Loong announced at the National Day Rally that his government intended to introduce a new law called the Maintenance of Racial Harmony Act to 'consolidate its powers to deal with racial issues'. According to Lee, the proposed law would include ' "softer" measures that can

order someone who has caused offence to stop doing it, and to make amends by learning more about the other race and mending ties with them'. See Aqil Haziq Mahmud, 'NDR 2021: New Racial Harmony Law Planned, Offenders Can Be Ordered to Learn about Another Race, Says PM Lee', CNA, 29 August 2021, www.channelnewsasia.com/singapore/race-religion-harmony-law-pm-lee-2143181 (accessed 15 September 2024). At the time of this book's publication, the Maintenance of Racial Harmony Bill had just been introduced to Parliament by the Minister for Home Affairs during the 2024 Committee of Supply debates and is likely to eventually become law. Also see epilogue, n. 29.

54 Chua, 'Multiculturalism in Singapore', p. 61; also see Walid Jumblatt Abdullah, 'Managing Minorities in Competitive Authoritarian States: Multiracialism and the Hijab Issue in Singapore', *Indonesia and the Malay World*, 44.129 (2016), 211–28.

55 'Yang Di-Pertuan Negara's Speech: Debate on the Address' (Singapore: Hansard, 1965).

56 See Syed Muhd Khairudin Aljunied, *Colonialism, Violence and Muslims in Southeast Asia: The Maria Hertogh Controversy and Its Aftermath* (London: Routledge, 2010); and Dayang Istiaisyah bte Hussin, 'Textual Construction of a Nation: The Use of Merger and Separation', *Asian Journal of Social Science*, 29.3 (2001), 401–30.

57 R. S. Milne, 'Singapore's Exit from Malaysia: The Consequences of Ambiguity', *Asian Survey*, 6.3 (1966), 175–84.

58 National Heritage Board, 'National Pledge', www.nhb.gov.sg/what-we-do/our-work/community-engagement/education/resources/national-symbols/national-pledge (accessed 15 September 2024).

59 Abdullah, 'Managing Minorities in Competitive Authoritarian States', p. 216.

60 Hussin Mutalib argues, rather generously, that multiracialism views ethnic diversity as a problem to be mitigated whilst multiculturalism views ethnic diversity as a strength. There are good reasons to reject this somewhat false dichotomy, but the first half sums up the limits of Singaporean multiracialism and the state's view on racial diversity quite well. Hussin Mutalib, *Singapore Malays: Being Ethnic Minority and Muslim in a Global City-State* (Abingdon: Routledge, 2012), pp. 115–17.

61 Chua Beng Huat, 'Singapore: Multiracial Harmony as Public Good', in *Ethnicity in Asia*, ed. Colin Mackerras (London: Routledge, 2003), pp. 101–7.

62 Chua Beng Huat, 'Being Chinese under Official Multiculturalism in Singapore', *Asian Ethnicity*, 10.3 (2009), 239–50 (p. 244).

63 Benjamin, 'The Cultural Logic', p. 115.

64 Bridget Anderson, *Us and Them? The Dangerous Politics of Immigration Control* (Oxford: Oxford University Press, 2013), p. 36.

65 John S. Furnivall, *Colonial Policy and Practice: A Comparative Study of Burma and Netherlands India* (Cambridge: Cambridge University Press, 1948), p. 311.

66 Daniel P. S. Goh, 'From Colonial Pluralism to Postcolonial Multiculturalism: Race, State Formation and the Question of Cultural Diversity in Malaysia and Singapore. Race and Multiculturalism in Malaysia and Singapore',

Sociology Compass, 2.1 (2008), 232–52 (p. 235). See also John Clammer, 'The Institutionalization of Ethnicity: The Culture of Ethnicity in Singapore', *Ethnic and Racial Studies*, 5.2 (1982), 127–39; and Daniel P. S. Goh, Matilda Gabrielpillai, Philip Holden, and Gaik Cheng Khoo, eds, *Race and Multiculturalism in Malaysia and Singapore* (London: Routledge, 2009).

67 Housing & Development Board, 'Ethnic Integration Policy and SPR Quota', 2017, www.hdb.gov.sg/cs/infoweb/residential/buying-a-flat/buying-procedure-for-resale-flats/plan-source-and-contract/planning-considerations/eip-spr-quota (accessed 19 September 2024).

68 Travis Lim, Chan-Hoong Leong, and Farzaana Suliman, 'Managing Singapore's Residential Diversity through Ethnic Integration Policy', *Equality, Diversity and Inclusion: An International Journal*, 39.2 (2019), 109–25 (p. 111).

69 'Parliamentary Debates: Official Report' (Singapore: Hansard, 2021).

70 Tharman Shanmugaratnam, 'An Investigative Interview: Singapore 50 Years after Independence – 45th St Gallen Symposium', 2015, www.youtube.com/watch?v=hpwPciW74b8 (accessed 19 September 2024).

71 Tharman Shanmugaratnam, 'Building Common Ground: A Conversation with Tharman Shanmugaratnam', 2023, www.youtube.com/watch?v=jPwYVZfznn0 (accessed 19 September 2024).

72 'Yang Di-Pertuan Negara's Speech: Debate on the Address'.

73 'Parliamentary Debates: Official Report' (Singapore: Hansard, 2021); Davina Tham, 'Minorities Bear "Direct and Real" Financial Burden from Ethnic Integration Policy for Public Housing: Pritam Singh', 27 June 2021, https://lkyspp.nus.edu.sg/docs/default-source/ips/cna_minorities-bear-direct-and-real-financial-burden-from-ethnic-integration-policy-for-public-housing--pritam-singh_270621.pdf (accessed 19 September 2024).

74 Chua Beng Huat, 'Race Relations and Public Housing Policy in Singapore', *Journal of Architectural and Planning Research*, 8.4 (1991), 343–54; Giok Ling Ooi, Sharon Siddique, and Kay Cheng Soh, *The Management of Ethnic Relations in Public Housing Estates* (Singapore: Times Academic Press, 1993).

75 The repeated use of the term *racial balance* in state discourse is important. There is a sense of equity to the notion of balance that suggests the current ethnic make-up of the nation is fair. There is also a sense that this reflects a natural state of affairs that helps both to *obscure* the fact that the government actively chooses to maintain these ethnic proportions through a racialized immigration policy and to *justify* its decision to do so by making it appear as if the nation would be thrust into an 'unnatural' and unsettled state were the ethnic proportions ever to shift.

76 Xinyi Lu, 'Forum: Careful Approach Taken to Manage Racial Balance', *The Straits Times*, 10 November 2020, www.straitstimes.com/opinion/forum/forum-careful-approach-taken-to-manage-racial-balance (accessed 15 September 2024).

77 See for example Lee Hsien Loong, 'National Day Rally 2010', 2010, National Archives of Singapore, www.pmo.gov.sg/Newsroom/National-Day-Rally-2010 (accessed 19 September 2024).

78 'Parliamentary Debates: Official Report' (Singapore: Hansard, 2013); see also gov.sg, 'What Are the Racial Proportions among Singapore Citizens?', 10 December 2019, www.gov.sg/article/what-are-the-racial-proportions-among-singapore-citizens (accessed 15 September 2024).

79 Amir Hussain, 'We Will Maintain Racial Balance among S'poreans: PM Lee', *TODAY*, 9 February 2013, www.todayonline.com/singapore/we-will-maintain-racial-balance-among-sporeans-pm-lee (accessed 15 September 2024).

80 See Mark R. Frost, 'An Unsettled Majority: Immigration and the Racial "Balance" in Multicultural Singapore', *Journal of Ethnic and Migration Studies*, 47.16 (2021), 3729–51; and Kamaludeen Mohamed Nasir and Bryan S. Turner, eds, *The Future of Singapore: Population, Society and the Nature of the State* (New York: Routledge, 2014).

81 See Sharon Siddique, 'The Phenomenology of Ethnicity: A Singapore Case-Study', *SOJOURN: Journal of Social Issues in Southeast Asia*, 5.1 (1990), 35–62; and Chua Beng Huat, 'Racial Singaporeans: Absence after the Hyphen', in *Southeast Asian Identities: Culture and the Politics of Representation in Indonesia, Malaysia, Singapore, and Thailand*, ed. Joel S. Kahn (Singapore: Institute of Southeast Asian Studies, 1998), pp. 28–50.

82 See Nirmala Purushotam, *Negotiating Multiculturalism: Disciplining Difference in Singapore* (Berlin: Mouton de Gruyter, 2000).

83 Lionel Wee, 'Language Politics and Global City', *Discourse: Studies in the Cultural Politics of Education*, 35.5 (2014), 649–60 (p. 651).

84 Chua, 'The Cultural Logic of a Capitalist Single-Party State, Singapore', p. 340.

85 This explains why despite the Eurasian community (which does not have an associated mother tongue, unlike the Chinese, Malay, and Indian communities) asking on multiple occasions for English to be recognized as its mother tongue, the state refuses to engage with the notion – English must stay symbolically dissociated from all ethnic communities so as to remain a neutral and therefore fair language. See Lionel Wee, 'When English Is Not a Mother Tongue: Linguistic Ownership and the Eurasian Community in Singapore', *Journal of Multilingual and Multicultural Development*, 23.4 (2002), 282–95.

86 See Stuart Hall, *Policing the Crisis: Mugging, the State, and Law and Order* (London: Macmillan, 1978), p. 394.

87 See, for example, Navene Elangovan, 'NDR 2021: Malay Community Has Made Significant Progress, Says PM Lee, but "Worrying Trends" in Home Ownership, Education Remain', *TODAY*, 2021, www.todayonline.com/singapore/ndr-2021-malay-community-has-made-significant-progress-says-pm-lee-worrying-trends-home (accessed 15 September 2024); Adrian Lim, 'National Day Rally 2019: Singapore Malays a Model for Other Muslim and Minority Communities', *The Straits Times*, 18 August 2019, www.straitstimes.com/politics/national-day-rally-2019-singapore-malays-a-model-for-other-muslim-and-minority-communities (accessed 15 September 2024); and Justin Ong, 'National Day Rally 2021: "Entirely Baseless" to Claim There Is Chinese Privilege in S'pore, Says PM Lee', *The Straits Times*, 30 August 2021, www.straitstimes.com/singapore/politics/national-day-rally-2021-all-races-treated-equally-in-spore-with-no-special (accessed 15 September 2024). Also see Chapter 2, n. 74.

88 This sensibility – ensuring that the main ethnic groups are all equally repre-
    sented – also extends to straight allies whom Pink Dot chooses to be its ambas-
    sadors. See Mano, 'Disarming as a Tactic'.

89 Lionel Wee, 'Linguistic Chutzpah and the Speak Good Singlish Movement',
    World Englishes, 33.1 (2014), 85–99 (p. 214); Michael Hill and Kwen Fee
    Lian, *The Politics of Nation Building and Citizenship in Singapore* (London:
    Routledge, 1995), p. 188.

90 Lee Kuan Yew, 'Transcript of the Prime Minister's Speech at the Opening of
    the Seminar on "Education and Nationbuilding"', 1966, National Archives
    of Singapore, www.nas.gov.sg/archivesonline/data/pdfdoc/lky19661227.pdf
    (accessed 19 September 2024).

91 Holidays Act, https://sso.agc.gov.sg/Bills-Supp/33-1968/Published/19680
    715?DocDate=19680715 (accessed 19 September 2024).

92 George Baylon Radics and Vineeta Sinha, 'Regulation of Religion and Granting
    of Public Holidays: The Case of Tai Pucam in Singapore', *Asian Journal of
    Social Science*, 46.4–5 (2018), 524–48 (p. 540).

93 Charles Taylor, 'The Politics of Recognition', in *Multiculturalism: Examining
    the Politics of Recognition*, ed. Amy Gutmann (Princeton: Princeton University
    Press, 1994), pp. 25–73.

94 Kwame Anthony Appiah, 'Identity, Authenticity, Survival: Multicultural
    Societies and Social Reproduction', in *Multiculturalism: Examining the Politics
    of Recognition*, ed. Amy Gutmann (Princeton: Princeton University Press,
    1994), pp. 149–63.

95 Lois McNay, *Against Recognition* (Cambridge: Polity Press, 2008), p. 65; also
    see Elizabeth A. Povinelli, *The Cunning of Recognition: Indigenous Alterities
    and the Making of Australian Multiculturalism* (Durham: Duke University
    Press, 2002).

96 I do not delve much further into the CMIO model in the book but its stubborn
    maintenance in state discourse reflects its investment in the assumption that these
    racial categories will remain largely stable and not mingle or coalesce through
    heterosexual coupling or family formation. Lee Kuan Yew, for instance, was
    not shy of asserting this view, saying: 'My expectation is there will always be a
    small group of the adventurous in all the ethnic groups, perhaps those who are
    less egotistical, who marry across ethnic lines. But they will probably be in the
    minority. Therefore the chances are that if you come back to Singapore a cen-
    tury from now, you would find people more or less the same.' In reality, both the
    internal heterogeneity within racial categories as well as coupling across racial
    categories have put increasing pressure on the CMIO model's claim to represent
    the nation accurately. See Raj K. Vasil, *Governing Singapore: Democracy and
    National Development* (Singapore: Eastern Universities Press, 1984), p. 15. See
    also Zarine L. Rocha, 'Multiplicity within Singularity: Racial Categorization
    and Recognizing "Mixed Race" in Singapore', *Journal of Current Southeast
    Asian Affairs*, 30.3 (2011), 95–131; Zarine L. Rocha and Brenda S. A. Yeoh,
    'Managing the Complexities of Race: Eurasians, Classification and Mixed
    Racial Identities in Singapore', *Journal of Ethnic and Migration Studies*, 47.4
    (2021), 878–94; and Siddique, 'The Phenomenology of Ethnicity'.

97 See Purushotam, *Negotiating Multiculturalism*, for how ethnic groups are assigned a 'mother tongue'.

98 Stuart Hall, 'Race, the Floating Signifier: What More Is There to Say about "Race"?', in *Selected Writings on Race and Difference*, ed. Paul Gilroy and Ruth Wilson Gilmore (Durham: Duke University Press, 2021), pp. 359–73 (p. 359).

99 The current Leader of the Opposition, Pritam Singh, is an example of both the flexibility and absurdity of this racialization. Strictly speaking, he is minoritized multifold by the CMIO system of racialization. But one would be hard pressed to find anyone in the country who would entertain the suggestion that he is not a legitimate member of the nation. This is, of course, in part because of extra-racial factors such as socio-economic status, class markers, and prominent social position, but it demonstrates how the racialization obtained within the CMIO system is a flexible and contextual one.

100 Chua, 'Multiculturalism in Singapore'.

101 Jeanette Tan, 'Monday #sgroundup: Filipinos in Singapore Drop IDay Celebration Plans after Abuse', Yahoo News, 26 May 2014, https://sg.news.yahoo.com/blogs/what-is-buzzing/monday--sgroundup--filipinos-in-singapore-drop-iday-celebration-plans-after-abuse-100522799.html (accessed 15 September 2024); Audrey Tan, 'Filipinos' Event Axed for First Time in 20 Years', *The Straits Times*, 28 May 2014, https://eresources.nlb.gov.sg/newspapers/digitised/issue/straitstimes20140528-1 (accessed 19 September 2024).

102 As an aside, whilst there is no coherent reason as to why iconicity is relevant to this discussion in the first place, it is difficult to take seriously conservatives' suggestion that what is essentially quite a generic brown-tiled mall stuffed to the brim with luxury brands is in any sense 'iconic'.

103 American Association of Singapore, 'Fourth of July', American Association of Singapore, www.aasingapore.com/4th-of-july (accessed 8 April 2023).

104 Lee Kuan Yew, *The Singapore Story: Memoirs of Lee Kuan Yew* (Singapore: Singapore Press Holdings, 1998), p. 17.

105 See Jaclyn Ling-Chien Neo, 'Malay Nationalism, Islamic Supremacy and the Constitutional Bargain in the Multi-Ethnic Composition of Malaysia', *International Journal on Minority and Group Rights*, 13.1 (2006), 95–118.

106 Chan et al., *Singapore's Multiculturalism*, pp. 173–201.

107 Elaine Lynn-Ee Ho and Laavanya Kathiravelu, 'More than Race: A Comparative Analysis of "New" Indian and Chinese Migration in Singapore', *Ethnic and Racial Studies*, 45.4 (2022), 636–55; Elaine Lynn-Ee Ho, *Citizens in Motion: Emigration, Immigration, and Re-Migration across China's Borders* (Stanford: Stanford University Press, 2019); Sylvia Ang, 'The "New Chinatown": The Racialization of Newly Arrived Chinese Migrants in Singapore', *Journal of Ethnic and Migration Studies*, 44.7 (2018), 1177–94.

108 Ho and Kathiravelu, 'More than Race', p. 650.

109 Valluvan, *The Clamour of Nationalism*, p. 36.

110 Anna Triandafyllidou, 'Nationalism in the 21st Century: Neo-Tribal or Plural?', *Nations and Nationalism*, 26.4 (2020), 792–806.

111 Anderson, *Imagined Communities*, p. 6.
112 Baudrillard, *The Perfect Crime*, p. 53.
113 Valluvan, *The Clamour of Nationalism*, p. 34.
114 'Speech to Parliament on Reading of Penal Code (Amendment) Bill'.
115 See, for example, Lee Hsien Loong, 'Transcript of Singapore Tech Forum 2020 Keynote Speech: Technology as Singapore's Strategic National Priority', Prime Minister's Office, 2020, www.pmo.gov.sg/Newsroom/Dialogue-by-PM-Lee-Hsien-Loong-at-the-Singapore-Tech-Forum (accessed 15 September 2024).
116 Valluvan, *The Clamour of Nationalism*, p. 38.
117 See, for example, Chris K. K. Tan, *Stand Up for Singapore? National Belonging among Gay Men in the Lion City* (London: Routledge, 2022).
118 Walid Jumblatt Bin Abdullah, 'The Politics of Compromise: Analyzing the Repeal of Section 377A in Singapore', *Pacific Affairs*, 96.1 (2023), 105–18.
119 'Speech to Parliament on Reading of Penal Code (Amendment) Bill'.
120 Fareed Zakaria and Lee Kuan Yew, 'Culture Is Destiny: A Conversation with Lee Kuan Yew', *Foreign Affairs*, 73.2 (1994), 109–26 (p. 113).
121 Weiss, 'Who Sets Social Policy in Metropolis?', p. 285.
122 Mathew Mathews, 'Traditional View of Family Likely to Persist in Singapore', *The Straits Times*, 24 March 2015, www.straitstimes.com/opinion/traditional-view-of-family-likely-to-persist-in-singapore (accessed 15 September 2024).
123 Tan and Lee, 'Imagining the Gay Community', p. 185.
124 Lee, *The Singapore Story*, p. 16.
125 Kenneth Paul Tan, 'Civic Society and the New Economy in Patriarchal Singapore: Emasculating the Political, Feminizing the Public', *Crossroads: An Interdisciplinary Journal of Southeast Asian Studies*, 15.2 (2001), 95–122.
126 Lee, *The Singapore Story*, p. 16.
127 Whilst there is insufficient space to adequately theorize this in the book, I think it is intriguing – somewhat oddly specific – that Lee feels the need to elaborate that Raman was a 'Tamil Brahmin'. In some sense, the Brahmin caste category is doing a lot of heavy lifting in Lee's explanation as to why he deferred to Raman in a matter that concerned Chinese manliness. It speaks to the way caste, too, is a live category in the formation of racial hierarchies and the broader enterprise of racialization. Amongst other works that have sought to address this specific relationality, see for example Rahul Rao, 'Is the Homo in Homocapitalism the Caste in Caste Capitalism and the Racial in Racial Capitalism?', *South Atlantic Quarterly*, 123.1 (2024), 79–103; Rahul Rao, 'Gandhi Falling … and Rising', *Journal of Historical Geography*, 82 (2023), 1–10; Anjali Arondekar, 'Go (Away) West!', *GLQ: A Journal of Lesbian and Gay Studies*, 28.3 (2022), 463–71; and Bhimrao Ramji Ambedkar and Arundhati Roy, *Annihilation of Caste*, ed. S. Anand, annotated critical edition (London: Verso, 2014).
128 Again, whilst the limits of this book foreclose theorizing this in much greater depth, one could open the question as to how, if exhibiting a lack of manliness is supposedly unbecoming specifically amongst Chinese men, this matrix could possibly set the stage for racially minoritized brown men to be feminized or otherwise rendered inadequate. Relatedly, it is also worth noting that whilst

the co-constitution of heteronormativity along axes of racial, gendered, and class vectors can produce substantively different sets of expectations, not all will necessarily be equally politically relevant at a given moment. For instance, Lee is clearly aware that both Chinese and non-Chinese people will have seen him transgress the expectations of Chinese masculinity; nonetheless, he is concerned not by what the people of Singapore or people abroad might think but specifically by what Chinese people might think. Perhaps this betrays an inadvertent racial primacy – that is normally otherwise obscured – in determining the heteronormative expectations that *really* matter in the context of the putative multicultural nation and the state's formal discourse. Also see Chapter 4, n. 93.

129 Lee, *The Singapore Story*, p. 16.
130 Tan, 'Civic Society and the New Economy'.
131 Anderson, *Imagined Communities*, p. 6.
132 Gellner, *Nations and Nationalism*, p. 55.

2

Three faces of the straight nation

The work of vulnerability

Singapore's state-led nation-building project operates with a considerable degree of coherence. Part of the reason this is possible is the scale at which government functions in the country. It is a small city-state without multiple levels of government – the same national government that formulates laws and policies in Parliament is also the local government that resolves municipal issues such as keeping the drains clear outside people's houses. As a consequence, the 'economic growth and improved material life' that people have benefited from is both experienced and rationalized as a direct result of the PAP government's policies, political decisions, and concomitant rhetoric.[1] This direct and consolidated form of government has led to Cherian George christening Singapore an 'air-conditioned nation' and 'a society with a unique blend of comfort and central control'.[2]

It is difficult to discount the inordinately large shadow of the PAP government in the production of Singaporean subjectivity. The PAP has formed the government since independence with an unbroken overwhelming parliamentary majority – and its domination of the political sphere has spread to include other state apparatus.[3] The administrative and civil service has been aligned with the PAP's governing logics and political rationalizations chiefly 'by exposing senior bureaucrats to party ideology'.[4] Senior civil servants and military leaders are regularly recruited into the party and quickly offered positions within government, with public and military service framed as the perfect training grounds for eventual political leadership.[5] Taken together with its near-exclusive stewardship of the nation-building project, it is tempting to read the PAP as synonymous with the state because of how it has permeated so many elements of it. But I would prefer to resist an entirely functionalist reading and so I read the production of subjectivity in Singapore as the result of a set of state decisions, policies, and rhetoric whilst at the same time keeping intentionality out of the calculus. Put differently, I consider the production of Singaporean subjectivity as the processual consequence of state power – bearing in mind, of course, that 'the exercising of power consists of "the conduct of conduct" '.[6] The reason this is important is that whilst the nation-building project is a state- and PAP government-driven project, the specific exclusions of nationalism are not necessarily state-driven, and to understand nationalism as such would be to misread it.

There are moments in *Imagined Communities* where, *contra* his general enthusiasm for the nation, Anderson suggests that it exerts its greatest hold in the moments it is under threat. Whilst he does not excavate this seam as much as he could have, he points out that 'the great wars of this [twentieth] century are extraordinary not so much in the unprecedented scale on which they permitted people to kill, as in the colossal numbers persuaded to lay down their lives'.[7] Gopal Balakrishnan goes further than Anderson's allusion to argue that '[o]nly in struggle does the nation cease to be an informal, contestable and taken-for-granted frame of reference, and become a community which seizes hold of the imagination'.[8] What unites both Balakrishnan and Anderson here is that their analyses are both post hoc readings of the nation, proceeding from the assumption that the nation as an entity already exists.

Unlike Anderson and Balakrishnan, Lee Kuan Yew was convinced that newly independent Singapore did not have a comparable depository of affect that a nation ought to command – and this was a key driver of his desire to create a majority home-owning population in Singapore. The idea was that in the absence of the powerful imaginary frame given by the abstract concept of the nation that Anderson and Balakrishnan both reference, owning one's home would give Singaporeans something material to defend. Lee Hsien Loong's glib comment in 2008 that 'public housing in Singapore is really "national housing" '[9] was thus a continuation of a consistent state conviction that has remained largely unchanged from Lee Kuan Yew's early position regarding home ownership and the nation. This compression effectively scales the nation down and produces, through the generation of the potential loss of one's home and family, an acute sense of vulnerability at the individual level that collectively multiplies back into the nation's psyche – or what William Walters terms 'domopolitics'.[10]

There are three major sites of heteronormativity in Singapore I want to examine: public housing, the heterosexual nuclear family, and the military. In this chapter, I am interested in how these interlinked sites are embedded within the domopolitical nation-building project and produce a certain subject position between them that Singaporean citizens are invited to occupy – one that is gendered, racialized, and classed in its own right. The affects of vulnerability that circulate within the nation-building project rationalize National Service (NS) – the policy of conscription where all men upon turning 18 must serve up to two years in the military.[11] But it is not just the survival of the nation that has concerned the state since independence, it is also its regeneration, and this has led to a gendered bifurcation of national service.

Whilst men are expected to contribute to the nation's survival through their participation in military defence as part of the formal NS programme, women are expected to contribute to the nation's reproduction by marrying and bearing children. This is the gendered dimension of domopolitics where women are 'constructed as responsible for the maintenance and reproduction' of the nation as home.[12] Put differently, it is the 'gendered call to patriotic duty: military service for men and maternal duty for women'[13] – one that is inflected by a latent logic of heterosexuality and heterosexual coupling. It is also precisely because the responsibility of reproducing the nation is laid at the door of women that these same logics can rationalize 'migrant women's reproductive practices as a legitimate and necessary site of securitised state intervention, as part of a broader project [of] constructing the national "home" '.[14] As we will be familiar with by now, heteronormativity, in its co-constitution with other forms of difference, can produce substantively different expectations for different people – and this is one manifestation of how the circulation of heteronormativity resolves into different sets of gendered expectations. Into this set-up one can insert the prototypical heterosexual nuclear family and their home, which gives the abstract concept of the nation both a material dimension to be protected and reproduced as well as a psychic dimension through which it can be imagined and rationalized.

Singapore's massive public housing programme is run by the HDB – the country's sole public housing authority and a statutory board under the auspices of the Ministry of National Development (MND). The vast majority of Singaporeans live in HDB flats that, importantly, they own. For Lee, home ownership was crucial because it would 'give all parents whose sons would have to do national service a stake in the Singapore their sons had to defend' and 'this sense of ownership was vital for our new society which had no deep roots in a common historical experience'.[15] The affects of ownership are thus central to the materialization of the nation because it ostensibly gives members something material and specific to protect and defend in the name of the nation – the nation is both expressed and experienced through the materiality of home ownership and kinship. Both are specified by heteronormative logics. Access to public housing is largely contingent on heterosexual coupling and the formation of a heterosexual 'family nucleus', and kinship is defined in strict terms that reify the heterosexual nuclear family above all other forms of kin and social relations. As such, the triad of defence, domesticity, and the family functions on a heteronormative, gendered logic that can render queerness incompatible, out of step, with the nation.

There is a certain logic of compression where the HDB flat becomes a scalar substitute for the nation. The EIP, which governs the ethnic distribution of every HDB block and precinct, does not simply ensure an ethnic mix. It also works to materialize the nation in domestic, residential spaces. In this way, nationalism and its politics are compressed into the HDB flat and one's home. Defending the nation is defending one's home is defending one's flat and is defending the heterosexual nuclear family. Of course, it is likely that people will have developed their own varied affective and emotional investments that they then deposit into their imaginary of the nation, but what I am specifying here is the set of logics that functions as part of a political rationality connecting heteronormativity with nationalism.

Placing the HDB flat, the individual's home, at the centre of the nation-building project buttresses the 'psychosocial working of the national home, a characterisation of deep homeliness through which yearnings for care and fortification alike are threaded'.[16] Many of the logics associated with the home, such as 'the home as *our* place, where we belong naturally, and where, by definition, others do not ... home as a place we must protect',[17] transfer easily onto the nationalist imperative that relies on a continual 'Othering that determine[s] to some significant degree and intensity the *interior* content of a nation's claim to being'.[18] Where nationalism functions on assaying an imagined threat, its domopolitical dimension can muster vulnerability. Thus, the warmth of inclusion[19] is juxtaposed with the apparent necessity of exclusion of various threats, activating the 'Us vs. Them'[20] mode of political rationality and parsing it through the conceptual frame of the home.

Unlike most postcolonial nations where nationalism operates, at least in its initial iterations, with a liberatory anti-colonial timbre as the product of some kind of revolutionary victory, in Singapore it is shot through with vulnerability, precarity, and paranoia. The Singaporean nation is marked by severance, splinter, rupture; and it narrates its independence in a melancholic way – akin to that of a child suddenly orphaned, cut adrift, and forced to find a way to survive. The iconic image associated with the moment of independence on 9 August 1965 is Lee Kuan Yew welling up with tears on national television as he announced Singapore's separation from Malaysia.[21] At the press conference following his proclamation of independence, Lee said 'every time we look back at this moment when we signed this agreement, which severed Singapore from Malaysia, it will be a moment of anguish because all my life I have believed in merger and the unity of these two territories.'[22] It was at this point, having described his anguish, that Lee began to tear up and asked for a short pause – which he later explained was because 'at that moment, my emotions overwhelmed me'.[23] The image of Lee crying whilst declaring Singapore's independence has become entwined with how the Singaporean nation is imagined through a 'popularised belief in the nation's essential conditions of resource poverty and vulnerability'.[24]

Singapore's story as an independent postcolonial state is thus narrated not from the rock of anti-colonial liberation and jubilation but from the shifting sands of grief and uncertainty. It is narrated not in the major key of triumph but in the minor key of remorse at an 'unjust break-up'.[25] Instead of independence as an exultant act of self-determination, or the product of what Partha Chatterjee calls 'anti-colonial nationalism',[26] Singapore simply 'had independence thrust upon it'.[27] Consequently:

> Singapore's post-colonial condition is marked officially not by [its] merger with Malaysia in 1963, which was supposed to liberate [Singapore] from the British empire – [its] proper colonisers – but by [its] separation from Malaysia in 1965. Thus signposted, Singapore's independence is regarded as a dangerous predicament, and [its] post-colonial condition has been constantly spooked ever since by multiple threats of failed nationhood – of which colonialism was notably not one.[28]

Lee's personal anguish has been aggrandized into the Singaporean nation as 'a consequence of the way [Singaporeans] narrate our history'.[29] Or, to be precise, the way the state narrates history.

In 2015, Singapore's 50th year of independence since separating from Malaysia, Lee Hsien Loong was asked whether he worried about Singapore continuing to thrive. Lee responded:

> We worry all the time. People say we are paranoid, which I suppose we are and we need to be. Because you are at a higher level, you expect to be at a higher level. You don't expect to go back to where you were in the 1960s. And yet, it is not natural that you stay at this place … It's an entirely unnatural state of affairs and one which we should count our blessings for, if not every day, at least every election.[30]

The prime minister's remarks were not out of the ordinary. In fact, they strongly echoed a parliamentary speech he had previously made when he said:

> We are a tiny, multi-racial, multireligious, one little red dot out of so many red dots in the middle of Southeast Asia, lack land, lack air space, lack sea space, lack water, sometimes, also run short of sand and granite, operating in a fast-changing competitive global environment against very powerful competitors … Our model is 'paranoid' government – a government which worries all the time, which plays a crucial role in this system … Will Singapore survive, much less prosper, without a capable team in charge? How did we get here? With strong political leadership and effective government.[31]

Paranoia, worry, with the constant humming of potential self-annihilation in the background, is implanted in the nation.

Prior to its becoming an independent country in 1965, Lee Kuan Yew had dismissed the idea of an independent Singapore as a 'political, economic and geographical absurdity'.[32] Nearly 60 years on, that sentiment continues to linger amongst government leaders – a kind of impostor syndrome rooted in the suspicion that an independent Singapore reflects 'an unnatural state of affairs' and is only one wrong decision away from realizing its supposed ludicrousness.[33] Ministers regularly remind Singaporeans of the nation's fragility in various ways, constantly recalling and reinscribing the anterior absurdity that Singapore's continued existence defies on a daily basis. As George summarizes pithily, 'Singapore's expulsion from the Malaysian federation in August 1965, together with its tiny size, has given its leaders an acute sense of national vulnerability, which they believe can be compensated for only through discipline and order.'[34]

Setting aside for the moment the distinct political legitimating function of resting in a constant state of paranoia, it would be a mistake to read the government's perpetuation of this sense of vulnerability as mere rhetoric; rather, it emerges out of a larger affective landscape of unease as a consequence of Singapore's narration of its own history. Paranoia and the perpetuation of worry are important nodes in the circuit through which nationalism is transmitted, and they shape Singaporean nationalism in a particular way. Besieged by the insecurity of being a small state surrounded by much larger ones, Singapore's default mode of operation is the realist/realpolitik approach captured well in the retired Singaporean diplomat Bilahari Kausikan's insistence that '[s]mall countries can manoeuvre only in the interstices between the relationships of major powers'.[35] To what extent this is the case is presumably a question that will excite international relations scholars more than me, but I find Amitav Acharya's point that 'realism and power balancing can also be a form of "cheap talk", a profoundly legitimizing rhetoric, easier to sell to a domestic audience which expects its leaders to be hardnosed defenders of the national interest' a valuable one.[36] What is more relevant for us is not how Singapore's political choices are determined by being a small and vulnerable state but how these states of diminutiveness and vulnerability are marshalled as devices to rationalize particular political choices in service of the nation. The work of vulnerability, in other words. It is not so much whether Singapore is always on the verge of a potential crisis, such that it might not 'stay at this place' any longer, but how 'crisis' as a state of affairs is invoked as a political rationality to entertain a sense of paranoia around the internal integrity of the nation.[37]

In and of itself, it is not particularly noteworthy that paranoia is baked into the operation of nationalism. After all, we know that nationalism can amplify itself through a fear of the nation's erosion; its British invocation, for instance, has long been constructed as something that implicitly 'assists in the process of making Britain great again'[38] – a prophetic formulation that Donald Trump and his far-right cabal appropriated all the way to the White House in 2016 and again in 2024. It must also be noted that in the present nationalist moment, nationalism has indeed been operating more frequently in the defensive mode of 'Little Englander' nationalism that imagines a certain loss that must be staunched at the soonest.[39] This is a 'politics of rearguard anxiety that styles itself as the voice of provincial white respectability versus deracinated metropolitan decadence'.[40] However, even though affects of vulnerability and insecurity can and do function as key nodes of transference in the circulation of nationalism, they operate against the backdrop of an anterior imperial might. This is why 'again' and 'back' are the crucial operative words in the nationalist shibboleths 'Make America Great Again'[41] and 'Take Back Control'[42] – they trade on a certain nostalgia for an imagined and rightful past greatness. Nationalism's machinations of xenology that follow in the wake of this starting point thus function as a reassertion of supremacy and superiority.

As a consequence of the way its national history is narrated, however, Singaporean nationalism does not quite have the luxury of this wellspring of imagined superiority to draw upon. It does not seek to reassert a certain supremacy because, simply put, there was none to begin with – a crucial contingency in the development of nationalistic currents in Singapore. Far from being an apologist argument in defence of Singaporean nationalism, this distinction is worth making because it helps explain how nationalism in Singapore is configured differently as a result of its roots not in imperialistic self-assertion but in the insecurity of insignificance. The xenology that flows as a consequence of the paranoia surrounding being returned to 'where [we] were in the 1960s',[43] as well as that temporal location being cast as a period of turmoil and chaos, vulnerability and strife, leads to nationalism in Singapore being rationalized as a necessity that guides governance in Singapore.

In August 1998, Indonesian president Jusuf Habibie could not have known how significant his condescending throwaway comment about Singapore would eventually become. Asked about bilateral relations between Singapore and Indonesia, Habibie complained he did not feel Singapore was friendly enough before pointing at a map and saying 'It's okay with me, but there are 211 million people [here in Indonesia]. All the green [area] is Indonesia. And that red dot is Singapore.'[44] Within weeks, prime minister Goh Chok Tong sought to reclaim the term by appropriating Habibie's turn of phrase in his National Day Rally speech. Referring to Singapore's ability to render Indonesia assistance during the Asian financial crisis, he said: 'Singapore will help Indonesia within the limits of our ability ... After all we are only three million people. Just a little red dot on the map. Where is the capacity to help 211 million people?'.[45]

Ever since then, the phrase *little red dot* has been invoked by Singaporean leaders as a point of pride, in the sense of a country punching well above its weight. At the same time, it keeps the currents of vulnerability circulating amongst the population by keeping the potentiality of littleness and insignificance alive in the background. It functions as a reminder of both Singapore's precocious and 'unnatural state of affairs' and the risk that Singapore could well 'go back to where [it was] in the 1960s'.[46] Reflecting on Habibie's comments five years later, Lee Hsien Loong remarked that '[it] was a vivid and valuable reminder that we are indeed very small and very vulnerable. The little red dot has entered the psyche of every Singaporean, and become a permanent part of our vocabulary, for which we are grateful.'[47] The state's embrace of the *little red dot* moniker is a prime example of how vulnerability is not only inscribed into the nation but is worn like a badge on its sleeve; and its representation on the map reflects how the nation imagines itself.

Thongchai Winichakul shows how one of the afterlives of the colonial venture is the instrument of the map and practices of mapping as a technology through which the nation's 'geo-body' is defined.[48] Representing the nation's geo-body is important not just in terms of legitimizing the nation but also in legitimizing the nation against other nations.[49] Thongchai's thoughtful study persuaded Anderson to modify his own theory of the nation to read the act of setting the boundaries of the colonial state with its concomitant cartographical practices, census-taking, and attendant racializations as crucial to defining the imagination of the nation in postcolonial nation-states.[50] The imagination of the Singaporean nation, however, occurs not through the representation of its geo-body on the map but through the very impossibility of its representation – the fact that it is so small it cannot be represented. It accentuates the sense of vulnerability around the nation that is harnessed as adversity – producing a nation that is perpetually in crisis and encouraging the sense of paranoia around it. Singapore is therefore always cast as caught in an existential struggle with the discourses of scarcity and lack figuring as master discourses in the nation's political rationalities that legitimize a host of policy decisions. The PAP government's classic refrain is that 'we have no natural resources other than our human resources'. At the same time, the people of this same population are also essentialized in ways that cast them as riven apart by fundamental divisions that only the state can manage and mitigate. The vulnerability the state produces and actively circulates simultaneously sets itself up as the only agent capable of protecting Singaporeans from themselves.[51]

Instead of explaining its political dominance away as the result of an undemocratic, authoritarian regime or through a simple 'false consciousness' thesis, this is a better explanation for why the PAP's overbearing style of governance has, to all intents and purposes, worked and kept it in power. There is plenty of warranted criticism of the PAP's authoritarian or 'soft' authoritarian style, and how it sets out to undermine its political opponents.[52] It has certainly engaged in its fair share of chicanery: its parliamentary dominance means that it 'has been able to amend the constitution without much obstruction, introducing multimember constituencies, unelected parliamentary membership, and other institutional changes that have, in effect, strengthened the [PAP] government's electoral dominance and control of parliament'.[53] It is also true that whilst Singapore has the formal features of a liberal democracy built on the Westminster parliamentary system, it severely anti-politicizes the public sphere, eschews many of the substantive features of liberal democratic political systems such as the right to protest, and often actively suppresses activism and other civil society efforts.[54] Nonetheless, one must always grant the devil his due and it would be disingenuous to avoid engaging with the reality that a significant number of people, election upon election, have continued to grant the PAP a strong popular mandate. One might take strong issue with the exact magnitude of this mandate and its translation into parliamentary dominance – and with good reason. For example, despite a national vote share that normally hovers around 60–70 per cent, the PAP has always occupied at least 80 per cent of parliamentary seats and often higher. Nonetheless, it is difficult to dispute that the PAP retains the popular support of a signifiant number of Singaporeans.

Whatever one thinks, then, about the PAP government, which has ruled Singapore since independence, one must also contend with the fact that popular support for it is a defining feature of Singapore's political landscape. In their longitudinal analysis of voting pattern fluctuations, Bilveer Singh, Walid Jumblatt Abdullah, and Felix Tan show that, under the right circumstances, Singaporeans are more than willing to vote against the PAP.[55] Lee Kuan Yew recognized this as early as 1984, lamenting that Singaporeans had 'acquired the ability to play brinkmanship with their votes, and that they are in fact sending messages to the government without amounting to the removal of the PAP itself'.[56] The fact that the PAP has in any event formed the government at every election suggests that a sizeable proportion of Singaporeans want the PAP in power.

Of course, it is possible to interrogate what informs that desire and Yao Souchou's argument is persuasive in this regard, suggesting that 'traumatized by history of its own telling, it is only too tempting [for many Singaporeans] to turn to a political form in which conflict and division have no place, where national history is also the history of the ruling party under a leader of powerful personality.'[57] Perpetuating a constant sense of crisis places the government's paternalistic, high-handed style as offering a kind of comforting parental reassurance in the sea of uncertainty that is constantly buffeting Singapore. It is a mode of governance that has persisted since the founding of the nation, and here it is impossible to ignore the shadow of Lee Kuan Yew, which looms large over Singapore's nation-building project.

There is a strong tradition of Foucauldian genealogical scholarship that demonstrates how the state is often metonymized as a household with citizens requiring the guidance of a patriarchal figure.[58] Lee was the patriarchal figure in Singapore's nascence as a nation – the strict father who constantly spoke in a stern but loving voice. Perhaps no moment typified this more than the 1980 Fullerton election rally, now the stuff of Singaporean lore, when he declared 'Let there be no mistakes about it. Whoever governs Singapore must have that iron in him. Or give it up. This is not a game of cards – this is your life and mine. I spent a whole lifetime building this. And as long as I'm in charge, nobody's going to knock it down.'[59] The fact that it was raining only added to the theatre of the moment. Whilst those gathered began to take shelter under their umbrellas, Lee paid no heed to the downpour and continued without missing a beat – playing the role of the strong resilient father, perfectly exemplifying his point about having that 'iron'. Like the family patriarch who was convinced he knew best, Lee was unabashed about guiding with a strong hand, intruding into the private sphere of the individual, shaping people's behaviour as one might do with one's children. In the 1986 National Day Rally, for example, he said:

> I am accused often of interfering in private lives of citizens. Yes, if I did not, had I not done that, we wouldn't be here today. We'd be the old Singapore ... And I say without the slightest remorse, that we wouldn't be here, we would not have made economic progress, if we had not intervened on very personal matters – who your neighbour is, how you live, the noise you make, how you spit or where you spit or what language you use. Had we not done that and done it effectively, we would not be here today. It was fundamental social and cultural changes that brought us here.[60]

Casting himself and his government in the image of the strict father figure also meant simultaneously emasculating and infantilizing the general public – ostensibly for its own good. It is exactly this infantilization of the population, characterizing it as beset by division and strife, 'that makes possible the state's heroic self-definitions'.[61] The sense of security that Lee offered the nation as the father figure who would always protect his children was encapsulated in his final National Day Rally in 1988 before he stepped down as prime minister. In a comment meant to assuage the fear that the nation's protector was vacating his position, he declared: 'even from my sick bed, even if you are going to lower me into the grave, and I feel that something is going wrong, I'll get up'.[62] Lee was the Weberian 'charismatic leader' and a figure who represented the amalgamation of party, government, and state.[63]

The vulnerability generated by the state is thus mitigated by the state – initially personally through Lee Kuan Yew, and subsequently since by the PAP through its metonymic association. Even though Lee died in 2015, the sense of a paternal government attempting to herd an infantilized Singaporean population has not dissipated. Lee's son, Lee Hsien Loong, who was the country's third prime minister from 2004 to 2024 presented a direct hereditary lineage and thus naturally channelled some of Lee Kuan Yew's authority as the nation's symbolic father. But beyond a biological link, the tendency to invoke Lee's paternal voice endures with the current cohort of cabinet ministers who constantly seek to demonstrate their own genealogies to him by articulating how extensively they worked with him or interacted with him or embody his 'values' – and thereby channel his authority as the anointed protector of the nation.[64] In this sense, Lee Kuan Yew continues to animate the Singaporean lifeworld. He does not need to rise from the grave because his political descendants never fail to conjure him up and speak in his voice – a continuous moment of prosopopoeia that only works to 'stunt the growth of an already immature citizenry'.[65]

The state's propagation of heteronormativity and its role in Singaporean nationalism must be located within these domopolitical currents of vulnerability, paranoia, and crisis. Since independence, survival and regeneration of the nation have been foremost concerns of the state. One's duty to the nation is split along gendered lines: 'military service for men and maternal duty for women'.[66] In other words, the heteronormative expectations produced as a function of nationalism are co-constituted by gender differences. Other differences, too, multiply into these sets of expectations. For it is not all women who are meant to reproduce.

The call to repopulate the nation is inflected by Lee Kuan Yew's dalliance with eugenics in the 1980s, which came to a head in what was termed the Great Marriage Debate in 1983. Propelled by a deep conviction in biological essentialism and the general view 'that intelligence (and by extension, social and professional success), was largely [hereditary] and determined by genes',[67] Lee argued that graduate women should be encouraged to have more children so that their intelligence would be transmitted to their offspring, whilst in the same breath he also lamented the fact that the poor and those with less formal education were having more children.[68] Warning of a future that would comprise a floundering economy, poor public services, and a society on the brink of collapse, he 'linked these negative consequences directly to the alleged genetic inferiority of those parents having the combination of both low education and high fertility'.[69] Geraldine Heng and Janadas Devan sum up his hysterical logic:

> Within a few generations, the quality of Singapore's population would measurably decline, with a tiny minority of intelligent persons being increasingly swamped by a seething, proliferating mass of the unintelligent, untalented, and genetically inferior: industry would suffer, technology deteriorate, leadership disappear, and Singapore lose its competitive edge in the world.[70]

There are stark racial and class dimensions to Lee's exhortation, as well as a firm belief in biological essentialism that demonstrates how the expression of heteronormativity that structures subjectivity in Singapore is further specified by other rationalities such as racial, gender, and class differences. These beliefs translated into legislation and policy most explicitly with the government's introduction of the Graduate Mothers' Scheme. Under the scheme:

> children of graduate mothers [gained] priority admission to schools. Women who were better-educated – defined as those with at least five [GCE] O-level passes – could also get generous tax benefits if they had children, with tax breaks of 5, 10 and 15 per cent of earned income respectively for the first, second and third child ...

> Other women, however, were paid to Stop At Two or even at one. Women below 30 who agreed to sterilisation after the first or second child could get a cash grant of $10,000 – provided both the parents did not have any O-level passes, and earned less than $1,500 a month together. If she went on to have another child, she would have to repay the $10,000 cash grant with 10 per cent compound interest a year.[71]

The scheme resulted in massive public blowback and also encountered internal resistance within Lee's government, particularly among ministers who were themselves married to non-graduates, and was very quickly abandoned.[72] But the logic of 'encouraging the "right" people to populate the city-state remains to this day', with tertiary-educated women consistently singled out for not reproducing sufficiently, and less educated and poor women constantly chided for having too many children.[73] There is a racialized dimension that complements the classed dimension to the selective logic of the state's pronatalist encouragement, with Malay Singaporeans in particular discouraged from having 'too many' children. As Teo puts it, in plenty of political discourse this is framed as a national problem where 'the Malay family form requires intervention, to curb early marriage and perhaps even fertility'.[74] Whilst comprehensively unwinding the racialized, classed, and gendered logics in the state's domopolitical vision of reproducing the nation is perhaps beyond this book's scope, it is still worth noting how racialized and classed logics are embedded into the circulation of heteronormative reproduction.

What motivated Lee's dalliance with eugenics was, not unlike other political leaders who bought into it, a distinct preoccupation with the survival of the nation.[75] In his view, 'the loss of [graduate mothers'] progeny was a loss to the nation's talent pool' that would eventually lead to its ruination.[76] In this way, heteronormativity is co-constituted by its gendered expectations of men and women, its classed and racialized expectations of the highly educated and less well-off, and the relentless maintenance of the heterosexual nuclear family unit, bound up with the vulnerability and paranoia that lie at the heart of the Singaporean nation. The particular performance of heterosexuality that is scripted into Singaporean subjectivity is rationalized as integral to the survival and replication of the nation. Queerness – failing to correctly recite from this hymn sheet of heterosexuality – therefore becomes a threat to the nation. Postcolonial Singaporean nationalism brings together all this baggage of history as well as insecurities of the nation to assemble queered people in the position of the delinquent subject in the straight nation.

At the affective junction of the home, military, and family

Teo argues that 'for all the talk of family values, and community traditions, the family is effectively treated as an *individual* unit' in Singapore.[77] The significance the sign of the family occupies in the national imaginary is held up by the primacy of heteronormativity humming in the background, and it is through the institution of the heterosexual nuclear family that citizens are taught to imagine the nation. One of the most significant ways that the family as an abstract concept is specified and possibilities of family formation are curated is through the HDB. Specifically, this is achieved through its policies that set the parameters around who is eligible to purchase public housing in the country.

After Singapore was granted self-government by the British colonial regime in 1959, one of the biggest immediate challenges the newly elected PAP government faced was housing Singapore's burgeoning population. People were living in overcrowded shophouses,[78] residential quarters, and villages that were crammed to their limits.[79] If the Singaporean government was already committed to instituting a public housing programme in 1959, independence in 1965 only further strengthened that resolve. For Lee Kuan

Yew, an adequately housed population was crucial in ensuring Singapore's social and political stability. Reflecting on his decision, he said:

> I wanted a home-owning society. I had seen the contrast between the blocks of low-cost rental apartments, badly misused and poorly maintained, and those of house-proud owners, and was convinced that if every family owned its home, the country would be more stable.
>
> [...]
>
> After independence in 1965, I was troubled by Singapore's completely urban electorate. I had seen how voters in capital cities always tended to vote against the government of the day and was determined that our householders should become homeowners, otherwise we would not have political stability. My other important motive was to give all parents whose sons would have to do national service a stake in the Singapore their sons had to defend. If the soldier's family did not own their home, he would soon conclude he would be fighting to protect the properties of the wealthy. I believed this sense of ownership was vital for our new society which had no deep roots in a common historical experience.[80]

Chua Beng Huat argues that 'the greatest potential legitimacy that can be gained by a government is through direct provision of housing because its efforts and results would be most visible'.[81] The PAP government in Singapore has done just that. The national public housing programme 'stands as [its] signal achievement' – demonstrative of its commitment to meeting the material needs of Singaporeans and 'a foundation of its legitimacy and longevity in parliamentary power'.[82]

The project to build public housing first started in 1927 through the Singapore Improvement Trust (SIT), which was established under the British colonial government. But the SIT was a poorly funded, underwhelming institution that never proved capable of sufficiently meeting the population's housing needs. It was replaced by the HDB in 1960, and this marked the nascence of public housing as an institution in Singapore.[83] Except for the actual construction of the apartment blocks, which is outsourced to private construction companies, the HDB handles everything housing-related including the planning, design, allocation, and pricing of flats. Public housing is not constructed as a legal entitlement in Singapore and as such, the HDB is free to act like any other private real-estate developer; it can set eligibility conditions, contractual terms, and make executive decisions as to the number of new housing projects to be built.[84] Within three decades of its establishment, by the mid-1990s, more than 85 per cent of Singapore's population lived in HDB flats. The HDB had essentially become 'the monopolistic and universal housing provider for the nation'.[85]

If one pays attention to Lee Kuan Yew's early sentiments, one will notice that his motivation behind creating a large public housing programme was never simply to provide people with housing per se. Simply putting a roof over people's heads was not good enough; it needed to be accompanied by the affective and material reality of owning their homes. But this conviction did not arise from an ideological belief in the universal provision and decommodification of housing.[86] Rather, Lee understood that the effect of widespread home ownership would be the 'expansion of commitment to the prevalent social order by the development of personal stakes in its survival'.[87] It would steadily enmesh more and more people with the national enterprise – the nation as a political project could also become a personal project. Thus, in his assessment, the formation of the HDB was 'crucial, life and death. If we failed, we would not be re-elected. This was the first year of office of [the] PAP.'[88] The provision of public housing was in this way intertwined with both Lee's own political fortunes and the survival of the nation.

In 1964, the HDB introduced the home ownership scheme where individuals could purchase their HDB flat. All HDB flats would be sold on a 99-year lease whilst the land itself remained in the state's perpetual ownership. This material distinction between the land and the flat built on the land meant the state still retained a legal backstop to resettle and compensate any owner if (re)development was judged necessary. The Land Acquisition Act passed in 1966 buttressed this and allowed the state to take into possession any land it judged necessary for national development with compensation fixed by the statute or the market rate – whichever happened to be lower.[89]

With the introduction of the 99-year lease and the home ownership scheme, instead of renting from the state, residents could now choose to buy their flats and – importantly – experience owning their flats.[90] Initially, the home ownership scheme had difficulties getting off the ground because many people did not have enough money to make the down-payment. But once the government found an elegant workaround that involved using personal retirement savings to solve this capital constraint, home ownership rates soared. By the late 1980s, 90 per cent of public housing residents owned their homes.[91]

Owning something that, for many, was easily the most expensive asset they would ever purchase or possess in their entire lives meant they had a far greater material stake in a future where Singapore not only survived as an independent country but also grew economically.[92] Significantly, this 'sense of ownership' that Lee Kuan Yew so desired simultaneously brought into being entirely new possibilities of loss. After all, one can only lose something one possesses. Near-universal home ownership meant almost every Singaporean now had something precious to lose – and, therefore, something precious to defend. Like this, the patriotic injunction to treat one's country as one's home is inscribed into the lives of Singaporeans through the figuration of the HDB flat. It was precisely for this reason that in addition to buoying the young PAP government's political legitimacy, Lee also saw the provision of public housing and its concomitant home ownership as vital – albeit indirectly – to Singapore's defence and security.

Whilst Singapore does have a small professional military, it has largely been formed of a conscript force since conscription was introduced in 1967. As such, the small number of professional soldiers notwithstanding, the nation's defence is contingent on the willingness of mostly male Singaporean citizens to bear a weapon, wield it, and potentially kill or be 'persuaded to lay down their lives' for the nation.[93] In Anderson's telling, such an act requires a depth of feeling that can only arise from the belief that one is acting in service of something much larger and more powerful than oneself – and the conceptual frame of the nation provides this. Lee, however, could not countenance this, fearing that '[i]f the soldier's family did not own their home, he would soon conclude he would be fighting to protect the properties of the wealthy'.[94]

Singapore's somewhat reluctant arrival at independence is worth bearing in mind here. As Lee put it:

> In the first place, we did not want to be Singaporean. We wanted to be Malayans. Then the idea was extended and we decided to become Malaysians. But twenty-three months of Malaysia – a traumatic experience for all parties in Malaysia – ended rather abruptly with our being Singaporeans.[95]

Whilst the question of Singapore as a sovereign state was settled when it separated from Malaysia in 1965, the question of Singapore as a nation was far less straightforward. In Singapore's early years, Lee Kuan Yew was convinced – either out of cynicism or realism, or perhaps both – that a Herderian national spirit did not exist in the minds of people for whom *Singaporean* had hardly carried any meaning as an imagined community on its own. Expecting citizens to place their lives on the line in defence of a nation-state they could barely imagine was a fool's errand as far as he was concerned. Using home ownership as a modality through which one would own a small part of the nation amounted to an atomized materialization of the nation. The abstract totality of the national imaginary was broken down into individual HDB flat-sized parcels such that in defending Singapore, one was doing so whilst imagining and defending the home one owned. In this way, the defence of Singapore became the sum total of individuals protecting their individual homes. By massively expanding public housing and the attendant affects of home ownership, citizens were coaxed into having skin in the game, so to speak.

At this point, one could draw attention to the gendered configuration of affects here. Technically, it would only apply to Singaporean males, since conscription only applies to Singaporean men. This is true to a certain extent. But it is worth remembering that the individual is also a relational being – in a relation to one's family, for instance. As such, even though it is only male citizens (and a small number of women who choose to join the military as professional soldiers) who must contend with the possibility of losing their own lives, this potentiality of loss is also imbricated within every Singaporean family. It is from this potentiality that nationalism, and a collective stake in the stable futurity of the nation, springs forth. In this way, public housing is tied to the defence and continued existence of Singapore itself. Whilst this began as a relatively weak connection in the immediate post-1965 years, it was strengthened over the decades by two processes occurring in parallel. First, the home ownership scheme gradually induced the affects of ownership in an ever-growing number of people and new families; second, successive generations of Singaporean males were undertaking NS. Whereas, initially, enlisted soldiers were not likely to be homeowners themselves – it was far more likely that their parents owned the HDB flats – as they grew older and purchased their own HDB flats, their own stake in the country via public housing deepened.

The state's formulation of the HDB flat as a parcel of the nation has remained consistent. In a speech he gave in 2011, Lee Kuan Yew's remarks on home ownership showed that his thinking had barely shifted – he was steadfastly convinced of its importance to Singapore and its role in nation-building. He said:

> Our families own their homes and are rooted to Singapore. Owning their homes gives everybody a sense of ownership. Moreover, with NS, every family must have a stake in a property to defend.
>
> [...]
>
> Singaporeans know that their HDB flats are valuable. As Singapore prospers, the value of their HDB homes also appreciate[s]. Home ownership motivates Singaporeans to work hard and to aspire for a better future for their family, to upgrade to better and bigger flats.[96]

He also attributed the country's security and stability to its high home ownership rates, saying:

> We have created a property-owning democracy, that's why we have stability in Singapore. You want people to defend this country, you must give them a stake. They are not going to defend this country for Far East Properties or Hong Leong or whoever. You own this home. You will fight for your family and yourself.[97]

Similarly, prime minister Lee Hsien Loong alluded to the idea of a 'stake in the nation' in 2018 whilst discussing public housing and home owner-ship[98] – demonstrating the depth of the state's belief that 'home owner-ship, in giving the people a greater stake in the nation, will induce in them a greater measure of [belonging]'.[99] Addressing the country at the 2018 National Day Rally,[100] Lee reiterated the first PAP government's rationale for home ownership, saying: 'They wanted every citizen to benefit from the country's growth and prosperity, and to have a valuable stake that would be theirs that they would defend, if necessary, with their lives.'[101]

Lee Kuan Yew was convinced that without a common collective his-torical reservoir they could draw from, Singapore did not possess a suf-ficiently powerful abstract national imaginary of the style that Anderson and contemporaries claimed could move its citizens to give their lives or take another's. The affect of home ownership thus functions as a modality that substitutes the materiality of the citizen's home into this void. In this way, the affect of ownership, of having a stake in the stable futurity of the country, functions as a wellspring from which a feeling of belonging springs forth to protect the territory named Singapore. And this is what Lee had in mind when he suggested it was imperative that Singaporeans own their homes so that they would be ready to defend the country and to 'fight for [their] family and [themselves]'.[102]

One of life's basic needs is shelter – a roof over our heads – and public housing in Singapore certainly fulfils that need. But it also does much more. Personal survival is also intertwined with the country's survival – the coun-try's defence rests on its citizen army's willingness to protect it, aided by the affect and knowledge that one is defending one's property. Housing, and owning one's flat, are thus crucial on a national scale because they engen-der a feeling of something to lose – affects that are materially crystallized through the concrete walls of one's HDB flat. For the Singaporean gov-ernment, from Lee Kuan Yew's to the current one, nationalism flows from materiality rather than a more abstract notion of nation. Defending one's home is something to be taken literally. Through home ownership, and by inducing its affect in the majority of the population, the collective act of defending the nation is transformed into a personal one – literally protecting one's property. One could read this as the ultimate neoliberal transforma-tion of citizenship.

As of 2017, more than 80 per cent of Singaporeans reside in public hous-ing, which marks it out as a significant node in the production of a particu-lar Singaporean subjectivity. Public housing has been transformed into a ubiquitous national symbol and access to it constitutes a marker of citizen-ship.[103] At the 2018 National Day Rally, Lee Hsien Loong remarked that '[i]t is the Singaporean norm ... Public housing in Singapore is really "national housing"'.[104] The HDB and public housing are thus contained within the formation of the national imaginary,[105] as well as the establishment and maintenance of the government's legitimacy.[106] This also means that the HDB – in setting eligibility conditions – effectively pronounces upon the legitimacy of family formations as well by offering housing, and the attendant affect of home ownership, only to particularly configured households.

The production of the affects of ownership occurs through a complex web of relations that means individuals pay for their homes with their own money but are often able to do so without actually suffering a significant reduction in their monthly disposable income. At the core of the web that generates this sense of ownership is the Central Provident Fund (CPF) scheme – Singapore's compulsory national savings scheme. The CPF scheme requires that every citizen pay a proportion of their monthly salary into their personal CPF savings account. Employers are also similarly required to contribute an amount as a proportion of their employees' salaries.[107] The money accumulated in one's CPF savings is basically meant to be an individual pension plan that provides one with an income after retirement, so it can only be withdrawn upon retirement.

When it was first instituted by the British colonial regime, the CPF scheme was an individual pension plan where employee and employer each contributed an amount equalling 3 per cent of the employee's salary to their CPF account, with the accumulated funds to be withdrawn upon retirement at 55. That is no longer the case. Since Singapore's independence in 1965, the CPF scheme has been tweaked and modified in a number of ways. Currently, a proportion of it is ringfenced for personal healthcare spending and individuals can further choose to invest a proportion of their CPF savings in certain government-approved bonds or securities.

The most significant modification to the CPF scheme with regard to public housing, however, occurred in 1968, when the CPF Act was amended to allow Singaporeans to use their CPF savings to purchase public housing.[108] With this change, both the down-payment and mortgage repayments could be paid directly from one's CPF account – and this opened an entirely new set of affective possibilities in the realm of home ownership. When the HDB had first offered residents the option of buying their flats on a fixed 99-year lease, reception was poor. Lee Kuan Yew recounts that '[t]he HDB offered buyers housing loans in 1964, at a low interest rate with repayment periods of up to 15 years, but the scheme did not take off. Prospective buyers could not raise the down payment of 20 percent of the selling price.'[109] Because of the difficulties they faced raising sufficient capital to finance their potential purchase, only about 13.6 per cent of public housing tenants opted to purchase their homes in 1964. After the 1968 amendment, however, home ownership rates increased dramatically. 'In 1968 alone, 44 per cent of all public-housing applicants elected to "buy" their flats. By 1970, 63 per cent applied to buy, and in 1986 the figure reached 90 per cent.'[110] Given the choice between spending their CPF savings on buying a home for themselves and having that money sit in their CPF savings account until retirement, the vast majority of Singaporeans chose to purchase HDB flats.[111]

In this almost magical way, the CPF scheme produces the affects of home ownership without imposing very much of a material economic cost to the individual. On the one hand, because the money comes from a personal account bearing their name, citizens develop a genuine sense of ownership – the kind of ownership that arises from paying for something using one's own money. Yet, at the same time, because their monthly CPF contribution would have been deducted from their monthly salary and would have been inaccessible till retirement anyway, they crucially do not experience a reduction in their disposable income and daily consumption. Most people – especially dual-income households – are able to meet the demands of their mortgage repayment schedule without having to dip into their personal savings – mostly because they work out beforehand the type of flat they can afford based on their ability to service their mortgage using their CPF savings.[112] In this way, the affects of ownership are produced without much of the material cost of ownership, the pleasure of consumption is produced without the cost of consumption, and a near-universal state of home ownership is conjured up through the sorcery of compulsory savings.

The sexual contingencies of home ownership

The eligibility conditions set around public housing regulate its access – they delimit who is able to purchase a HDB flat and who is left out of the picture. Because of the very high cost of residential property in the private property market,[113] notwithstanding the small minority that can afford housing on the private market, the HDB is effectively the universal provider of housing for Singaporeans.[114] As such, its eligibility conditions do much more than merely regulate access. Through insistence on the formation of a family nucleus, and then the definition of what counts as a family nucleus, the form of the family is idealized, regulated, and realized through public housing. In this way, by setting conditions around access to what is effectively a shared national practice, the HDB aids in the reproduction of heteronormativity by pronouncing upon the legitimacy of familial forms in relation to the nation.

Generally, only Singaporean citizens or permanent residents who are 21 and above, and who intend to form a nuclear family either with their parents or a marital partner of the opposite sex qualify to buy public housing from the HDB.[115] The condition of marriage shows the heteronormative force embedded within Singapore's public housing policy by tying domesticity to a specific form of heterosexual coupling and family formation; and it is through this that heteronormativity is reproduced and reinforced. Heterosexual marriage thus functions as a fulcrum upon which contrasting degrees of access to public housing, a vital public good and marker of belonging, are balanced. Depending on how one engages with it, the balance either tilts towards or away from one.

As a concept and institution, marriage acquires an additional layer of meaning. But it is insufficient to simply trace the interaction of public housing eligibility conditions with family formation and demonstrate how access to public housing depends on whether an individual chooses to get married. The crucial question here is not whether one engages with the institution of marriage or chooses to form a family nucleus. Rather, we should interrogate the frame that enshrines these apparent choices and ask, in the first place, who is able to engage with the institution of marriage and who is precluded? Only by posing this question is the full heteronormative force embedded within public housing policy made clear because it is not possible to proffer an answer to this question without becoming aware of the fact that the institution of marriage in Singapore is only made available to heterosexual couples. Non-heterosexual coupling does not figure as a possibility in the eyes of the state. Thus, it is not just the creation of a family nucleus that is being promoted; it is specifically heterosexual coupling and the heterosexual nuclear family that are reified through the eligibility conditions that are set up around public housing.[116]

The universality of public housing in Singapore and its nomination as 'national housing' means housing policy is a particularly salient mechanism through which the state exerts a disciplinary force on familial forms.[117] It is 'through public housing that the state signifies and institutionalizes most strongly its [heteronormative] vision of the ideal family'.[118] Here, one sees the disciplining function of Foucauldian power where its functioning is contingent on subjects' participation in their subjection.[119] Disciplinary power is exercised not by a state that exists up above, but through a processual interaction. The citizen-subject retains the freedom to make a choice. But it is the freedom of a false choice, for the matrix within which these choices are inscribed has already been delimited by the state according to a heteronormative logic that privileges married heterosexual couples and the formation of heterosexual nuclear families. This is the precise effect of the policies and eligibility conditions that envelop public housing.

It is beside the point whether the policies surrounding public housing have actually achieved the state's intended effect in terms of encouraging heterosexual coupling and nuclear family formation to reproduce the nation. On the contrary, the country's demographic trends show that the total fertility rate has remained below the replacement rate of 2.1 and is on a consistent downward slope.[120] In and of themselves, then, the policies have failed. Yet, in their existence, they inscribe a certain normality and contribute to producing a shared Singaporean script. One is free to deviate from this script but does so knowing full well that one is deviating from what it is to be a 'normal' Singaporean. If we accept that the HDB flat and the affects of home ownership are crucial to the sustenance of the nation, then we should be hypersensitive to the operation of inclusion/exclusion in this sphere. For, taking seriously the state's position that public housing is a Singaporean norm, it follows that those who cannot or do not have access to public housing are presumed not to be a part of that norm, presumed not to belong or to have done enough to belong to the nation. This is the lot of queered people.

To be fair, there are some exceptions to the heteronormative policies that allow some queered folks space to navigate these restrictions around accessing public housing. One of the most obvious ways is through the Joint Singles Scheme (JSS) – a relatively new scheme – which allows unmarried adults above 35 to purchase their own flat, albeit from a very limited pool.[121] Yet, in this formula, the queered subject is still an exception that the state has deigned to cater to through a specific scheme and whose needs are deprioritized in relation to heterosexual couples because the latter reflect a commitment to promoting family formation. To debate the extent of exceptionalism is to risk missing the state's production of the exception in the first place. The significance of the HDB's eligibility conditions is that they normalize heterosexual coupling – marking it out as a distinct norm against which other forms of coupling (or lack thereof) become deviant.

Nonetheless, it is true that the JSS creates some affordances for queered people to access public housing – even if on different terms and at a different life stage than heterosexual couples. It is certainly the case, then, that the HDB policy of 'allowing a single person and/or groups of single people above a certain age group to legally apply and buy a public flat … has also unwittingly sanctioned the blossoming of new domestic non-heteronormative sexual partnerships'.[122] Home ownership is still conceptualized through a heteronormative lens but 'although a hegemonic discourse of heteronormative home ownership continues to prevail, the new government policy has unwittingly made possible non-heteronormative domesticity'.[123] Arguments in this vein that point out how queered individuals have found ways to cope with the astringencies of the state are thus certainly not wrong. But instead of paying attention to how some queered subjects are able to sidestep the state's heteronormative strictures, I want to focus for a moment on the production of queer subjectivity.

In the case of LGBT couples, for example, the JSS has allowed some LGBT couples access to forms of domesticity previously unavailable to them.

But they have had to attain this through the occupation of a veiled subject position by essentially pretending to be two unmarried heterosexual singles. One could open the dossier of institutional legibility here by thinking about how the state reads and recognizes subjects – a move that is contingent on subjects being rendered legible in particular ways.[124] We know that whilst, on the face of it, LGBT couples are ineligible to purchase a HDB flat, the JSS provides sufficient cover for them to do so – by buying a flat as two singles instead. In other words, as long as LGBT couples maintain an institutional visibility as two singles, the state is unable to read them otherwise. In fact, because marriage in Singapore is restricted to heterosexuals, the state has no mechanism that would make non-heterosexual coupling legible to it – it is therefore not capable of reading LGBT couples as anything other than two unmarried heterosexual people. But marriage as the institution that makes heterosexuality legible also means that a heterosexual couple only become legible as such if they get married. Thus, two heterosexuals who wish to co-habit without getting married would similarly not be able to purchase a HDB flat except through the JSS – just like an LGBT couple and other queered subjects. As I have previously intimated in the introduction, heterosexuality and heteronormativity are not the same thing. The elevation of a particular expression of heterosexuality leads to the queering of multiple groups, not just LGBT people; it means that straight people too can be governed by it in ways that place them in particular straitjackets by demanding that they express heterosexuality according to a fixed script of straightness.

Buying a home whilst posing as two single people is a creative way to defy the state's heteronormative home ownership rules but it does nothing to change the fact that they are compelled to beat a path around the state in the first place – in a way that married heterosexual couples do not have to. It is only in masking queerness, in hiding it from the eye of the state, that queered subjects are able to access public housing. These different possibilities of 'non-heteronormative domesticity' thus still do not quite resolve the real problem: that the 'hegemonic discourse of heteronormative home ownership continues to prevail'.[125] It is in the very act of having to mask queerness, one's deviance from the norm, that Singaporean subjectivity is always-already beyond the queered subject. What it also shows is how the operation of heteronormativity and its attendant logics can minoritize a range of people – LGBT people, single individuals, co-habiting heterosexuals, and more – who are queered as a result.

Locating the three faces of heteronormativity – public housing, marriage, and heterosexual nuclear family formation, as well as the military – in the national imaginary reveals the ways in which the nation is produced and protected through the HDB flat, through its distinctive towers, which traverse virtually the entire country. Gazing out the window of one's flat at hundreds of similar flats, knowing that each probably houses a heterosexual couple or nuclear family, knowing that marriage was a similar condition of purchase, knowing that each flat belongs to at least one person ostensibly willing to give their life to protect it, there is a powerful sense of uniformity that insists it is normal simply because it is how everyone else in Singapore lives as well.[126] The window of the HDB flat thus becomes a window into a heteronormative lifeworld that appears dominant, maintaining the illusion of a straight nation, and continuing to render it a 'value precisely equivalent to reality'.[127]

Notes

1 Chua Beng Huat, *Liberalism Disavowed: Communitarianism and State Capitalism in Singapore* (Ithaca: Cornell University Press, 2017), p. 51.
2 Cherian George, *Air-Conditioned Nation Revisited: Essays on Singapore Politics* (Singapore: Ethos Books, 2020), p. 19.
3 Terence Chong, 'Embodying Society's Best: Hegel and the Singapore State', *Journal of Contemporary Asia*, 36.3 (2006), 283–304 (p. 284).
4 Hill and Lian, *The Politics of Nation Building*, p. 23; also see Vasil, *Governing Singapore*, p. 57.
5 See, for example, Michael D. Barr, *The Ruling Elite of Singapore: Networks of Power and Influence* (London: I.B. Tauris, 2014); Michael D. Barr and Zlatko Skrbiš, *Constructing Singapore: Elitism, Ethnicity and the Nation-Building Project* (Copenhagen: NIAS, 2009).
6 Michel Foucault, *Dits et écrits 1954–1988* (Paris: Gallimard, 1994), Vol. IV (1980–88), p. 237.
7 Anderson, *Imagined Communities*, p. 144.
8 Gopal Balakrishnan, ed., *Mapping the Nation* (London: Verso, 1996), p. 210.
9 Lee Hsien Loong, 'National Day Rally 2018', 2018, National Archives of Singapore, www.nas.gov.sg/archivesonline/audiovisual_records/record-details/472db30e-7d02-11e9-a894-001a4a5ba61b (accessed 27 September 2024).
10 William Walters, 'Secure Borders, Safe Haven, Domopolitics', *Citizenship Studies*, 8.3 (2004), 237–60 (p. 240).
11 All fit, able-bodied, male citizens are conscripted into the Singapore Armed Forces upon turning 18. A small number are posted to the police and civil defence forces. They serve for a period of up to two years after which they return to their civilian lives and are assigned to a reserve unit. Reserve forces can be recalled for up to 40 days of training per year for up to 10 years after completing NS. Whilst conscription applies only to male Singaporean citizens, female citizens can (and some do) choose to enlist in the military full time.
12 Gwyneth Lonergan, 'Reproducing the "National Home": Gendering Domopolitics', *Citizenship Studies*, 22.1 (2018), 1–18 (p. 2). See also Carole Pateman, *The Disorder of Women: Democracy, Feminism and Political*

Theory (Cambridge: Polity Press, 1989); and Ruth Lister, *Citizenship: Feminist Perspectives* (Basingstoke: Palgrave Macmillan, 2003).

13 Tang and Quah, 'Heteronormativity and Sexuality Politics', p. 651; see also Yuval-Davis, *Gender & Nation*.

14 Lonergan, 'Reproducing the "National Home"', p. 2.

15 Lee Kuan Yew, *From Third World to First: The Singapore Story, 1965–2000* (New York: HarperCollins, 2000), pp. 95–96.

16 Valluvan, *The Clamour of Nationalism*, p. 175.

17 Walters, 'Secure Borders', p. 241.

18 Valluvan, *The Clamour of Nationalism*, p. 34.

19 William E. Connolly, *The Ethos of Pluralization* (Minneapolis: University of Minnesota Press, 1995).

20 Daiva K. Stasiulis, 'International Migration, Rights, and the Decline of "Actually Existing Liberal Democracy"', *Journal of Ethnic and Migration Studies*, 23.2 (1997), 197–214 (p. 203).

21 'Prime Minister Lee Kuan Yew (Right) Holding a Press Conference to Announce the Separation of Singapore from Malaysia', National Archives of Singapore, 1965, www.nas.gov.sg/archivesonline/photographs/record-details/61b36405-1162-11e3-83d5-0050568939ad (accessed 4 October 2024).

22 Lee, *The Singapore Story*, pp. 15–16.

23 Ibid., p. 16.

24 Kenneth Paul Tan, 'The Ideology of Pragmatism: Neo-Liberal Globalisation and Political Authoritarianism in Singapore', *Journal of Contemporary Asia*, 42.1 (2012), 67–92 (p. 72).

25 Hussin, 'Textual Construction of a Nation', p. 419.

26 Partha Chatterjee, 'Whose Imagined Community?', in *Mapping the Nation*, ed. Gopal Balakrishnan (London: Verso, 1996), pp. 214–25 (p. 216).

27 Lee, *The Singapore Story*, p. 22.

28 Alfian Sa'at, Faris Joraimi, and Siew Min Sai, 'Introduction', in *Raffles Renounced: Towards a Merdeka History*, ed. Alfian Sa'at, Faris Joraimi, and Siew Min Sai (Singapore: Ethos Books, 2021), pp. 11–16 (p. 13).

29 Ibid., p. 13.

30 Lee Hsien Loong, 'Transcript of Dialogue with Prime Minister Lee Hsien Loong at the SG50+ Conference on 2 July 2015', Prime Minister's Office, 2015, www.pmo.gov.sg/Newsroom/transcript-dialogue-prime-minister-lee-hsien-loong-sg50-conference-2-july-2015 (accessed 17 September 2024).

31 'Speech to Parliament on Civil Service Salary Revisions' (Singapore: Hansard, 2007).

32 'Transcript of the Broadcast on August 13 at 10.30 p.m. over Radio Singapore – Being a Speech Made by the Finance Minister, Dr. Goh Keng Swee, on July 26, before the United Nations Special Committee on Colonialism, and a Summary of the Case of the Singapore Government by the Prime Minister, Mr. Lee Kuan Yew, Disposing of Points Made by the Representatives of the 19 Singapore Assemblymen who Appeared before the Committee Earlier in the Morning of

the Same Day' (Radio Singapore, 1962), National Archives of Singapore, www. nas.gov.sg/archivesonline/speeches/record-details/73a9ee43-115d-11e3-83d5-0050568939ad (accessed 27 September 2024).

33 'Speech to Parliament on Civil Service Salary Revisions'.

34 Cherian George, 'Consolidating Authoritarian Rule: Calibrated Coercion in Singapore', *The Pacific Review*, 20.2 (2007), 127–45 (p. 132).

35 Bilahari Kausikan, 'The Arena: Southeast Asia in the Age of Great-Power Rivalry', *Foreign Affairs*, 16 February 2021, www.foreignaffairs.com/reviews/review-essay/2021-02-16/arena (accessed 17 September 2024).

36 Amitav Acharya, *Singapore's Foreign Policy: The Search for Regional Order* (Singapore: World Scientific Publishing, 2008), p. 9.

37 Lee, 'Transcript of Dialogue with Prime Minister Lee Hsien Loong at the SG50+ Conference on 2 July 2015'.

38 Gilroy, *There Ain't No Black in the Union Jack*, p. 46.

39 Paul Gilroy, Tony Sandset, Sindre Bangstad, and Gard Ringen Høibjerg, 'A Diagnosis of Contemporary Forms of Racism, Race and Nationalism: A Conversation with Professor Paul Gilroy', *Cultural Studies*, 33.2 (2019), 173–97.

40 Sivamohan Valluvan, 'Racist Apologism and the Refuge of Nation', *Ethnic and Racial Studies*, 2021, 466–77 (p. 471).

41 This phrase was first deployed during Ronald Reagan's 1980 presidential campaign. Donald Trump resurrected it in his 2016 presidential campaign and it has remained a key tenet of US nationalism since.

42 This is a popular phrase in the United Kingdom that was initially central to the Brexit campaign to leave the European Union and has now become a recurring trope in British nationalism.

43 Lee, 'Transcript of Dialogue with Prime Minister Lee Hsien Loong at the SG50+ Conference on 2 July 2015'.

44 Richard Borsuk and Reginald Chua, 'Singapore Strains Relations with Indonesia's President', *The Wall Street Journal*, 4 August 1998.

45 Goh Chok Tong, 'National Day Rally 1998', 1998, National Archives of Singapore, www.nas.gov.sg/archivesonline/speeches/record-details/771287e0-115d-11e3-83d5-0050568939ad (accessed 27 September 2024).

46 Lee, 'Transcript of Dialogue with Prime Minister Lee Hsien Loong at the SG50+ Conference on 2 July 2015'.

47 Lee Hsien Loong, 'Keynote Address by Deputy Prime Minister, Mr Lee Hsien Loong at the Network Conference 2003: Learning and Living the Singapore Story', 2003, National Archives of Singapore, www.nas.gov.sg/archivesonline/data/pdfdoc/2003050301.htm (accessed 27 September 2024); also see Buck Song Koh, *Brand Singapore: Nation Branding after Lee Kuan Yew, in a Divisive World*, 2nd edn (Singapore: Marshall Cavendish Business, 2017).

48 Thongchai Winichakul, *Siam Mapped: A History of the Geo-Body of a Nation* (Honolulu: University of Hawai'i Press, 1997).

49 Ibid., pp. 167–70.

50 Anderson, *Imagined Communities*, pp. 163–86.

51 Laavanya Kathiravelu, 'Rethinking Race: Beyond the CMIO Categorization', in *Living with Myths in Singapore*, ed. Kah Seng Loh, Pingtjin Thum, and Jack Meng-Tat Chia (Singapore: Ethos Books, 2017), pp. 159–68.

52 See for example Hussin Mutalib, 'Illiberal Democracy and the Future of Opposition in Singapore', *Third World Quarterly*, 21.2 (2000), 313–42; Tan, 'The Ideology of Pragmatism'; and George, 'Consolidating Authoritarian Rule'.

53 Tan, 'The Ideology of Pragmatism', p. 71.

54 See, for example, Terence Lee, 'The Politics of Civil Society in Singapore', *Asian Studies Review*, 26.1 (2002), 97–117; Giok Ling Ooi and Gillian Koh, eds, *State–Society Relations in Singapore* (Singapore: Eastern Universities Press for Institute of Policy Studies, 2003); and Garry Rodan, 'Embracing Electronic Media but Suppressing Civil Society: Authoritarian Consolidation in Singapore', *The Pacific Review*, 16.4 (2003), 503–24.

55 Bilveer Singh, Walid Jumblatt Abdullah, and Felix Tan, *Unmasking Singapore's 2020 General Elections: COVID-19 and the Evolving Political Landscape* (Singapore: World Scientific, 2021).

56 Cited in Chua Beng Huat, 'Political Space: Has It Shrunk since the '60s?', in *Space, Spaces and Spacing: The Substation Conference 1995*, ed. Weng Choy Lee (Singapore: The Substation, 1996), pp. 20–26 (p. 24).

57 Souchou Yao, *Singapore: The State and the Culture of Excess* (London: Routledge, 2007), p. 45.

58 Mitchell Dean, *Governmentality: Power and Rule in Modern Society* (Thousand Oaks: Sage, 1999), p. 201.

59 rubatirabbit, 'Lee Kuan Yew versus the SIA Strikers', YouTube, 2015, www.youtube.com/watch?v=ytMXSLeqFMY (accessed 17 September 2024).

60 Lee Kuan Yew, 'National Day Rally 1986', 1986, National Archives of Singapore, www.nas.gov.sg/archivesonline/audiovisual_records/record-details/48aabfb1-1164-11e3-83d5-0050568939ad (accessed 27 September 2024).

61 Kenneth Paul Tan, 'Who's Afraid of Catherine Lim? The State in Patriarchal Singapore', *Asian Studies Review*, 33.1 (2009), 43–62 (p. 48).

62 Lee Kuan Yew, 'National Day Rally 1988', 1988, National Archives of Singapore, www.nas.gov.sg/archivesonline/audiovisual_records/record-details/d9d20500-9629-11e4-859c-0050568939ad (27 September 2024).

63 Max Weber, *From Max Weber: Essays in Sociology* (London: Routledge, 1991), p. 296.

64 Singapore's fourth prime minister, Lawrence Wong, is no exception in this regard. See Lawrence Wong, 'Lawrence Wong at the Joint Initiative "Grateful for the Present, Nurturing the Future" in Support of the Lee Kuan Yew Centennial Fund', Prime Minister's Office, 2023, www.pmo.gov.sg/Newsroom/DPM-Wong-at-the-Joint-Initiative-in-Support-of-the-LKY-Centennial-Fund (accessed 17 September 2024). See also Swee Keat Heng, 'Heng Swee Keat's Intimate Essay on the Red Box, & What Working for the Late Lee Kuan Yew Was Like', *Mothership*, 2015, https://mothership.sg/2018/12/red-box-heng-swee-keat-lky/ (accessed 17 September 2024).

65 Tan, 'Who's Afraid of Catherine Lim?', p. 58.
66 Tang and Quah, 'Heteronormativity and Sexuality Politics', p. 651.
67 C. K. Chan, 'Eugenics on the Rise: A Report from Singapore', *International Journal of Health Services*, 15.4 (1985), 707–12 (p. 708).
68 Diane K. Mauzy and R. S. Milne, *Singapore Politics under the People's Action Party* (London: Routledge, 2002), p. 55.
69 J. John Palen, 'Fertility and Eugenics: Singapore's Population Policies', *Population Research and Policy Review*, 5.1 (1986), 3–14 (p. 5).
70 Geraldine Heng and Janadas Devan, 'State Fatherhood: The Politics of Nationalism, Sexuality, and Race in Singapore', in *Bewitching Women, Pious Men: Gender and Body Politics in Southeast Asia*, ed. Aihwa Ong and Michael G. Peletz (Berkeley: University of California Press, 1995), pp. 195–215.
71 Chua Mui Hoong and Rachel Chang, 'Did Mr Lee Kuan Yew Create a Singapore in His Own Image?', *The Straits Times*, 24 March 2015, www.straitstimes.com/singapore/did-mr-lee-kuan-yew-create-a-singapore-in-his-own-image (accessed 17 September 2024).
72 Ibid.
73 Oswin, *Global City Futures*, p. 90.
74 Teo, *Neoliberal Morality in Singapore*, p. 109. This is an example of a racialized problem that is often addressed in the Malay language segment of the prime minister's National Day Rally speech. See Chapter 1, n. 87.
75 Whilst beyond the scope of the book, it is worth emphasizing that, as with all things eugenics, there is also a strong racial dimension to it – in this case, an obsession with the maintenance of a Chinese-majority population.
76 Youyenn Teo, 'Shaping the Singapore Family, Producing the State and Society', *Economy and Society*, 39.3 (2010), 337–59 (p. 339).
77 Teo, *Neoliberal Morality in Singapore*, p. 113.
78 The shophouse is a building type relatively specific to Singapore, Malaysia, and some other parts of Southeast Asia. It is normally a two- or three-storey building comprising shop premises on the ground floor and residential dwellings on the upper floor(s).
79 See, for example, Brenda S. A. Yeoh, 'From Colonial Neglect to Post-Independence Heritage: The Housing Landscape in the Central Area of Singapore', *City & Society*, 12.1 (2000), 103–24; and Kah Seng Loh, *Squatters into Citizens: The 1961 Bukit Ho Swee Fire and the Making of Modern Singapore* (Copenhagen: NIAS Press, 2013).
80 Lee, *From Third World to First*, pp. 95–96.
81 Chua, *Political Legitimacy and Housing*, p. 2; also see Kenneth Paul Tan, *Singapore: Identity, Brand, Power* (Cambridge: Cambridge University Press, 2018).
82 Chua, *Liberalism Disavowed*, p. 75.
83 Belinda K. P. Yuen, Ho Pin Teo, and Giok Ling Ooi, *Singapore Housing: An Annotated Bibliography* (Singapore: NUS Press, 1999).
84 Chua, *Political Legitimacy and Housing*; also see Yuen et al., *Singapore Housing*.

85 Chua, *Liberalism Disavowed*, p. 75.

86 See, for example, Iván Szelényi, *Urban Inequalities under State Socialism* (Oxford: Oxford University Press, 1983).

87 John Agnew, 'Home Ownership and the Capitalist Order', in *Urbanization and Urban Planning in Capitalist Society*, ed. Michael Dear and Allen Scott (London: Methuen, 1981), pp. 457–80.

88 Han Fook Kwang, Warren Fernandez, and Sumiko Tan, *Lee Kuan Yew: The Man and His Ideas* (Singapore: Marshall Cavendish Editions, 2015), p. 334.

89 Centre for Liveable Cities, Singapore, *A Chance of a Lifetime: Lee Kuan Yew and the Physical Transformation of Singapore* (Singapore: Centre for Liveable Cities and the Lee Kuan Yew Centre for Innovative Cities, 2016), pp. 17–18.

90 Strictly speaking, given that the flats are bought on a fixed-term lease, they will return to the state upon expiry of the lease. This was not raised as an issue when the home ownership scheme was first rolled out, as 99 years into the future appeared a speck on the horizon. In recent times, however, there has been increasing public concern over the issue of 'lease decay', what will happen when the lease expires, and whether one substantively owns one's HDB flat. The government's response has generally been to reiterate that the purchaser still owns the flat, and that the fixed-term lease is there to ensure fairness in the distribution of public housing. See Lee, 'National Day Rally 2018'; Justin Ong, 'NDR 2018: Why Are HDB Leases 99 Years Long? PM Lee Explains', CNA, 19 August 2018, www.channelnewsasia.com/singapore/ndr-2018-hdb-lease-99-years-flat-national-day-rally-804611 (accessed 17 September 2024); and Ravi Philemon, 'PM Lee Chides Commentators who Claim 99-Year Leases on HDB Flats Are "Merely an Extended Rental"', Yahoo! Finance, 2018, https://sg.finance.yahoo.com/news/pm-lee-chides-commentators-claim-160729625.html (accessed 13 October 2023).

91 Chua, *Liberalism Disavowed*, p. 80.

92 It helps to think of the second half of this equation – the stake people had in economic growth – as the contextual background to Chua's theorization of pragmatism as a political rationality in Singapore. See Chua, *Communitarian Ideology*.

93 Anderson, *Imagined Communities*, p. 144.

94 Lee, *From Third World to First*, pp. 95–96.

95 Lee Kuan Yew, 'Transcript of Speech by the Prime Minister, Mr. Lee Kuan Yew, at the Reunion Dinner of St. Andrew's Old Boys' Association on 7th September, 1968', National Archives of Singapore, www.nas.gov.sg/archivesonline/data/pdfdoc/lky19680907.pdf (accessed 24 September 2024).

96 Lee Kuan Yew, 'Speech at Launch of Tanjong Pagar Town Council's Five-Year Masterplan and Opening of ABC Waters', 2011, National Archives of Singapore, www.nas.gov.sg/archivesonline/speeches/record-details/811c4c79-115d-11e3-83d5-0050568939ad (accessed 27 September 2024).

97 Han Fook Kwang, Zuraidah Ibrahim, Chua Mui Hoong, et al., *Lee Kuan Yew: Hard Truths to Keep Singapore Going* (Singapore: Straits Times Press, 2011), p. 201.

98 Royston Sim, 'PM: Home Ownership Gives Singaporeans a Stake in Nation', *The Straits Times*, 25 August 2018, www.straitstimes.com/politics/pm-home-ownership-gives-sporeans-a-stake-in-nation (accessed 17 September 2024).

99 Chua, *Political Legitimacy and Housing*, p. 20.

100 The National Day Rally is the most significant political speech of the year in Singapore. It is usually delivered by the prime minister in August shortly after National Day on 9 August.

101 Lee, 'National Day Rally 2018'.

102 Lee Kuan Yew, 'Speech at Launch of Tanjong Pagar Town Council's Five-Year Masterplan and Opening of ABC Waters'.

103 'HDB History and Towns', Housing & Development Board, 2017, www.hdb.gov.sg/about-us/history (accessed 27 September 2024).

104 Lee, 'National Day Rally 2018'.

105 See, for example, Hill and Lian, *The Politics of Nation Building*; and Tan, *Singapore*.

106 See Chua, *Political Legitimacy and Housing*.

107 Since 2016, CPF contribution rates have been pegged such that individuals contribute 20 per cent of their monthly salary and employers contribute a further 17 per cent.

108 In 1981 the CPF Act was further amended to include private residential property in addition to public housing.

109 Lee, *From Third World to First*, p. 96.

110 Chua, *Political Legitimacy and Housing*, p. 23.

111 Cedric Pugh, 'Housing and Development in Singapore', *Contemporary Southeast Asia*, 6 (1985), 275–307.

112 Chua, *Liberalism Disavowed*, pp. 79–80.

113 An apartment in a condominium would easily cost upwards of 1 million SGD (570,000 GBP) and a terraced house would cost more than 2 million SGD (1.13 million GBP).

114 Whilst a detailed exploration of this sits beyond the scope of the book, this is a good example of how heteronormativity can be inflected by class difference. For those in the relatively small minority who have sufficient wealth to buy on the private housing market, they are able to sidestep the heteronormative mechanisms of the state specifically in relation to public housing. In addition to the co-constitution of heteronormativity with other categories of difference producing substantively different heteronormative expectations, then, it also produces substantively different ways in which it is experienced.

115 Couples must register their marriage before or within three months of completing the purchase of the HDB flat.

116 Theresa Wong and Brenda S. A. Yeoh, *Fertility and the Family: An Overview of Pro-Natalist Population Policies in Singapore* (Singapore: Asian MetaCentre for Population and Sustainable Development Analysis, 2003), pp. 18–20.

117 Lee Hsien Loong, 'National Day Rally 2008', 2008, National Archives of Singapore, www.nas.gov.sg/archivesonline/speeches/record-details/7f764c0e-115d-11e3-83d5-0050568939ad (accessed 27 September 2024).

118 Teo, *Neoliberal Morality in Singapore*, p. 45.
119 Foucault, *Discipline and Punish*.
120 Department of Statistics Singapore, 'Total Fertility Rate', www.singstat.gov.sg/
-/media/files/visualising_data/infographics/population/total-fertility-rate.ashx
(accessed 27 September 2024).
121 Even so, it is worth noting that unmarried Singaporeans are limited to purchasing studios and two-room flats, which points towards a certain hierarchization
of space that rationalizes living configurations outside a heterosexual marriage
as less deserving or less in need of it.
122 Yue, 'Queer Singapore', pp. 6–7.
123 Lazar, 'Homonationalist Discourse', p. 424.
124 James C. Scott, *Seeing like a State: How Certain Schemes to Improve the
Human Condition Have Failed* (New Haven: Yale University Press, 2008).
125 Lazar, 'Homonationalist Discourse', p. 424.
126 Teo, 'Shaping the Singapore Family', p. 345.
127 Baudrillard, *The Perfect Crime*, p. 53.

3

The work of kinship

Focus on the family

In 2007, Lee Hsien Loong defended his government's decision to retain Section 377A of the Singapore Penal Code in Parliament by saying:[1]

> [LGBT people] are free to lead their lives, free to pursue their social activities. But there are restraints and we do not approve of them actively promoting their lifestyles to others or setting the tone for mainstream society. They live their lives. That is their personal life, it is their space. But the tone of the overall society, I think remains conventional, it remains straight, and we want it to remain so.
>
> [...]
>
> The family is the basic building block of our society. It has been so and, by policy, we have reinforced this and we want to keep it so. And by 'family' in Singapore, we mean one man one woman, marrying, having children and bringing up children within that framework of a stable family unit.[2]

Until its repeal on 3 January 2023, Section 377A, a law that criminalized sex between men, was one of the most visible legal manifestations of heteronormativity in Singapore. But it is only one piece of what we could call a system of heteronormative legalism. By this, I mean to suggest the way in which the functioning of the law is premised on a certain set of heteronormative kinship logics.

Section 377A has understandably been the focal point of plenty of activist and academic attention in recent years.[3] But it is important to recognize that the operation of heteronormative legalism is far-reaching and goes well beyond one homophobic statute. There is a range of laws and policies that produce the systemic reification of a particular familial norm where heterosexual coupling and reproduction within the heterosexual nuclear family unit are naturalized – and are, as such, central to the operation of 'heteronormative familism'.[4] In other words, the heterosexual nuclear family that is consecrated as the default Singaporean family unit lies at the core of an entire set of laws and policies in Singapore. Besides the moments where it is explicitly constructed in state rhetoric as the only legitimate familial form, it is also produced at the nexus of various laws and policies that privilege heterosexual coupling and childbearing as a process nestled within that structure. As a fundamental presupposition of how social life in Singapore is organized, the ubiquity of heterosexual coupling and the heterosexual nuclear family functions as common sense – a self-evident truth that needs no further justification – and is crucial to how citizenship in Singapore is constituted.

Family does significant conceptual work as a sign in Singapore's political imaginary. It is typically shorthand to index a specific familial formation – 'one man one woman, marrying, having children and bringing up children within that framework of a stable family unit', as the prime minister had made clear in 2007.[5] Put differently, 'the Singapore family is a nuclear one, built around an opposite-sex cisgender couple, full stop'.[6] Lee was neither the first nor the last government leader to speak about the family in these plainly heteronormative terms. In plenty of extant scholarship on the family in Singapore, not only is this point taken for granted, it is taken as a 'natural' fact worth actively defending.[7] The sociologist Paulin Tay Straughan, for example, has argued that 'to continue to thrive and capitalise on the tremendous opportunities of our global geopolitical position, we must first ensure that our social order continues to facilitate family life' where *family* reflexively refers to the heterosexual nuclear family.[8] Oswin rightly observes that:

> much of the existing wealth of literature (particularly that which is policy-oriented) on the family within Singapore studies commends the government's efforts to reform the family [as the heterosexual nuclear family], depicting its initiatives as facilitating the liberation of women and the creation of the reliable workforce that has attracted multinational capital to the city-state while fostering social harmony and responsibility.[9]

The abstract concept of family is thus specified through the reification of the nuclear family unit and, as we have seen in the previous chapter, household formation that inextricably links heterosexual coupling with marriage and the nuclear family.

But Lee's remarks are also an example of how the image of the Singaporean family is frequently conceptually mobilized against queerness. When the topic of LGBT rights is broached, the normative place of the heterosexual nuclear family in the national imaginary is reasserted as a way of militating against their potential advancement – LGBT rights are rendered incompatible with the maintenance of the Singaporean family unit. When the topic of access to housing for unmarried people is raised, it is positioned as contradicting the objective of heterosexual nuclear family formation and reproduction, and thus its deprioritization is justified – those who are willing and able to participate in the heteronormative spectacle are rationalized as more deserving of their own roof over their heads.[10] We should thus remain alert to how, whilst stating that the 'tone' of Singaporean society is 'conventional' and 'straight', Lee also added that 'we want it to remain that way'.[11]

There is a sleight of hand in the expression of volition – the state is not agnostic in this matter but maintains an active investment in keeping Singapore a straight nation by design. Such an investment in heteronormativity does more than minoritize LGBT lives alone. It nominates a specific path and lifeworld – built around the heterosexual nuclear family – as the 'right' way of living in Singapore. Contained in this assertion is a powerful delegitimizing function that minoritizes many people who express or experience kinship differently.

In *Antigone's Claim*, Judith Butler introduces us to Antigone as a figure 'caught in a web of relations that produce no coherent position within kinship'.[12] Instead, Antigone is caught in an unstable position, occupying multiple kinship positions at once and thus unable to be placed on the nominal roll of kinship. Kinship, Butler reminds us, 'is not simply a situation that [Antigone] is in but a set of practices that she also performs, relations that are reinstituted in time precisely through the practice of their repetition'.[13] Kinship is something Antigone does rather than something that merely is – it is actively produced through a relational process between people instead of simply existing a priori. *Antigone's Claim* shows how, together with the incest taboo, the vocabulary of kinship draws from the inventory of heteronormativity to produce relations within a heterosexual matrix.[14] In Singapore, where the state regularly presses kinship into its service, and where subjectivity is set up as a function of kinship, Butler's Antigone looms large as a spectre of queerness. She is replicated in the lives of multiple queered individuals in Singapore 'because of the state's chronic inability to imagine forms of kinship outside of the heteronormative linguistic categories that structure it'.[15]

The circulation of heteronormativity relies heavily on the state's reification of the heterosexual nuclear family unit as the only legitimate form of kinship such that the Singaporean family unit is understood in a very narrow sense premised upon recognizing ontological kinship relations. Implicit in this understanding is the presumption that 'kinship derives from biological processes – reproduction, birth, and sexual intercourse – which yield indissoluble relations, that is, relations of *being*, not *doing*'.[16] In the state's field of vision, then, for social relations to be legible within the frame of kinship, they must be locatable within the nomenclature of ontological kinship relations – even if the individuals in question aren't necessarily biologically related. That is to say, it is the linguistic categories of kinship (i.e. father, mother, son, daughter etc.), and being able to occupy one of these categories, that legitimize social relations such that they are recognized as kinship relations. Obligations of care (relations of doing) are embedded within the nuclear family (relations of being) and made into a duty between family members rather than a state obligation between state and citizen. There is thus plenty at stake in the contestation of legibility – which social relations are legible as kinship relations – because of the obligations that the state parks in the lot of the family.

I want to make visible the centrality of heteronormative familism and the work that kinship is conceptually made to do in service of the nation. I argue that the social relations contained by and within the heteronormative structures of kinship are elevated and made to matter as all-important social ties around which membership of the nation is imagined. Amongst other things, Antigone's story is a story of the limits of kinship and its constitutive inability to distinguish between relations of being and relations of doing. Citizenship in Singapore works on the basis of this slippage. Persistently understanding the family unit not only as a site containing relations of being, but as a site where these relations of being are also expected to be relations of doing, is crucial to the workings of heteronormativity in Singapore.

One of the ways subjectivity in Singapore is structured is through heteronormativity's reproduction in the neatness of the assumed overlap between relations of being and relations of doing. Those for whom these relations do not properly overlap are queered as a consequence; they are unable to derive the care they need from within the heterosexual nuclear family and are often left marginalized because care is institutionally imagined within heteronormative kinship structures.[17] I argue that heteronormative familism hierarchizes social relations and is a key modality through which heteronormativity works to structure subjectivity in Singapore. Kinship ties are assumed to be repositories of support and care freely available to everyone. They are elevated above other social ties that lie outside of the heteronormative nuclear family, which are relegated in terms of relative importance – meaning that those who are estranged from or lack access to these structures of kinship are subjectivized differently and queered by the operation of heteronormativity. Dismantling this regime and expanding the vocabulary of kinship necessarily requires challenging the tenets of heteronormative familism as well as the reification of the nuclear family unit as a privileged nest of relations.

Heteronormative familism, legalism, and looking beyond the law

On 17 December 2018, the High Court of Singapore delivered a landmark decision in *UKM* v. *Attorney-General*. This was an application made by a Singaporean gay man living with his long-term male partner to legally adopt his biological son, who had been conceived through a surrogate overseas in the USA. The court granted the adoption order and, in doing so, indirectly presided over the formation of the first officially recognized same-sex family unit in the country. In and of itself, the formation of a same-sex family unit is not particularly novel. Sharon Quah, for example, has documented how people in Singapore have worked around the model of the heterosexual nuclear family and parented in diverse ways ranging from divorced or unwed single parents to same-sex parenting units.[18] Quah suggests that 'Singaporeans have never been distant from diverse kin practices organised in ways that do not conform to the narrow familial model of a "traditional" family.'[19] However, just as non-heterosexual couples can purchase HDB flats but are read by the state as two individuals, non-heterosexual nuclear familial forms exist but cannot be recognized as such by the state because it does not have the necessary syntax to read a same-sex family unit as one.

UKM v. *Attorney-General* was significant because it was the first time the state recognized a same-sex family unit as such. In other words, even though many in Singapore parent in a variety of family forms, *UKM* v. *Attorney-General* was the first state-legible same-sex configuration of the dual-parent unit. At the same time, it is worth noting how, even though it did challenge the image of the heterosexual couple at the apex of the nuclear family, the court's decision in *UKM* v. *Attorney-General* was rationalized through the logics of heteronormative familism. I am not suggesting this was a bad thing – particularly for the child at the centre of this bureaucratic tussle, this was a compassionate and sensible outcome. But it is worth remaining alert to the grounds upon which the court's decision was rationalized because of how it centres the importance of the nuclear familial structure in organizing Singaporean society.

The case of *UKM* v. *Attorney-General* involved two men who had been in a long-term relationship since 1998 and had been living together since 2003. In 2012, the couple decided they wanted to have a child.[20] Whilst exploring the options available to them with regard to adoption, they discovered that the Adoption of Children Act did not allow a joint adoption by same-sex couples, and also mandates that a man can only adopt a male child.[21]

It is worth dwelling for a moment on the exact formulation of the laws governing the adoption of children in Singapore and how they function on a particular heteronormative logic. Section 3(3) of the Adoption of Children Act states that 'Where an application for an adoption order is made by 2 spouses jointly, the court may make the order authorising the 2 spouses jointly to adopt an infant.'[22] Whilst same-sex couples are neither explicitly mentioned nor barred from adopting children, that exclusion emanates from the semantic field of *spouses* within the law. This hinges on Section 12(1) of the Women's Charter, which states that '[a] marriage solemnised in Singapore or elsewhere between persons who, at the date of the marriage, are not respectively male and female is void'.[23] The direct consequence of Section 12(1) is that marriage as a legal institution in Singapore is restricted to heterosexual couples alone. It is helpful to think of marriage here as the formal process by which the state bestows upon an individual the status of spouse – a process that only heterosexual couples can participate in. The legal category of spouse therefore becomes available only to married heterosexual people. Because the marriage franchise is limited in this way, same-sex spouses are unable to adopt children – they are illegible by virtue of the fact that in the state's heteronormative syntax, same-sex spouses present as a logical impossibility – a contradiction in terms that cannot be reconciled. Thus, in the case of *UKM* v. *Attorney-General*, only the child's biological father could make the application to officially adopt the child – because the law has neither the capacity nor the affordance to accommodate a joint adoption application by a same-sex couple.

This is an illustration of how heteronormativity is produced as an instantiation of heteronormative legalism. Whereas homophobia is easily recognizable because it manifests as an express disavowal, such as in Section 377A, that explicitly outlawed sex between men, heteronormativity is produced through a network of meanings and relations that pronounce upon each other. Here, it is produced at the interstices of Section 3(3) and Section 12(1) where a particular form of heterosexuality – heterosexual coupling – is marked as legitimate. This is also how queerness is invisibilized and produced through any deviation from the normative, visible, performance of heterosexuality through coupling and marriage.

Again, one could read this as illustrative of how heteronormativity can govern straight people as well by demanding of them a certain expression of heterosexuality. Similar to how they would not be eligible to purchase a HDB flat as a couple, neither would an unmarried heterosexual couple be able to adopt a child under Section 3(3) of the Adoption of Children Act. They, too, are queered in a similar way to the same-sex couple in *UKM* v. *Attorney-General* because their coupledom is deemed incompatible with the strictures of heteronormativity. Of course, they do not necessarily experience their minoritization in the same way – heteronormativity is, after all, co-constituted by a variety of other differences in addition to sexual difference. But both are queered by the operation of heteronormativity in the sense that both a same-sex couple and an unmarried heterosexual couple are produced as non-ideal subjects. It is in this sense that '[t]he queer subject within straight culture ... deviates and is made socially present as a deviant' in ways that exceed identity categories.[24]

A similar invisibilizing gesture occurs obliquely in Section 4(3) of the Adoption of Children Act, which states:

> An adoption order shall not be made in any case where the sole applicant is a male and the infant in respect of whom the application is made is a female unless the court is satisfied that there are special circumstances which justify as an exceptional measure the making of an adoption order.[25]

This subsection presumably exists to protect the child and prevent potential sexual abuse. On the face of it, this is not something that appears to require contestation. Indeed, protecting the child's safety is a valid reason for enacting a law. What is equally salient, however, is what the child is presumed to require protection from, and the terms along which that threat is constructed. The parameters of Section 4(3) where a sole male applicant cannot adopt a female infant reside upon a certain regulation of rogue heterosexual desire. To be precise, it seeks to regulate male heterosexual desire that could potentially endanger a female child's personal safety. But this is also the limit of Section 4(3) – only male heterosexual desire is made visible for policing whilst other forms of desire remain invisible and illegible in the law's heteronormative grid. To be clear, this is neither an argument for the removal of Section 4(3) nor an argument that it should necessarily be expanded to incorporate non-heterosexual desire into its regulatory framework. Rather, it is to illustrate how heterosexuality and the logics of heteronormativity are embedded within the language of the law, its own logics, presuppositions, and assumptions, and in this case the forms of desire that are taken as default and legible within it.

As a function of these myriad laws, plus the fact that surrogacy is not legal in Singapore, the couple involved in *UKM* v. *Attorney-General* turned to overseas surrogacy as their next best option. They picked the USA 'because of its well-established surrogacy laws', flew out to meet their surrogate, and their son was born in November 2013.[26] However, because the child was born in the USA, he was an American citizen when the couple returned with him to Singapore. Their application for the child to be granted Singaporean citizenship was rejected and they were advised by the MSF that 'their prospects would be enhanced if the child was legally adopted'.[27] For this reason, in December 2014, the biological father of the child applied to legally adopt him as a single parent. This first application was dismissed before being reversed on appeal.

In their grounds for decision, the appeal judges lay out the difficulty before them in granting the adoption order:

> On balance, it seems appropriate that we attribute significant weight to the concern not to violate the public policy against the formation of same-sex family units on account of its rational connection to the present dispute and

the degree to which this policy would be violated should an adoption order be made. However, having regard to all the circumstances before us, we think that neither of these reasons is sufficiently powerful to enable us to ignore the statutory imperative to promote the welfare of the Child, and, indeed, to regard his welfare as first and paramount ... With not insignificant difficulty, therefore, we conclude that an adoption order ought to be made in this case.

In arriving at this conclusion, we feel compelled to underscore two points. First, our decision is a decision on the particular facts of this case, and should not be taken as an endorsement of what the appellant and his partner set out to do. As we have mentioned at [209] above, our decision was reached through an application of the law as we understood it to be, and not on the basis of our sympathies for the position of either party ... given that the appellant's use of surrogacy was such a critical step in his path to obtaining an adoption order, it is somewhat unsatisfactory that in the end, we could place no weight on that conduct either way due to the equivocality of the materials presented.[28]

Clearly, the judges are aware of what is at stake. They acknowledge that existing public policy militates 'against the formation of same-sex family units' and the fact that in granting the adoption order, their decision would be violating that policy. It is precisely these conditions that have created the 'not insignificant difficulty' before them. They also make clear that their decision was made on the 'particular facts' of this case, which limits its use as a precedent in future proceedings. The imperative to prioritize the child's welfare was ultimately given priority in this instance but it is clear that the decision should be read as an exception to Singapore's heteronormative legal landscape.

The *UKM* v. *Attorney-General* case was one where the constitutive logics of heteronormative legalism and familism were made to turn upon themselves. One expectation (the child should be raised within the structure of a dual-parent family unit) was brought into conflict with another (that the two parents in this family unit ought to be an opposite-sex couple). The heteronormative logics of coupling and kinship configurations were brought into a mutually exclusive tension. The result of the judgment was that whilst the image of heterosexual coupling as the only legitimate form of coupling was temporarily excepted, this exception also simultaneously reified the structure of the nuclear family. That is to say, heteronormative familism itself rationalized the exception to one of its own constitutive logics of heterosexual coupling. In this way, whilst the courts legitimized the formation of a same-sex family unit, by drawing from the vocabulary of heteronormative kinship it simultaneously reinforced the conceptual legitimacy of the family as well as its place at the centre of Singaporean society.

In the immediate aftermath of the High Court's decision, the MSF released a statement saying that it respected the court's decision but 'had opposed the appeal because, amongst other [reasons], the adoption would be contrary to public policy against the formation of same-sex family units'.[29] It added that it would review its existing family policies.[30] Minister for Social and Family Development Desmond Lee also suggested that 'since the courts have recognised that the adoption violates the public policy against the formation of same-sex family units, it may be harder for future applicants doing the same to argue that they did not intentionally set out to do so'.[31] It is difficult not to take this as a kind of ominous warning to other couples who might have been considering a similar route to adoption.

Lynette Chua explains how one of the constraints in resisting heteronormativity in Singapore is the ineffectiveness of what she terms 'judicial activism'.[32] She highlights how 'Singapore's judiciary lacks a record of upholding constitutional liberties over state interests' and how, on the rare occasions the court does favour constitutional liberties, the government typically responds by amending the necessary laws or even the Constitution to foreclose the possibility of similar decisions in future.[33]

As Chua's argument presaged, within a month of the judgment in *UKM* v. *Attorney-General*, the Minister for Social and Family Development stated in Parliament that:

> while the welfare of the child should always be a very important consideration in adoption proceedings, we are looking at whether the Adoption of Children Act needs to be amended[34] so that a better balance can be struck when important public policy considerations are involved.[35]

He also doubled down on the state's definition of family by restating the heteronormative nuclear family as the paradigmatic familial form:

> While we recognise that there are increasingly diverse forms of families and households in Singapore, the prevailing social norm in our society is still that of a man and woman marrying, and having and bringing up children within a stable family unit. This is also the family structure that the Government encourages. Most of us would agree that it is ideal for children to grow up in families anchored by strong and stable marriages. This is reflected in the differentiation we maintain in policies and benefits to encourage and support parenthood within marriage.[36]

Emancipation from heteronormative familism, therefore, is unlikely to arrive exclusively via judicial means or contestations in the legal arena. The grip that it has on the Singaporean political imagination as well as the dynamics of parliamentary power mean that it is difficult for heteronormative familism to be resolved exclusively through the judiciary. This, of course, does not mean that unjust laws should not be challenged. On the contrary, it reiterates the importance of broad activist pressure and community organizing towards more than just judicial recourse so that that any gains are not short-lived.

Take Section 377A, for instance. The prime minister's comments in 2007 'identified only one possible reason for the existence of [Section 377A] itself – the symbolic "signalling" that homosexuals are not to actively promote their "lifestyles" or to "set the tone" for mainstream society'.[37] Even though the prime minister sought to assure gay men that the law would not be enforced in private situations involving consenting adults, its spectre remained hanging over them. The law also indexed all sexual minorities as illegitimate, and legitimized plenty of blatant bigotry. In that context, challenging Section 377A in court as well as the consistent activist and community work that called on the government to repeal it were important in building pressure and signalling to sexual minorities that there was strength in numbers.[38]

That being said, particularly in the aftermath of Section 377A having become an artefact in the legal archives, it is important to appreciate that heteronormativity and heteronormative familism are much more than a problem of 'legal classification'.[39] Katherine Franke thus cautions LGBT people and community organizers against 'looking to law as at once the source of our oppression and the key to our liberation'.[40] Getting rid of Section 377A was therefore a necessary but insufficient move in contesting the regime of heteronormative legalism that works to maintain the heterosexual nuclear family at the core of Singaporean society. Because liberation will not come from 'securing legal rights and recognition by the state',[41] and because of the general ineffectiveness of judicial activism in Singapore's political system, pushing for constitutional or legal reform alone will be insufficient in undoing heteronormativity. It was necessary because, to put it simply, some laws are wrong and should be publicly condemned as such until they have been expunged. But it is insufficient because the workings of heteronormativity constitute more than the 'exclusionary politics of homosexuality'[42] – they also constitute the inclusionary politics of heterosexuality, particularly around the family. Whilst Section 377A was a clearly discriminatory law, we have also seen other laws that do the work of propagating and enforcing heteronormativity without the naked homophobia contained in Section 377A.

The point of this analysis is neither to work out how one can be included instead of being excluded nor to find out how to be shut in with heteronormativity instead of being shut out by it. It is to decipher the inclusion/exclusion operation – in other words, to examine *both* the exclusionary politics of homosexuality and queerness *and* the inclusionary politics of heterosexuality and heteronormative familism. In this spirit, 'we can and ought to go further to interrogate the more general politics of intimate regulation of which this contest is only part' and investigate what is at stake in the elevation of the heteronormative family.[43]

The politics of kinship

The reification of the nuclear family substitutes kinship for the state as the main reservoir of welfare, aid, and care in the national imaginary. Lee Kuan Yew summarized this viewpoint succinctly, saying:

> As a student I grew up in Great Britain, immediately after the war. Back then, the Beveridge Plan was in place, according to which the British should be cared for from the cradle to the grave. I witnessed how this system failed. When I went back to Singapore, where the British had introduced the same system, I silently ushered in the volte-face and said: No, no. First you rely on your family and when the family has used up all its resources, I help you.[44]

Leaving aside Lee's *l'état, c'est moi* moment, his comments capture the positioning of the family as the institution primarily responsible for supporting and caring for individuals. State intervention in the form of economic aid is thus deferred and calibrated to kick in only after familial ties have been entirely exhausted economically.[45] Melinda Cooper locates the rekindling of the family as a moral and economic institution within a larger, global neoliberal current, arguing that '[t]he notion that private family obligations should ultimately take the place of welfare transfers [is] supplemented by the idea that the state should take an active pedagogical role in cultivating proper family values among the welfare and non-welfare population alike.[46] In addition to government leaders frequently telling Singaporeans that the duty of care is a non-negotiable, obligatory function of kinship, the state's pedagogical role is also accomplished by the process of calibrating economic aid to commence as a last resort, only after familial aid had been used up. As Lee put it, the state would help only 'when the family has used up *all* its resources'.[47] The expectations loaded upon kinship are such that any kind of support – financial or otherwise – that could be wrung out of it ought to be extracted from it first before the state can be expected to step in.[48] Calibrating aid in this manner, putting into practice the welfare state's 'volte-face' and helping only when the family is no longer able to, performs the state's work in policing kinship – teaching everyone that these are the obligations of kinship in Singapore.[49]

The discourse of 'family responsibility' as well as the rhetoric of 'self-reliance' is not uniquely Singaporean – it is a project that parallels Thatcherism in the UK and Reaganism in the USA.[50] The difference in Singapore's iteration, however, is that the obligation of care is further rationalized as a form of filial piety, initially via the generic discourse of 'Asian values'.[51] Lee Kuan Yew was not shy about insisting that the family unit was emblematic of some primordial Asian identity, saying that 'Eastern societies believe that the individual exists in the context of his family. He is

not pristine and separate ... The ruler or the government does not try to provide for a person what the family best provides.'[52] The West is caricatured
as the source of excessive individualism that supposedly stands in contrast
to Asian communitarian sensibilities. Together with a kind of defiant reassertion of an Asian civilizational identity that insists Singapore is different
and better than the West, 'the idea that there is something fundamental
and organic about Singaporean culture that should lead to behaviours different from those in the West ... [and that they] are part of what makes
Singaporean society and Singaporeans unique and good' has become a key
part of Singaporean subjectivity.[53] This remains the case even if the overt
rhetorical reliance on the 'Asian values' discourse has diminished since the
turn of the millennium. Whilst *Asian values* has fallen out of fashion and is
hardly bandied about in political rhetoric any more, the sign of the family
still does plenty of work in terms of the individual's obligation in relation
to the family, rationalizing this in contrast to the 'Western' obsession with
'individualism', and making it a core tenet of being Singaporean.[54] In other
words, kinship, familial obligations, and caring for family continue to be
cast discursively as central to what it means to be a proper Singaporean –
and this is codified in multiple ways materially.

The Maintenance of Parents Act, for example, requires adult children to
provide their parents with a monthly allowance once they are above 60 or
suffering from mental or physical infirmities.[55] Whilst a few hundred people
have exercised their rights and actually taken their children to court to force
a monthly allowance in recent years,[56] the significance of the Act is twofold.
Legally, it establishes the principle that 'the private family (rather than the
state) should serve as the primary source of economic security' by making it
an obligation for children to materially provide for their elderly parents.[57]
But, as with Section 377A, it has a pedagogical function – it teaches individuals to see themselves as the rightful source of economic security for
their elderly parents. The state absents itself from this equation. In this way,
the primary duty of care and caregiving is translated from a public good
into a private good and imbricated firmly within heteronormative kinship
structures.

Another way the notion of the family as the primary site of care is reinforced is through the disbursement of the Proximity Housing Grant – an
additional subsidy that the government provides specifically to those who
choose to buy an HDB flat within a 2-km radius of their parents' homes.
The rationale behind this policy is to encourage families to 'live with or close
to each other for mutual care and support'.[58] Keeping multigenerational
nuclear family structures in close physical proximity like this facilitates caregiving duties between them.[59] The idea is that initially, with grandparents
living nearby, they will be able to care for their young grandchildren whilst

their parents are both away at work; then, subsequently, as the grandparents themselves grow older, their adult children will be close by to provide the care that old age may render necessary.[60] Making it easier for families to live close to one another is not necessarily a bad thing but it is noteworthy how the state has once again subtracted itself and the public provision of support and care from this neat equation of family responsibility. Implicit in these configurations is the notion that the responsibility for care and mutual support lies within kinship structures, between individuals and their respective families, rather than being something that everyone should be entitled to as a public provision organized by the state.

Here, it would be remiss to gloss over the strongly gendered dimension to this move. The imbrication of care into the kinship structures of the heterosexual nuclear family is primarily targeted at women who are meant to take on the domestic work of caring and household responsibilities. We have already seen previously how the 'gendered call to patriotic duty' assigns 'military service for men and maternal duty for women'.[61] Whilst men are assigned the role of protector and defender of the nation, women are held responsible for caring for and reproducing the nation.[62] The stark difference in parental leave, where mothers are entitled to 16 weeks of maternity leave whilst fathers are entitled to two weeks of paternity leave,[63] is one indication of whom the state expects to primarily carry out the work of caring for and parenting the child.[64] Thus, whilst women in Singapore are encouraged to work, this does not absolve them of simultaneously shouldering caring responsibilities and other domestic work – women who hold a job are essentially expected to also manage housework and look after whoever needs caring for in the family.

One of the things the state does to facilitate this arrangement is to grant working mothers who employ foreign domestic workers (live-in help) additional tax relief through the Foreign Domestic Worker Levy Relief, which 'is given to encourage married women to stay in the workforce'.[65] Importantly, this relief is made available only to women who have expressed their heterosexuality correctly by engaging with the institution of marriage – thus, only married or divorced women qualify. Men or single unmarried women are ineligible – even if they do have children and have hired a domestic worker to help with caregiving duties. The relief provides Singaporean women with financial incentive to continue working whilst outsourcing the caregiving and household duties that have been loaded upon them onto a foreign domestic worker for a relatively small sum of money.

The co-constitutive and interactive nature of heteronormativity is once again evident here. Foreign domestic workers are typically brown migrant women from poor families in Southeast Asia or South Asia and they live with their employer throughout their duration of employment, carrying out the work of running the household, cooking, cleaning, caring for children, and so on. What the Foreign Domestic Worker Levy Relief does, therefore, is to essentially provide Singaporean women with the opportunity to relieve themselves of the effects of the nation's patriarchal logics by transferring some of its burden onto another woman. The gendered expectations that obtain from the smooth operation of heteronormativity in Singapore where a woman is encouraged to work whilst also remaining responsible for child-care and other household duties can be reconciled through recourse to a racialized, gendered, and classed practice where a brown woman in a lower socio-economic class position is employed to perform the household work that the Singaporean woman is herself unable to do.

At the same time, the racialization and classism buried in the heart of Singaporean nationalism that dictates who is or is not suitable to reproduce the nation mark these foreign domestic workers out as incompatible with the nation. For, whilst they are employed to carry out household duties and child-care in Singapore, these women are themselves legally barred from bearing children as a condition of their work visas. In this way, the heteronormative politics of kinship in Singapore that encourage reproduction of the nation also rely on the very denial of reproduction for a certain constituency of women to maintain the supposed integrity and purity of the nation. Chapter 4 explores the xenological machinations of heteronormativity in greater detail but it is helpful to mention here to understand how this is one of the gendered expectations placed on women by the state – the 'structural context in which women are encouraged to be employed formally and full-time, and yet given primary responsibility for overseeing housework and childcare'.[66] It is less a critique of individual Singaporean women than a critique of the state that has actively created and sustained these structural conditions that rely on a certain configuration of heteronormative expectations. And it is vital to understand this heteronormative expectation that structures Singaporean subjectivity as being constituted out of an interaction with racial, gender, and class differences as well as sexual normativity.

Kinship's queers

Despite lionizing kinship in its rhetoric, we should remain alert to how the state structures and defines kinship in a very specific sense that limits what it means to relate to another as family, who counts as family, and what family looks like. Whilst Lee Hsien Loong stated this in no uncertain terms in 2007, whittling the bounds of kinship in this way such that *family* is limited to the heterosexual nuclear family was the culmination of a process of shaping the family that began decades ago.[67]

Prior to independence in 1965, multigenerational and communal forms of living were common and this was reflected in household configurations at the time.[68] With many living in kampungs (villages), people oriented their social and economic lives around their extended families, in-laws, and other kith and kin who lived either close by or in the same household as them. After independence, however, a series of government interventions worked to orient citizens away from affiliations with one's extended family and limit them to the nuclear family. The historian Loh Kah Seng argues that the new PAP government 'inherited the colonial regime's fixation with over-crowding, insanitation and spatial control', which led to the institution of what was effectively a universal public housing programme administered by the HDB.[69]

In part, this move was motivated by a logic of capital accumulation. Minister for Finance Goh Keng Swee argued that 'the extended family sys-tem could be an obstacle to economic growth because it discouraged one who has to share the fruit of his or her labour with others in the family to strive harder'.[70] But in the fixation on the nuclear family, one might also detect some of the pressures of compactness attributable to an acute aware-ness of smallness. As we saw previously in Chapter 2, the nation is imagined as a land-scarce little red dot lacking a geo-body – small to the point of being unrepresentable on a map. Within such an imagination, sprawling, extended families living in large households, creating extended networks of economic and social interdependence, can be rationalized psychically and physically as luxuries that Singapore cannot afford to accommodate. The smallness of imagination thus aids in calcifying and materializing the idea of the nuclear family as the 'building block of society'.[71]

Living in and amongst large extended families was effectively curtailed by newly built flats that were designed to accommodate the nuclear family unit. Christopher Tremewan argues that what followed was a:

> [f]orced resettlement in HDB flats [that] not only split up communities but, as the flats were designed for nuclear families, also split up generations and ensured that the nuclear family became the basic social unit. Thus, HDB resi-dents were moved from an extended family context with an active community life of mutual support and a sense of local identity and security into serried ranks of self-contained concrete boxes.[72]

As a consequence, across the country social ties and kinship structures began to be dissolved and remade in the image of the heterosexual nuclear family.[73] Making marriage the precondition to purchasing public housing meant that marriage became the point where two individuals would typi-cally leave their existing households (and respective nuclear families) to form their own 'core family nucleus'.[74] The result has been the naturaliza-tion of a distinctive Singaporean script where marriage, housing, and fam-ily formation are bound together. It also contributes to narrowly defining *family* as the heterosexual nuclear family unit in the Singaporean imaginary.

In this way, the state's 'monopoly of housing provision has been used to shore up the family institution, which the government has ideologically adopted formally as the "fundamental" institution of society'.[75] This is 'one of the most significant means by which the state's heteronormative imagination of family is continually reinscribed and reproduced'.[76]

A word of clarification is warranted at this point because in pointing out how the heteronormative nuclear family has been actively shaped and constructed at the expense of older, more expansive household configurations, there is a risk of inadvertently romanticizing them. Whilst I suggest the vast, near-universal public housing programme functioning on a set of heteronormative and familial logics that render multiple groups of people queer has its own set of problems, I am not suggesting that pre-independence, pre-HDB modes of living and configurations of familial life were necessarily any better. In fact, it is possible and perhaps even likely that such modes of living could have been experienced as decidedly *more* heteronormative than the present. After all, living in large communal houses with one's extended family in close proximity subjects one to multiple degrees of surveillance and informal regimes of monitoring. The heteronormative gaze of the state might have nominally been less intense because it did not superimpose the form of the heterosexual nuclear family unit onto household configurations. But such settings also left one open to a different gaze – or gazes, to be precise – for it left one more exposed to lateral surveillance via the 'peer-to-peer surveillance of spouses, friends and relatives'.[77]

Large communal settings meant a distinct lack of private spaces for queered people – particularly LGBT people – to retreat into, away from heteronormative spaces. In a similar sense to John D'Emilio's argument that capitalism created new possibilities of gay life because it freed the individual from material dependence on the family,[78] the public housing programme and its attendant policies that broke up large communal living settings have also inadvertently created new affordances of 'non-heteronormative domesticity'.[79] But as I contended in Chapter 2 in relation to the JSS, which allows some queered people access to HDB flats, it is significant that these affordances rely on queerness being masked and rendered illegible within a heteronormative matrix of relations. Similarly, it is equally significant here that the instrument of rationalization for housing reform was the heterosexual nuclear family – the institution whose preservation and reification are also responsible for rendering queer those who are unable to be neatly positioned within it.

The positioning of the heterosexual nuclear family as the rightful exclusive site of care and support can render queer various forms of social relations that cannot be inscribed within the 'core family nucleus'.[80] It is in this sense that heteronormativity can render various people queer along varying logics of difference beyond sexual difference alone. The logics of heter-onormative familism can position queered individuals outside the nation – in the space of the counter-nation – and this category of people provides fodder for imagining the nation as 'the container for the remaining entity of belonging'.[81]

From the outset, I have argued that *queer* should be understood as more than an identity category or position. It is more than a synonym or a catch-all term for LGBT people. Without understanding queerness as political, the way heteronormativity governs both heterosexual people and other non-normative sexualities is missed.[82] Whilst there is a substantive body of critical scholar-ship spanning multiple disciplines that analyses various forms of inequities arising out of the obsessive maintenance of the nuclear family in Singapore, they have elided a focus on heteronormativity. Amongst feminist scholars, Teo, for example, draws out the implications of gendered inequalities that are contained within the discourse of 'family values'.[83] Heng and Devan show in their seminal essay how the state's obsession with the reproduction of the nuclear family both at the individual and national level is shot through with racial, gendered, and class differences. It has led, they argue, to an objective of 'the regeneration of the country's population … in such rations of race and class as would faithfully mirror the population's original composition at the nation's founding moment'.[84] Other scholars in political science and public policy show how the family works to further the exclusion of sexual minor-ities.[85] All this existing work thus shows how the governance of sexuality and the maintenance of a familial norm produce various forms of exclusion, but they do not quite identify heteronormativity as the force that produces these exclusions, resulting in a distinct lack of analytical attention paid to the ways in which heteronormativity governs the lives of many people, including straight people.

Again, not everyone who is queered in this sense experiences its effects in the same way. The weight of heteronormativity presses down differently on different people, some of whom are able to bear it better than others depend-ing on the various identity categories and social positions that they happen to occupy. But the distribution of queerness and its attendant effects is not some-thing that is balanced solely on a homo-/heterosexual binary, not least because ' "nonnormative" procreation patterns and family structures of people who are labelled heterosexual have also been used to regulate and exclude *them*'.[86]

Producing the radial limits of the Singaporean nation

By the late 1980s, the public housing programme meant that the state had successfully crumbled larger communities into far smaller, isolated units literally built to house the heterosexual nuclear family. Together with the latent force of heteronormativity that emanated from housing and family policies, it meant that 'the [heterosexual] nuclear family became the basic social unit' organizing social relations in Singapore at the expense of other social ties that could not be inscribed within the heterosexual nuclear family unit.[87] As Timothy Austin puts it, 'what the citizen gained in running water, electricity, and a better roof, [they] lost in mutual, neighbourhood support groups and community spirit'.[88] Of course, the images of 'community spirit' and 'support groups' that Austin invokes here were not necessarily experienced in a universally positive way.[89] The line between mutual support and mutual surveillance, community spirit and coercive spirit, can be a blurry one. And whilst neighbourly support and a community spirit might well be nice, it is debatable whether many would prefer it over the provision of clean running water, stable electricity, and a good roof. Though, of course, it wouldn't be unreasonable to want both – utilities and communities.

But it is not very helpful to invoke 'the citizen' as an abstract individual, because whether 'the citizen' experiences the breaking up of older living configurations as a loss of mutual support or as gaining access to new modes of privacy is inflected by their individual inhabited contexts. Ultimately, I am not very interested in advancing a critique that is rooted in nostalgia and a valorization of the communal setting of the kampung. The problem with the HDB housing programme was less to do with how it broke up extended families and other living arrangements and more to do with the fact that it actively legitimized one dominant living arrangement – the individualized heterosexual nuclear family – at the expense of others. The trouble, in other words, was it effectively made the heterosexual nuclear family the universal living arrangement for the vast majority of Singaporeans.

The effect of the state centring the family unit in the national imaginary both through housing policy and through other forms of policies and rhetoric is that the nation is imagined as a tessellation of uniform family units that simultaneously constricts the salience and significance of relating to others outside of these units. The physical walls of the HDB flat can extend out of the material confines of the flat and shape the social lives of its inhabitants.[90] It is in this sense that heteronormative familism, with its obsessive fetishization of the family unit as well as its superimposition of the heterosexual nuclear family structure upon household formations, has effectively foreclosed lateral connections across members of the putative Singaporean nation. Subjectivity is shot through by heteronormative familism such that the ideal subject position is always positioned vis-à-vis one's family. As I detail further in the next chapter, the notion of a civilizational identity in opposition to the 'West' and an essentialized Asian disposition to communitarianism limited to the family inducts care into the familial sphere and, specifically, the nuclear family unit. The apotheosis of the reification of the family unit is the concomitant erasure of connections and obligations between individuals outside kinship structures; and it ensures care becomes a private kinship obligation rather than a public obligation that the state is responsible for providing and ensuring.

Tracing the lineaments of heteronormativity in Singapore is expectedly a complex task. But it should be clear by now that one of the major founts of its imbrication with the production of subjectivity in Singapore is the heterosexual nuclear family and how it is marshalled in relation to domesticity and domestic affairs. Here, we should remain alive to the polysemy in *domestic*. In one sense, it refers to one's home, residence, the private sphere; but in another sense, it refers to a country's internal affairs and the public sphere. In Singapore, both these meanings are inextricably intertwined – the domestic sphere is constituted by (heteronormative) domesticity.

The imagination of the Singaporean nation is formed in the heteronormative familial space of one's HDB flat. In this way, it is the 'building block' of the nation and what it means to be a 'normal' Singaporean.[91] Its near-universal ubiquity functions as a microcosm of the nation and a proxy for the Singaporean lifeworld. Singaporeans know what to expect when they walk around any public housing neighbourhood in the country – exactly whatever they would expect to encounter in their own public housing neighbourhood. HDB housing neighbourhoods are centrally and comprehensively planned down to the level of the precinct (a cluster of a few apartment blocks) such that every town is adequately and similarly furnished in terms of public amenities such as children's playgrounds, bus stations, shopping malls, markets, food centres, religious sites of worship, and so on.[92]

The visible exchangeability and uniformity of amenities, facilities, and resources within one's domestic space creates a sense of 'this is what it is like for everyone else' – subtly reinforcing the heteronormative space of the HDB flat as the Singaporean way of life. In this way, 'spatial distributions effectively [equate] the nation with the heterosexual "normal" space', testifying to how sexuality can become a prism through which a sense of nationhood – belonging, and non-belonging – is articulated.[93] Heteronormative familism is thus reproduced through the HDB flat, through the rhetoric surrounding the families that inhabit it, through the conditions that adjudicate when one is eligible to leave one's family's flat and purchase a flat of one's own, and through a set of policies that place heterosexual nuclear families within the flat together with the attendant obligations of kinship.

In producing Singaporean subjectivity through the totalizing power of heteronormative familism, it is not just minoritized sexualities who are queered. Oswin's reminder resounds here, reminding us of how 'that which is cast as foreign to the domestic can and ought to be interrogated as also often queer'.[94] If heteronormativity is responsible for maintaining the form of the family, in Singapore it is combined with the state's insistence on the centrality of kinship arising out of a particular Asian civilizational identity that the nation is imagined to be a part of. The result is a peculiarly Singaporean version of mutual obligation where the citizen-subject is only expected to be responsible for their kin whilst other social relations are rendered illegible and vacated of any mutual obligation. When one bothers to look, it becomes evident that what the state claims is an imagined community is, in fact, a composition of disparate family units, neatly assembled in their respective households across the entire island where the radial limits of one's obligations terminate at the limits of one's kinship groupings. Whilst 'in the privacy of its flat, each family lives with its own material excess or deprivation, surfeit or hunger, happiness or depression, according to its own financial circumstances',[95] other obligations – moral, financial, or otherwise – to other fellow citizens are obfuscated and elided, apparently non-existent.

Given how Singaporean subjectivity is set up and made contingent on heteronormative familism, it is not surprising that sexual minorities try to demonstrate their compatibility with kinship structures in a display of 'strategic normativity'.[96] In Chapter 5, I explore how the social movement Pink Dot foregrounds the notion that non-normative sexualities are not incompatible with heteronormative familism. They insist that they can fit into extant familial forms and meet the obligations built into kinship ties. This is essentially the logic that convinced the High Court to grant the adoption order in *UKM* v. *Attorney-General*; and this is the logic that many minoritized sexualities, activists, and community organizers have resorted to in the hope that the ideal Singaporean subject position could be adjusted to accommodate them. I can understand why taking this position can seem appealing, but I want to suggest that this is insufficient in detaching one from the clutches of heteronormativity.

As Shane Phelan argues, 'the heterosexual formulation of kinship that defines gays and lesbians (as well as unmarried adults) as either outside kin networks or unable to form new ones ... suggests that kinship will have to be rethought'.[97] Thus, even if the operation of heteronormative familism in Singapore could be edited to accommodate sexual minorities who were able to fit into extant kin relations, such a move would continue to reify ontological kin relations and hierarchize them above other social relations. The people who do not or cannot find a place for themselves within kinship structures, for whatever reason, will continue to remain queered. Instead, we need to change the constitution of kinship itself. After all, the problem is not to find a way to make Antigone legible; it is to transform the very frame within which her legibility is made to matter in the first place.

Notes

1 This was the speech where Lee declared that what the legal scholar Michael Hor termed '*pax homosexualis*'. The prime minister said that even though Section 377A would be retained, it would not be proactively enforced. See Michael Hor, 'Enforcement of 377A: Entering the Twilight Zone', in Yue and Jun Zubillaga-Pow, *Queer Singapore: Illiberal Citizenship and Mediated Cultures*, pp. 45–58 (pp. 55–56). Before Section 377A was repealed in 2022, at least two former Attorney-Generals raised serious concerns over this détente with regard to its constitutionality and whether it impinged on prosecutorial discretion. See V. K. Rajah, 'Section 377A: An Impotent Anachronism', *The Straits Times*, 30 September 2018, www.straitstimes.com/opinion/section-377a-an-impotent-anachronism (accessed 23 September 2024); and Walter Sim, 'Walter Woon, Tommy Koh Differ on 377A Anti-Gay Sex Law at NUS Forum', *The Straits Times*, 19 January 2016, www.straitstimes.com/singapore/walter-woon-tommy-koh-differ-on-377a-anti-gay-sex-law-at-nus-forum (accessed 23 September 2024).
2 'Speech to Parliament on Reading of Penal Code (Amendment) Bill'.
3 See, for example, George Baylon Radics, 'Section 377A in Singapore and the (De)Criminalization of Homosexuality', *Reconstructions*, 15.2 (2015); Radics, 'Decolonizing Singapore's Sex Laws'; Pablo Ciocchini and George Baylon Radics, eds, *Criminal Legalities in the Global South: Cultural Dynamics, Political Tensions, and Institutional Practices* (Abingdon: Routledge, 2019); Alfred Chua, 'Veteran Diplomat Tommy Koh Calls on S'pore's Gay Community to Mount Challenge against S377A', *TODAY*, 7 September 2018; and Lynette J. Chua, 'Collective Litigation and the Constitutional Challenges to Decriminalizing Homosexuality in Singapore', *Journal of Law and Society*, 44.3 (2017), 433–55.
4 Cho, 'Deferred Futures', p. 245.
5 'Speech to Parliament on Reading of Penal Code (Amendment) Bill'.
6 Oswin, *Global City Futures*, p. 85.
7 See, for example, Stella R. Quah, *Family in Singapore: Sociological Perspectives* (Singapore: Times Academic Press, 1994); Paulin Tay Straughan, *The Social Contradictions of the Normal Family: Challenges to the Ideology*, Department of Sociology Working Papers, 135 (Singapore: Department of Sociology, National University of Singapore, 1999); Mathews, 'Traditional View of Family'; Chan et al., *Singapore's Multiculturalism*; and Paulin Tay Straughan, *Marriage Dissolution in Singapore: Revisiting Family Values and Ideology in Marriage* (Leiden: Brill, 2009).
8 Straughan, *Marriage Dissolution in Singapore*, p. 121.
9 Natalie Oswin, 'Sexual Citizenship in Singapore: Heteronormativity and the Cultural Politics of Population', *Intersections: Gender and Sexuality in Asia and the Pacific*, 36 (2014) http://intersections.anu.edu.au/issue36/oswin.htm#t8 (accessed 20 November 2021).
10 Janice Lim, 'The Big Read in Short: Revisiting the Link between Family Formation and Housing Policies', *TODAY*, 13 March 2021, www.todayonline.com/big-read/big-read-short-revisiting-link-between-family-formation-and-housing-policies (accessed 23 September 2024).

11 'Speech to Parliament on Reading of Penal Code (Amendment) Bill'.

12 Judith Butler, *Antigone's Claim: Kinship between Life and Death* (New York: Columbia University Press, 2012), p. 57.

13 Ibid., p. 58.

14 Ibid., pp. 71–72; see also Gayle Rubin, 'The Traffic in Women: Notes on the Political Economy of "Sex"', in *Toward an Anthropology of Women*, ed. Rayna R. Reiter (New York: Monthly Review Press, 1975), pp. 157–210.

15 Mano, 'Rethinking the Heteronormative Foundations of Kinship', p. 148.

16 David Murray Schneider, *A Critique of the Study of Kinship* (Ann Arbor: University of Michigan Press, 1984), p. 131, emphasis in original.

17 Teo, *Neoliberal Morality in Singapore*.

18 Sharon Ee Ling Quah, *Perspectives on Marital Dissolution: Divorce Biographies in Singapore* (Singapore: Springer, 2015).

19 Tang and Quah, 'Heteronormativity and Sexuality Politics', p. 652.

20 Rachel Au-yong, 'Family Life Takes Shape for Gay Couple after Adoption Ruling', *The Straits Times*, 23 December 2018, www.straitstimes.com/singapore/family-life-takes-shape-for-gay-couple-after-adoption-ruling (accessed 26 September 2024).

21 Adoption of Children Act 1939, https://sso.agc.gov.sg/Act/ACA1939# (accessed 26 September 2024).

22 Ibid.

23 Women's Charter 1961, available at https://sso.agc.gov.sg/act/wc1961?ProvIds=P13- (accessed 23 September 2024).

24 Ahmed, *Queer Phenomenology*, p. 21.

25 Adoption of Children Act.

26 Au-yong, 'Family Life Takes Shape'.

27 'Gay Father Permitted to Adopt Biological Son Born via Surrogacy, in First for Singapore', CNA, 17 December 2018, www.channelnewsasia.com/news/singapore/gay-father-adopt-surrogate-son-singapore-11039384 (accessed 30 January 2024).

28 Sundaresh Menon (Chief Justice), *UKM v. Attorney-General* [2018] SGHCF 18, pp. 143–44.

29 Fabian Koh, 'Ministry to Study if Policies Need to Be Reviewed after Court Allows Gay Singaporean to Adopt Surrogate Son', *The Straits Times*, 17 December 2018, www.straitstimes.com/singapore/ministry-to-study-if-policies-need-to-be-reviewed-after-court-allows-gay-singaporean-to (accessed 23 September 2024).

30 'Court Ruling on Gay Father's Adoption Appeal: MSF Says to Consider If Policies Need to Be Reviewed', CNA, 17 December 2018, www.channelnewsasia.com/singapore/gay-father-adoption-biological-son-high-court-decision-msf-914071 (accessed 30 January 2019).

31 'Gay Father's Adoption Appeal: MSF Responds to Concerns on Whether Case Sets a Precedent', CNA, 19 December 2018, www.channelnewsasia.com/singapore/gay-fathers-adoption-appeal-msf-responds-concerns-whether-case-sets-precedent-914606 (accessed 30 January 2024).

32 Chua, *Mobilizing Gay Singapore*, p. 32.

33 Ibid. The PAP government is able to do this because, since independence, it has held an overwhelming parliamentary supermajority. Internal party discipline is also very high, meaning that PAP MPs – with very rare exceptions – vote with the government.

34 In May 2022, the Singapore government introduced legislation in Parliament that overhauled the Adoption of Children Act. Amongst other changes, eligibility criteria were tightened and only (heterosexual) married couples were permitted to adopt. See Jalelah Abu Baker and See Kit Tang, 'Parliament Passes New Bill to Improve Adoption Laws and Practices', CNA, 9 May 2022, www.channelnewsasia.com/singapore/parliament-passes-new-bill-improve-adoption-laws-and-practices-2673671.

35 'Parliamentary Debates: Official Report' (Singapore: Hansard, 2019).

36 Ibid.

37 Hor, 'Enforcement of 377A', pp. 56–57.

38 See, for example, Lynette J. Chua, 'The Power of Legal Processes and Section 377A of the Penal Code: *Tan Eng Hong v. Attorney-General*', *Singapore Journal of Legal Studies*, 2012, 457–66; Chua, 'Collective Litigation'; Radics, 'Section 377A in Singapore and the (De)Criminalization of Homosexuality'; George Baylon Radics, 'Challenging Antisodomy Laws in Singapore and the Former British Colonies of ASEAN', *Journal of Human Rights*, 20.2 (2021), 211–27; and Chua, 'Veteran Diplomat Tommy Koh'.

39 Katherine M. Franke, 'The Domesticated Liberty of *Lawrence v. Texas*', *Columbia Law Review*, 104.5 (2004), 1399–1426 (p. 1419).

40 Ibid.

41 Ibid.

42 Oswin, 'Sexual Citizenship in Singapore', p. 3.

43 Ibid.

44 Matthias Nass, 'The World According to Two Old Friends: Lee Kuan Yew and Helmut Schmidt', *The Straits Times*, 22 September 2012, www.straitstimes.com/singapore/the-world-according-to-two-old-friends-lee-kuan-yew-and-helmut-schmidt (accessed 23 September 2024).

45 Teo, *Neoliberal Morality in Singapore*, pp. 113–15.

46 Melinda Cooper, *Family Values: Between Neoliberalism and the New Social Conservatism* (New York: Zone Books, 2017), p. 68.

47 Nass, 'The World According to Two Old Friends', emphasis mine.

48 Social workers, for instance, check that those who approach social-assistance institutions for help have reached out to their families and obtained whatever help they can from them.

49 Jacques Donzelot, *The Policing of Families* (Baltimore: Johns Hopkins University Press, 1979).

50 Cooper, *Family Values*, p. 68; Wendy Brown, *Undoing the Demos: Neoliberalism's Stealth Revolution* (New York: Zone Books, 2015), pp. 100–01.

51 Youyenn Teo, 'Gender Disarmed: How Gendered Policies Produce Gender-Neutral Politics in Singapore', *Signs: Journal of Women in Culture and Society*, 34.3 (2009), 533–58.

52 Zakaria and Lee, 'Culture Is Destiny', p. 113.

53 Teo, 'Gender Disarmed', pp. 548–49.

54 Mathews, 'Traditional View of Family'.

55 Maintenance of Parents Act 1995, https://sso.agc.gov.sg/Act/MPA1995 (accessed 27 September 2024).

56 Laura Elizabeth Philomin, '213 Cases Lodged with Commissioner for the Maintenance of Parents in 2014', *TODAY*, 25 November 2015, www.todayonline.com/singapore/213-cases-lodged-commissioner-maintenance-parents-2014 (accessed 23 September 2024).

57 Cooper, *Family Values*, p. 69.

58 HDB, 'Living with/near Parents or Child', www.hdb.gov.sg/residential/buying-a-flat/resale/financing/cpf-housing-grants/living-with-near-parents-or-child (accessed 22 November 2024).

59 As I previously mentioned in the introduction, grandparents can be read as part of a multigenerational nuclear family structure. The familial obligations of care operate within this structure and, in different contexts and at different times, fall on parents, grandparents, and children variably. The Maintenance of Parents Act, for example, codifies the expectation that adult children are responsible for the welfare of their parents, whilst the Proximity Housing Grant codifies the expectation that retired parents will take on the care of their working children's offspring. As I have previously suggested, it is important to keep in mind that all of these obligations operate within the nuclear family structure – even if it is multigenerational – and reflect the state's narrow, heteronormative view of kinship.

60 Youyenn Teo, 'Inequality for the Greater Good: Gendered State Rule in Singapore', *Critical Asian Studies*, 39.3 (2007), 423–45.

61 Tang and Quah, 'Heteronormativity and Sexuality Politics', p. 651; see also Yuval-Davis, *Gender & Nation*.

62 Yuval-Davis, *Gender & Nation*; Lynne A. Haney and Lisa Pollard, *Families of a New World: Gender, Politics, and State Development in a Global Context* (New York: Routledge, 2003); Heng and Devan, 'State Fatherhood'.

63 At the National Day Rally 2024, prime minister Lawrence Wong announced the government's intention to increase parental leave allowances from 1 April 2025. In addition to an increase in parental leave that can be shared between parents, paternity leave will increase to four weeks. See Lawrence Wong, 'National Day Rally 2024', 2024, Prime Minister's Office, www.pmo.gov.sg/Newsroom/National-Day-Rally-2024 (accessed 30 September 2024).

64 A brief note that this gendered dimension of reproduction and caring is also strongly racialized – female migrant workers are forbidden from becoming pregnant in Singapore on pain of deportation. Most migrant women work as domestic workers, and part of their job involves caring and child-rearing duties, especially whilst their employers are away at work. Thus, the heteronormative politics of kinship that assigns reproductive and maternal duties to Singaporean women also relies on the availability of migrant women to bear part of the load. Whilst female migrant workers, typically from poorer

countries in South/Southeast Asia, are crucial to keeping the circuits of care imbricated in kinship networks working, they are simultaneously interdicted from coupling with members of the nation or participating in the nation's reproduction. Chapter 4 analyses heteronormativity's capacity to xenologize.

65 Internal Revenue Authority of Singapore, 'Foreign Domestic Worker Levy (FDWL) Relief', www.iras.gov.sg/taxes/individual-income-tax/employees/deductions-for-individuals/personal-reliefs-and-tax-rebates/foreign-domestic-worker-levy-(fdwl)-relief (accessed 25 September 2024).

66 Teo, 'Inequality for the Greater Good', p. 429.

67 'Speech to Parliament on Reading of Penal Code (Amendment) Bill'.

68 Janet W. Salaff, *State and Family in Singapore: Restructuring a Developing Society* (Ithaca: Cornell University Press, 1988).

69 Loh Kah Seng, 'Black Areas: Urban Kampongs and Power Relations in Post-War Singapore Historiography', *SOJOURN: Journal of Social Issues in Southeast Asia*, 22.1 (2007), 1–29 (p. 12).

70 Goh Keng Swee, *The Economics of Modernization* (Singapore: Asia Pacific Press, 1972), p. 63.

71 'Speech to Parliament on Reading of Penal Code (Amendment) Bill'.

72 Christopher Tremewan, *The Political Economy of Social Control in Singapore* (London: Macmillan, 1994), p. 50.

73 Gregory Clancey, 'Toward a Spatial History of Emergency: Notes from Singapore', Asia Research Institute Working Paper Series no. 8 (Singapore: Asia Research Institute of the National University of Singapore, 2003).

74 HDB, 'Eligibility', *Eligibility*, 2017, www.hdb.gov.sg/cs/infoweb/residential/buying-a-flat/resale/eligibility- (accessed 22 November 2021).

75 Chua, *Political Legitimacy and Housing*, p. 141.

76 Mano, 'Rethinking the Heteronormative Foundations of Kinship', p. 148.

77 Mark Andrejevic, 'The Work of Watching One Another: Lateral Surveillance, Risk and Governance', *Surveillance & Society*, 3.2 (2005), 479–97 (p. 481); see also Thomas Mathiesen, 'The Viewer Society: Michel Foucault's "Panopticon" Revisited', *Theoretical Criminology*, 1.2 (1997), 215–34; Hee Jhee Jiow and Sofia Morales, 'Lateral Surveillance in Singapore', *Surveillance & Society*, 13.3–4 (2015), 327–37.

78 John D'Emilio, 'Capitalism and Gay Identity', in *The Lesbian and Gay Studies Reader*, ed. Henry Abelove, Michèle Aina Barale, and David M. Halperin (New York: Routledge, 1993), pp. 467–76.

79 Lazar, 'Homonationalist Discourse', p. 424.

80 HDB, 'Eligibility'.

81 Valluvan, *The Clamour of Nationalism*, p. 34.

82 Cohen, 'Punks, Bulldaggers, and Welfare Queens', p. 438.

83 Teo, 'Inequality for the Greater Good'; Lily Kong and Brenda S. A. Yeoh, *The Politics of Landscapes in Singapore: Constructions of 'Nation'* (Syracuse: Syracuse University Press, 2003).

84 Heng and Devan, 'State Fatherhood', p. 196; see also Nasir and Turner, *The Future of Singapore*.

85 Tan and Lee, 'Imagining the Gay Community'; Weiss, 'Who Sets Social Policy in Metropolis?'.

86 Cohen, 'Punks, Bulldaggers, and Welfare Queens', p. 447 (emphasis in original).

87 Tremewan, *The Political Economy of Social Control in Singapore*, p. 50.

88 Timothy Austin, 'Crime and Control', in *Management of Success: The Moulding of Modern Singapore*, ed. Kernial Singh Sandhu and Paul Wheatley (Singapore: Institute of Southeast Asian Studies, 1989), pp. 913–27 (pp. 918–19).

89 Ibid.

90 Riaz Hassan, *Families in Flats: A Study of Low Income Families in Public Housing* (Singapore: Singapore University Press, 1977), pp. 200–03.

91 'Speech to Parliament on Reading of Penal Code (Amendment) Bill'.

92 Aline K. Wong and Stephen H. K. Yeh, eds, *Housing a Nation: 25 Years of Public Housing in Singapore* (Singapore: HDB, 1985), pp. 56–112.

93 Anna Marie Smith, *New Right Discourse on Race and Sexuality* (Cambridge: Cambridge University Press, 1994), p. 25.

94 Oswin, 'The Modern Model Family at Home in Singapore', p. 265.

95 Chua, *Liberalism Disavowed*, p. 84.

96 Amy Brainer, *Queer Kinship and Family Change in Taiwan* (New Brunswick: Rutgers University Press, 2019), p. 83; see also Benedict J. L. Rowlett and Christian Go, 'Tracing Trans-Regional Discursive Flows in Pink Dot Hong Kong Promotional Videos: (Homo)Normativities and Nationalism, Activism and Ambivalence', *Journal of Language and Sexuality*, 10.2 (2021); Phillips, ' "We Aren't Really That Different" '.

97 Shane Phelan, *Sexual Strangers: Gays, Lesbians, and Dilemmas of Citizenship* (Philadelphia: Temple University Press, 2001), p. 157.

4

Xenologizing queerness

The queer–foreign communion

Because of how heteronormativity saturates Singaporean subjectivity and is constitutive of the nation, queerness can find itself marooned off its shores and in the space of the foreign. Put differently, queerness – as in all that exceeds the limits of reproductive, coupling, marriage-, and kinship-based expressions of heterosexuality – can be represented as incompatible with and even contradictory to the nation. Whilst consequently rendering people queer, it also positions them as counter-national in the sense of being antithetical to the nation, which is precisely why what is 'cast as foreign to the domestic can and ought to be interrogated as also often queer'.[1] Calling for a broader understanding of queerness that is not restricted to non-heterosexualities is therefore not merely an exercise in theoretical improvisation. Eschewing an analysis routed through identity categories in favour of an appraisal of how power is reified in normative assertions is a way of accounting for the many people who are queered by the same force that also minoritizes non-normative sexualities. In this chapter, I want to think about how queerness is xenologized, and how those who happen to be cast as foreign can have their incompatibility with the nation confirmed by being rendered queer and thus cast out of step with the straight nation.

At the same time, I am not saying that because queerness is placed in the space of the foreign, all non-citizens in Singapore are queered. To see how and when the foreign is rendered queer, we need to go beyond the formal categories of citizen/non-citizen. There is, of course, an advantage to occupying the category of the citizen. That is precisely what allows Pink Dot to mobilize nationalist discourses and attempt to imbricate LGBT people with the nation.[2] Pink Dot's basic claim is that since LGBT Singaporeans are also Singaporean citizens, they deserve to be treated fairly like other citizens and live lives free of discrimination. Occupying the formal category of citizen thus channels the authority of the state and gives LGBT citizens the capacity to try and address their exclusion from the nation. In other words, the force behind Pink Dot's demand for equality in terms of their lived experience flows from a nominally indisputable equality in their status as citizens. Even though queerness is xenologized and rendered foreign in relation to the nation, occupying the formal category of citizen provides LGBT Singaporeans with some claim to domesticity mediated by the nation. Essentially, were Pink Dot not organized by Singaporeans, it would not be able to draw on the vocabulary of the nation in the way that it does.

Nonetheless, despite the way the category of the citizen can be mobilized, the xenologization of queerness itself – as that which runs counter to the nation – does not map neatly onto the formal citizen/non-citizen division. Xenology operates less at the formal level of citizenship statuses and more in the sense of subjectivity and (in)compatibility with the straight nation. This opens the door to making visible how certain people can be rendered foreign – just as certain people can be rendered queer – and I suggest the formal category of citizenship is not the only mechanism that subjectivizes people to these ends. After all, as we have already seen, within the formal category of Singaporean citizens, some people are queered as a function of how subjectivity is set up at the intersections and interstices of laws, policies, and culture in Singapore. Queered citizens are subjectivized differently despite formally occupying the same category as other citizens and rendered out of step with the nation. It follows that where non-citizens are concerned, a similar logic prevails – not all non-citizens are xenologized to the same extent or cast as equally foreign.

To cast someone is to select them to play a particular role, to assign them a particular function in service of a script and a larger narrative. But to cast can also be understood as a way of moulding and fixing something in place in the way a plaster cast does. To cast as foreign can therefore be understood as producing the foreign according to a certain fixed script in service of a larger narrative. In that sense, I want to explore the way the spectre of the foreigner – the figure that is constructed as incompatible with the nation and cannot be domesticated as such – can be mediated by queerness. In what ways do those who are rendered irrevocably foreign in the sense of being positioned as incongruous with the nation have their incongruence confirmed by being queered? In other words, how does rendering someone queer assist in the work of casting them as foreign? Tugging at these threads, I turn to the paradigmatic figuration of the foreign in Singapore – the foreign worker.

If connecting queerness with the foreign like this appears idiosyncratic, it reflects the fact that the fields of migration studies and queer studies have not made common cause in Singapore. Lenore Lyons briefly gestured towards it in the early 2000s by highlighting how 'non-reproductively oriented sexualities are excluded from dominant representations of the Singaporean nation', identifying how foreign workers in particular are cast as having 'alien sexualities'.[3] Lyons' invocation of the alien was an invitation to open the register of sexuality in tandem with the dossiers of domesticity, xenology, and alienation, but with the exception of Oswin's *Global City Futures* that particular nexus has hardly been mined.[4]

It bears mentioning that within each of these spheres, there is plenty of very good scholarship. Extant work on migrants and migration in Singapore elaborates on the ways in which 'race', class, and gender are sites that produce the exclusions that foreign workers in particular experience. Taken together, these various exclusions produce a 'bifurcated labour' regime that manifests in a categorical distinction between 'foreign workers' and 'foreign talent',[5] as well as the different legal regimes that these categories are subjected to. The differentiated legislation that governs different categories of non-citizens creates a 'bifurcated governmentality that results in the constitution and embodiment of foreign workers and foreign talent in specific racialized and classed ways'.[6] Brenda Yeoh and Shirlena Huang's work highlights the gendered differentiations in the regulation of foreign workers' lives.[7] But there remains scant consideration of heteronormativity's role – the privileging and reification of a particular expression of heterosexuality – in producing and legitimizing these exclusions.

It is a similar story with queer studies in Singapore. Many scholars have articulated the multiple inequalities generated by the policing of sexuality and gender. Russell Heng's work documents many of the historical challenges that LGBT people in Singapore faced with community organizing and mobilizing.[8] Lynette Chua's *Mobilizing Gay Singapore* and Phillips' *Virtual Activism* are comprehensive ethnographic studies of the development of LGBT activism in the country.[9] Others identify various sites of resistance and advocacy that have emerged in Singapore more recently and draw out how the conceptual frame of the nation is invoked in debates over LGBT rights.[10] Yet none of them quite makes the move of identifying the centrality of heteronormativity in dominant imaginations of the nation and the consequent implications that this has for queerness writ large. By and large, existing critical scholarship shows how the governance of sexuality intersects with the nation. Some of it defends an assimilationist approach to activism and articulates how it has made gains. But there remains a general underappreciation for how the alliance between heteronormativity and the nation relies on xenologizing queerness. Taken together, these bodies of work help build strong critiques of state-sponsored assemblies of sexuality and gender in Singapore and help understand how migrant labour is used and exploited in various ways.

Oswin goes further and urges us to read Singapore as a 'straight space' by arguing that some non-citizens are rendered queer because they are excluded from the nation and its associated reproductive logics.[11]

I agree but I think we should take this argument to its end to fully draw out the connections between the nation and the counter-nation, the processes of domestication and xenologization, and the states of permanence and transience in the nation. To do this, it is insufficient to read Singapore merely as a straight *space* – we need to read it as a straight *nation*.

Being able to occupy the ideal subject position in Singapore hinges on the correct expression of a particular form of heterosexuality expressed through marriage and the heterosexual nuclear family. Many people are excluded from this process of subject formation and rendered queer as a result – they are made counter-national by being unable to occupy the ideal Singaporean subject position. Queerness is xenologized in this sense. I want to spend some time meditating on the common ground that can be forged between queerness and foreignness to make visible how those who are categorized as incompatible with the nation are governed by a set of interdictions that prevent them from expressing the specific form of heterosexuality that nationalism in Singapore demands – thus confirming their incompatibility.

As I suggested previously, all nations instantiate counter-nations. If the nation is a political project, then the counter-nation is formed through the coalescence of various minorities and others that are disclaimed by the very operation of those politics. Whilst some non-citizens are made available for domestication via integration into the nation, others are cast as permanently and irredeemably foreign. I would like to suggest that the irredeemability of foreignness can be sealed through the production of queerness.

Non-citizens and their dissimilitudes

The terms most commonly used in government and public discourse to refer to the non-citizen workforce in Singapore are 'foreign worker' and 'foreign talent'.[12] Even as both denote non-citizens working in Singapore, there are racial and class dimensions to the constitution and deployment of these terms. *Foreign talent* is a category that is primarily made up of white Euro-Americans in senior, well-paid positions. It is typically used 'for professionals, managers, and executives, usually for Western foreigners, but has gradually expanded to include some [middle class] Asians, such as Indian [professionals]'.[13] In contrast, *foreign worker* is used to refer to low-wage workers performing manual labour and working in the 'manufacturing, construction, service, and maritime sectors who come mainly from [poorer or developing countries in South/Southeast Asia]'.[14] The category that one is placed in has significant implications for how one is positioned in relation to the nation. The dissimilitude between how foreign talents and foreign workers are subjectivized is guided by a set of logics that lifts up the former whilst abasing the latter.

The distinctions and discriminations arising from this differentiation have been examined by scholars working in this particular intersection of migration and labour politics.[15] Whilst foreign talent are encouraged and afforded opportunities to settle in Singapore, to develop their futures here, and to build their families here, the foreign worker stands in diametric opposition to this. Foreign workers are treated as 'potentially disruptive to Singaporean society if left unregulated, [and] state policy is opposed to long-term immigration and directed at ensuring that this category of migrants remains a transient workforce, subject to repatriation during periods of economic downturns'.[16] They are 'temporarily inserted into highly gendered roles within the nation and regulated on a "use and discard" basis' with no possibility of permanence or long-term settlement in Singapore open to them.[17] The extent to which this bifurcation has become embedded in quotidian Singaporean life is such that:

> for someone living in Singapore, this sort of juxtaposition – where one group is held up as highly desirable and of which there is lots to say, and the rendering of the other group as largely a fact to be tolerated and best left out of dinner conversation – is continually reproduced as a taken-for-granted reality of everyday life.[18]

Not only is it taken for granted, it is also codified in legislation. Whereas foreign talent typically apply for an Employment Pass to work and reside in Singapore, it is the employers of foreign workers who apply on their behalf for a Work Permit. This Work Permit is tied to a specific employer and it is cancelled upon termination of employment. Employers are also compelled to repatriate foreign workers to their home country upon termination of employment, which means that foreign workers 'cannot therefore gain access to the local labour market' and look for new jobs.[19]

These pieces of legislation also effectively mean that foreign workers are permanent transients in a state of permanent transience, which forecloses the possibility of them achieving a semblance of permanence in the nation. This does not necessarily mean they do not live and work in Singapore for a long time – many foreign workers work in Singapore for a decade and more; but because of the threat and very real possibility of being repatriated at any given moment, it is not permanence in any reasonable sense but more like an extended period of precarity. Living with an axe hanging over one's head, unsure if its restraining cable might give way any second, is hardly comfortable – even if said axe never comes crashing down, it is experienced as incessantly difficult. Incidentally, this is also an approximate description of the affective landscape that many sexual minorities, and gay men in particular, were mired in whilst Section 377A remained in the Penal Code, which perhaps helps show how these struggles that have historically been fought separately and thought of as distinct have, in fact, potential lines of commonality.[20]

The Work Permit and Employment Pass distinction also contains a key difference in relation to the families of non-citizens, in that 'Employment Pass holders may bring in family members through the Dependant's Pass or Long-Term Social Visit Pass programmes – and this includes spouses, children, parents and parents-in-law – work permit holders have no such option.'[21]

Hence, for foreign talent, migration comes with the possibility of moving whilst retaining the integrity of their (nuclear) family – even if, in practice, not all might take this up. But nominally being able to participate in the circuits of heteronormative familism by migrating and living with their families in Singapore allows them to demonstrate their compatibility with Singaporean subjectivity. In stark contrast, as Work Permit holders, foreign workers are compelled to leave their families behind when they migrate to Singapore for work – further entrenching their transience because it forecloses the possibility of this group of people settling and building a long-term presence in the country with their families.

To be clear, I am not suggesting there is something inherently good about the nuclear family that necessarily elevates it above other forms of social relations in building one's life somewhere. Foreign workers may not necessarily want to migrate with their families but my point here is that they are necessarily removed from the circuits of heteronormative familism in ways that foreign talent are not. Because the state invests the heterosexual nuclear family with certain meanings, how one is positioned in relation to it carries implications for how one is subjectivized. As they are compelled to leave their families to live in Singapore outside familial structures, foreign workers are queered; turned into non-familial figures; and as such, never fully compatible with a nation that insulates itself from them through the law. If heteronormativity in Singapore calls for the expression of a particular form of heterosexuality that structures subjectivity in Singapore, those who are designated foreign workers are denied the very possibility of expressing themselves in this manner – even if they wanted to.

There is more. The Employment of Foreign Manpower Act (which applies solely to Work Permit holders) forbids foreign workers to form families in Singapore or to couple with Singaporean citizens or permanent residents. The Fourth Schedule of the Act sets out this injunction in unambiguous terms under the section termed 'Conduct':

The foreign employee shall not go through any form of marriage or apply to marry under any law, religion, custom or usage with a Singapore citizen or permanent resident in or outside Singapore, without the prior approval of the

Controller, while the foreign employee holds a work permit, and also after the foreign employee's work permit has expired or has been cancelled or revoked.

If the foreign employee is a female foreign employee, the foreign employee shall not become pregnant or deliver any child in Singapore during and after the validity period of her work permit, unless she is a work permit holder who is already married to a Singapore citizen or permanent resident with the approval of the Controller.

The foreign employee shall not be involved in any illegal, immoral or undesirable activities, including breaking up families in Singapore.[22]

This is perhaps the most visible manifestation of the racialized, gendered, and classed dimensions to the domopolitics that are embedded in nationalism and co-constitute heteronormativity in Singapore. Because the scope of the law is striking. The prohibition of foreign workers marrying another Singaporean citizen or permanent resident applies even if the individual in question is no longer holding a Work Permit, and extends to prohibit marrying Singaporeans beyond the physical borders of the country.

The clause that extends this prohibition even after their Work Permit has expired means that, from the moment they are categorized as a foreign worker and issued a Work Permit, they can never marry a Singaporean – they are permanently categorized as unsuitable and undesirable as part of the nation. For female Work Permit holders, a further condition applies – they are expressly prohibited from becoming pregnant, and to that end they are subject to mandatory six-monthly medical checks.[23] The six-month interval means that any pregnancy can be detected early enough such that the Work Permit holder can be repatriated in good time without delivering the child on Singaporean shores. The extensive work that goes into maintaining this biopolitic regime reflects the 'endemic nervousness', a continuing racialized anxiety, around who is allowed to reproduce the nation as well as the consequent membership of the nation.[24] The gendered dimension of heteronormative familism collides here with a racialized dimension in how female foreign workers are regulated. Whereas some women – university graduates, for example – are positioned as desirable reproducers of the nation, desperately coaxed to reproduce, as a function of the 'gendered call to patriotic duty', other women – brown foreign workers who typically come from poorer, less-developed countries in Southeast Asia or South Asia – are positioned as unsuitable and prevented by law from reproducing the nation on pain of deportation.[25]

Some might want to suggest that despite its expansive language, in practice the legal injunction against marriage cannot function as intended simply because foreign workers could opt to marry outside of Singapore.[26] Strictly speaking, this is correct. However, the Fourth Schedule also grants the state the right to cancel the foreign worker's Work Permit should they get married to a Singaporean citizen or permanent resident in another jurisdiction – thus making it difficult for them to re-enter and continue to work in Singapore. In other words, they would find it very difficult to live and make a living in Singapore legally. The riddle of enforceability across jurisdictions finds its solution in the necessity of employability. For foreign workers, then, the right to work in Singapore becomes contingent on rescinding the possibility of becoming part of the nation in the way that foreign talent can.

It is also worth noting how the Employment of Foreign Manpower Act not only refuses foreign workers the possibility of being incorporated into the nation but also actively casts them as potential sexual threats to the nation. Whilst the initial sections of the Fourth Schedule prohibit them from forming new heteronormative kin relations in Singapore, their threat is codified in the subsequent line that they must not engage 'in any illegal, immoral or undesirable activities, including breaking up families in Singapore'.[27] There are some echoes here of the logics that animate the Adoption of Children Act where male heterosexual desire, once extracted from the safe site of the heterosexual couple, becomes cast as dangerous and requiring regulation. Once again, together with the other sections in the Fourth Schedule, the law does important pedagogical work in signalling the undesirability and unsuitability of foreign workers within the nation; it also gestures towards the sexual danger that their incompatibility poses. This injunction against breaking up families reflects a certain anxiety about the foreign worker who, having been removed from the safe confines of the heterosexual nuclear family, is now sexually overdetermined as a threat to be policed, and the logics of sexual overdetermination are both gendered and racialized. Thus, the male foreign worker is produced as a sexual threat and a danger to Singaporean women in particular; the female foreign worker is produced as a temptress whose excessive sexuality could disrupt the institution of marriage and the sacrosanct Singaporean nuclear family unit.[28]

In contrast to foreign workers, foreign talent retain the possibility of coupling with Singaporean citizens or permanent residents and becoming members of the nation. In this sense, they are cast as potentially compatible with the nation. It is precisely this potentiality – the possibility that they might be suitable constituents of the nation – that grants them some relief from the full extent of xenology that non-citizens are exposed to. It is in this sense that not all non-citizens in Singapore are rendered equally foreign. The degree to which one is xenologized turns upon which subcategory of the foreign one occupies. As Oswin argues, 'While those migrants who fall under the category "foreign talent" are invited into the national family to help reproduce the nation, those who are characterized as "foreign workers" are excluded from Singapore society and rendered permanently extranational.'[29] But it also seems to me that it is perhaps worth pushing the argument further. Whilst the notion of extranational does convey a sense of being outside and beyond (*extra*) the scope of the nation, it does not carry much of a value judgement – the sensibility fundamentally powering nationalism that what is outside the nation is in fact an active threat that must be surveilled, policed, and regulated. In fact, reading them as extranational is very much akin to Anderson's theorization of the nation in which nationalism's exclusion is merely the quite banal side-effect of inclusion. The problem we have to contend with is that the extranational is what the national is predicated upon – the gesture of exclusion is both the condition and limit of inclusion. So we should be precise here in locating the force of exclusion being produced by the force of nationalism. Foreign workers are not rendered merely extra-national – they are rendered counter-national. It is precisely because they are rendered counter-national that they are denied the possibility of living a life that could meet the exigencies of heteronormativity in Singapore.

Differentiated domesticabilities

At the turn of the millennium, on 31 August 1999, the Singaporean government published *Manpower 21: Vision of a Talent Capital* – an economic restructuring report that was meant to serve as a 'strategic blueprint to support Singapore's transition into a knowledge economy'.[30] The *Manpower 21* report acknowledges that Singapore had 'achieved economic success in the past three decades, progressing from an entrepot to an industrialized nation', and that the country's industries had evolved from 'labour-intensive manufacturing to high value-added, technology-intensive production and services'.[31] The report then goes on to suggest that with other countries in the region competing in the same industries whilst providing access to larger markets and workforces at lower costs, for Singapore '[t]o stay ahead, we need to move higher up the value-chain and tap the next wave of development – by becoming a knowledge economy'.[32]

The broad idea contained in the *Manpower 21* report was to retain competitiveness 'by pursuing deregulation, attracting inward investments, and initiating the in-migration of workers of various skill levels'.[33] Thus, one of the key strategies articulated was to 'leverage on foreign manpower at all levels to enhance our economic growth' as part of a 'deliberate strategy to enable us to grow beyond what our indigenous resources can produce' through 'manpower augmentation policies'.[34] Foreign manpower was defined as comprising 'international talents who include specialist talents, creative talents and entrepreneurial talents; and general foreign workers who are less skilled or unskilled'.[35] Even though the *Manpower 21* report augured a restructuring of the economy, the logic of foreign labour as a supplement to the domestic workforce was not particularly new – this had been a long-standing policy since the 1970s. The first few years after Singapore's independence in 1965 were mainly spent on infrastructure planning, but once the country began to industrialize rapidly, its dependence on foreign labour grew.[36] Similar to the *Gastarbeiter* ('guest worker') programmes that became popular in postwar Germany particularly and western Europe more generally, the underlying principle was that these non-citizen workers would serve as a temporary boost to the citizen labour force, aid in terms of economic growth, before eventually returning to their home countries.

In 2006, this changed. At the National Day Rally, the prime minister intimated that Singapore needed to attract immigrants not just to work but to settle as well. He said:

> If we want our economy to grow ... then we need a growing population and not just numbers but also talents in every field in Singapore ... We have to promote our immigration programme overseas ... Then we can choose and have good ones, capable, able to make a contribution, join Singapore ... But more importantly, as a society, we as Singaporeans, each one of us, we have to welcome immigrants.
>
> [...]
>
> What we are short of is talent, and the more we can get our talent ... I think the better off we will be.[37]

The notion of remaining open to immigration and attracting talent so as to power the engines of economic growth had already begun to circulate a few years prior to 2006. What was significant, however, was the invitation for immigrants, specifically foreign talent, to settle and become Singaporean citizens. In other words, designating some non-citizens as waypoints on the path to economic growth was not new; what was new was their designation as suitable members and reproducers of the nation. Prior to 2006, the state's approach to population growth had consisted primarily of 'efforts at encouraging marriage and fertility' and a slew of pronatalist policies aimed at Singaporean citizens that had largely not worked for nearly three decades.[38] In fact, in the immediate years leading up to 2006, encouraging Singaporeans to marry and have children was the position that the PAP government had maintained. In his 2004 National Day Rally speech, for example, Lee spent a significant amount of time speaking about the 'national problem' of the falling birth rate and strongly urged Singaporeans to have more children.[39] By 2006, he had basically given up that exhortation – only briefly mentioning it before moving on to mount the argument for immigration as a tool of population growth. The 'association between "talent" and population growth through immigration' has been recognized as a 'striking innovation in government policy' but its significance in relation to the nation remains somewhat underappreciated.[40]

Whilst Lee's 2006 speech certainly 'signalled a shift towards a more aggressive pursuit of immigration', it also changed the meanings generated around immigrants, immigration, and the nation.[41] Until 2006, the reproduction and regeneration of the nation was largely an endogenous process – the responsibility of reproduction was placed squarely on the shoulders of citizens, people who were already members of the nation. Of course, there were immigration flows – as has been the case in Singapore for decades – but immigration was treated primarily as a strategy to augment the nation's workforce and drive economic growth. The 2006 National Day Rally signalled a shift where the process of regenerating the nation was no longer primarily endogenous – it actively incorporated exogenous elements too. Consequently, immigration was no longer solely a strategy of economic growth – it was also a strategy of reproducing the nation. Immigration was not aimed at merely augmenting the nation's workforce; it was also aimed at augmenting the nation itself. Of course, Lee did not mean that all non-citizens would be offered the chance to settle. For, if we pay attention, we detect an element of evaluation embedded in his words when he says 'we can *choose* and have *good ones*, capable, able to make a contribution, join Singapore'.[42]

This condition upon which the invitation to join the nation rests is crucial because it shows the expectations loaded onto non-citizens before they are seen as potential members of the Singaporean nation. By opening the dossiers of propriety and capability, and making them the conditions upon which non-citizens would be judged before being offered the opportunity to settle in Singapore, Lee was giving the rubrics that would subdivide the category of non-citizens. There were those who were appropriate and those who were not, those who could fit into the nation and those who could not, good ones and bad ones, foreign talent and foreign workers. Because of this resultant alliance formed between appropriate non-citizens and the nation's survival and futurity, foreign talent – particularly those who could form heterosexual families and help reproduce the nation – are 'cast as harbingers of a bright future'.[43] They are invited to migrate to Singapore with their families, encouraged to settle in the country, and become part of the nation.[44] They are granted a degree of permanence that is denied to foreign workers who are, in contrast, permanently maintained in a transient state, forbidden to migrate with their families or build a new one *in situ*, and disallowed from substantively becoming a part of the nation. Only when we recognize the racialized and classed dimensions of this move can we begin to see nationalism's inclusion/exclusion operation being put to work through the modality of heteronormativity that also furthers existing gender, racial, and class fault lines.

In its various iterations, the government's rhetoric around immigration elides the fact that 'Singapore takes in at least two radically different groups of migrant workers, and that migration means starkly different things for these two groups'.[45] For one, with their desirable racial and class categories, they are emblems of futurity; for the other, of lower class positions and from parts of Southeast and South Asia, they are signifiers of the impossibility of futurity itself – in the sense that they are cast as abjectly foreign and incompatible with the nation. This point was formally reinforced in 2013 when the government introduced a white paper that formally articulated what Lee had previously set in motion. It said '[w]e will continue to welcome immigrants who can contribute to Singapore, share our values and integrate into our society' owing to a chronically falling birth rate and '[t]o stop our citizen population from shrinking'.[46]

We should not gloss over the qualified welcome – it is not any immigrant that the state is looking to incorporate into the nation. Rather, in limiting the potential offer of citizenship to productive immigrants who share the nation's values and can integrate into Singaporean society, the national franchise is limited to those deemed compatible with an a-priori imagination of the nation. This is the category of people considered integrable where integration marks the process of domesticating the foreign. It is this potential propriety – the fact that, even though they are not (yet) citizens, they could be – that ensures they are not xenologized to the point of being categorized irredeemably foreign. It is important to be precise here. I am not saying that non-citizens who are classified as potentially integrable are not xenologized or are regarded as full citizens. Nationalism in Singapore exposes all non-citizens to some degree of xenology just for the fact that they are not Singaporean citizens. But through a combination of legislation and rhetoric, the state positions some non-citizens (foreign talent) as potentially integrable and domesticable whilst others (foreign workers) are positioned as unintegrable. Foreign talent's potential compatibility with the nation mitigates their foreignness. Foreign workers, on the other hand, do not have such a similar potential compatibility to proffer in response to their xenologization; and this is why they can be read as paradigmatic figures of the foreign.

Identifying this central premise in Singapore's immigration policy is an invitation to then ask how the quality of propriety is determined. That is to say, who is bestowed with the status of being potentially appropriate and integrable and who is classified as beyond integration? It helps that there is an official unit ostensibly responsible for this work, at least as far as the state is concerned – the National Integration Council (NIC). The Council was formed in 2009, three years after the state's policy shift to begin boosting Singapore's resident population via immigration. It states that it aims to 'facilitate social interactions between Singaporeans and newcomers, and raise awareness of Singapore society, norms, and values'.[47] As such, amongst other things, it sets out to '[h]elp newcomers adapt to the Singaporean way of life, including helping them better understand local cultures and social norms', as well as '[f]acilitate the formation of friendships and shared experiences among Singaporeans and non-locals, so as to foster mutual understanding and acceptance through their interactions'.[48]

The NIC is chaired by the Minister for Culture, Community and Youth, and can be read as a state-driven institutionalized attempt to programmatically domesticate the foreign in the image of the nation.[49] Significantly, this process is only targeted at, and offered to, immigrants who are on a pathway to gaining citizenship and settling in Singapore. Permanent residents and transient non-citizens are not made a part of this state integration project and are 'mostly left on their own'.[50] Their being in transience is an 'oft-quoted justification as to why this category of foreigners is not included in the government's integration efforts' – the idea being that since they are not going to become members of the nation, they do not need to be integrated or domesticated as such.[51]

It is not hard to see the inclusion/exclusion operation at work here where the state's programme driving the attempted inclusion of one group simultaneously engenders the exclusion of another. Yeoh points out that '[t]he drawing of unambiguous citizen/non-citizen lines dividing up the population – negotiable in that fulfilling residency requirements provides a means of crossing the divide – fixes the body of the nation and embeds an exclusive form of nationalism in a defined territory.'[52] In this formulation, the space for negotiating the citizen/non-citizen division lies in the pathway to residency that is opened only to some non-citizens. In addition to the pathway to formal citizenship, the state's integration programme administered through the NIC is another avenue that offers the possibility of crossing the divide that is set up between citizen/non-citizen subjectivities. The crossing of this divide thus does not lie solely in occupying the formal category of the citizen – though this is, of course, also relevant; it also lies in the programmatic domestication – integration – that is offered to some subjectivities but not to others on the basis of a presumed incompatibility with the nation.

Dormitories and the spectre of the counter-nation

In September 2008, Serangoon Gardens, an affluent, middle-class neighbourhood, found itself at the centre of a heated controversy. Early that month, it had been reported that the MND was considering converting Serangoon Gardens Technical School – a decommissioned school in the area – into a temporary dormitory for up to 1,000 foreign workers.[53] Upon learning this and that the proposed site would have been 'less than 10 m away from the nearest house along Burghley Drive' in the estate, Serangoon Gardens residents were deeply upset.[54] More than 600 residents signed and submitted a petition to the Minister for National Development which stated that the government's proposal would 'create security and social problems and spoil the ambience of the estate'.[55] Media reports carried far more forthright views that dispensed with the superficial courtesies of the petition's euphemistic expressions. Residents expressed 'their fears that the low-skilled foreigners [would] soil their parks, clog up their streets as well as violate their children and womenfolk'.[56] Others worried that '[these] workers often hung out in groups, and would spit and litter'.[57] Again, at this point, we should not miss that it was not all non-citizens who were the targets of fear and ire; rather, it was specifically brown foreign workers from relatively poorer communities than most in Singapore – those who are positioned in multiple ways as fundamentally incompatible and irreconcilable with the nation.

In the days that followed, this localized hysteria 'escalated into a national debate of sorts where [Serangoon Gardens] residents alongside other Singaporeans were in support of keeping foreign workers away from population centres'.[58] The MND eventually decided to press ahead with its plan but offered several mitigating measures. The number of migrant workers to be housed at the site was reduced from the initially reported 1,000 to 600. The site was set further back than initially proposed, such that there would be a 'buffer zone' between the quarters and Serangoon Gardens residents.[59] The entrance to the site from Burghley Drive within the neighbourhood was sealed off and – at a cost of 2 million SGD (1.17 million GBP) – an entirely new dedicated access road was constructed directly off the Central Expressway so that vehicles ferrying workers could enter and exit the dormitory premises without having to pass through the neighbourhood.[60] This was also meant to ensure, of course, that the workers living in the dormitory would not be able to enter the neighbourhood via Burghley Drive. The MND further strongly emphasized in public statements that the dormitory would be self-sufficient, with amenities including a provision shop available on site such that workers '[would] have little reason to leave it'.[61] Eventually, the dormitory opened to minimal fuss at the end of 2009 with some residents even conceding that their initial reaction might have, in fact, been somewhat over the top.[62]

The sentiments that swirled around Serangoon Gardens map neatly onto the larger nationalist sentiment in Singapore. As an op-ed in *The Straits Times* rightly observed, '[t]he Serangoon Gardens affair [was] just a micro-cosm of the larger debate on the extent to which Singaporeans [were] pre-pared to accommodate and co-exist with the foreigners imported to do the work they shun'.[63] The final clause lays out the parameters around which the figure of the foreign is constructed and tolerated. It is not all non-citizens that Singaporeans are unwilling to live with, it is not all non-citizens who are excluded from subjectivity, and it is not all non-citizens who are queered. It is particularly those who happen to fall under the category of foreign workers who are marginalized as irredeemably foreign. There is a strong racial, neocolonial element to the operation of xenology here, par-ticularly as a function of Singapore being one of the richest countries in the Southeast Asian region. In strikingly similar ways to how the colonial pro-ject functioned on *mission civilisatrice* logics and exploited people who were rationalized as inferior, foreign workers from generally poorer communities are rationalized and racialized as being of insufficient quality to be part of the nation, and in debt to Singapore for 'rescuing' them from the squalid conditions of their home countries.[64]

The Serangoon Gardens affair 'brought to the surface tensions that have lain latent for years and were formerly couched in platitudes'.[65] It showed how foreign workers were cast in the imagination as figures of sexual excess possessing 'alien sexualities'.[66] Much of the discussion around the foreign worker being allowed into sites of domesticity was racialized and gendered. It traded in 'orientalist discourses about dangerous male sexuality (coded around the "dark" bodies of construction workers from the Indian sub-continent) and lascivious female sexuality (coded around the bodies of poor rural women from South and Southeast Asia)'.[67] The episode thus laid bare the way in which low-wage foreign workers were regarded as 'mere eco-nomic actors, whose other human attributes could be suspended for the duration of their economic engagement in Singapore', and demonstrated how this figure of the foreign was regarded as intolerable within spaces of Singaporean domesticity.[68]

There is a strong connection between domesticity, heteronormativity and the consequent structuring of subjectivity in Singapore. But there are places where this triangulation is disrupted. These are places where the spectre of queerness – in the sense of disrupting the logics of heteronormativity and reproduction that structure the nation – looms large residually; places where the spectre of the *xenos* is too overwhelming to ignore because they are the collective residence of those who have been rendered irredeemably foreign and queer. Foreign worker dormitories – of the sort built in Serangoon Gardens – are one such place. We could think of these spaces as physical manifestations of the counter-nation – spaces that are treated as foreign because they run counter to the dominant imagination of the nation. Reading these spaces as part of the counter-nation allows us to make sense of the way they are policed, surveilled, and managed to keep the incompatible elements of the foreign inhabiting these spaces away from the rest of the nation.

We have previously seen the domopolitics that infuse subjectivity in Singapore to the extent that the prime minister christens HDB flats 'national housing'.[69] The eligibility conditions surrounding access to public housing that hinge on heterosexual marriage fuse subjectivity with heteronormativity; and the expected expression of heterosexuality in this specific way freights marriage with added meaning. Marriage also becomes a staging point for induction into the heteronormative national imaginary, and the junction point for the emanation of a new nuclear family unit. As a function of their Work Permit conditions, foreign workers cannot migrate to Singapore with their family or dependants and so they must necessarily leave their families when they come to work in Singapore, whether they want to or not. They live in Singapore as individuals outside the orbit of a familial nucleus because they live physically apart from their families. It is this removal from kinship circuits that are taken as foundational in this country that renders them incompatible with Singaporean subjectivity. Without the buffer of the family, they are imagined as racialized figures of threatening sexual excess – a threat that is further specified as it is routed through gender. Thus, the dark-skinned men who largely make up the male foreign workforce are imagined as dirty, overflowing with uncontrollable sexual urges, and a 'threat to the modesty of local girls and women'.[70] The brown women who largely work as domestic workers residing in their employers' homes are imagined as sexual threats – beguiling temptresses capable of sexually usurping the woman in the heterosexual nuclear family and undermining the family unit itself.

It is important to point out here that foreign workers are *produced* as heterosexual individuals 'without families' and therefore suspicious subjects because of the conditions of immigration the state imposes upon them. Like many people, these workers' families can be significant parts of their lives. They too are subject to the associated heteronormative familial logics – often in similar ways to Singaporeans, with similar obligations of care and support imbricated within these kinship networks. In fact, that is typically the reason many come to Singapore to work in the first place – to fulfil their obligations of care and to financially support their families in their home countries. The point I am trying to make therefore is not that these workers do not have nuclear families of their own; rather, they are necessarily removed from the nuclear family, and thus made to seem incompatible with the nation. Absent the nuclear family units, they become threats to the nation and are governed as such. Imagined as sexually overdetermined figures, they are irreconciliable with the nation and a presence to be militated against, which the Employment of Foreign Manpower Act takes great care to codify.

In the next chapter, we will encounter Pink Dot's famous refrain: 'supporting the freedom to love'.[71] It is a powerful phrase because it highlights the fact that minoritized sexualities in Singapore are not able to love legitimately and freely in the way that straight people can. It is a call to action that is generally associated with the difficulties that Singaporean sexual minorities face around coupling legitimately. But it also hums gently in the background here, showing the stakes of sexual intimacy in the machinations of xenology that render foreign workers queer, as well as the common cause that sexual politics and nationalism have yet to make. For what foreign workers are denied is precisely the freedom to love and the freedom to form families of their own in Singapore. Bracketing how many have their own families abroad, it is salient that they are expressly denied the possibility of love and family formation, and are governed in ways that others in Singapore are not. They are marginalized by the operation of heteronormativity – rendered queer and incompatible with the nation. To be clear, this is not to say that all foreign workers are indeed heterosexual or that they ought to couple, get married, have children, and so forth. Rather, I want to show how they are positioned by the state, through various pieces of legislation and categorizations, in relation to the heterosexual family unit that is invested with meaning where the nation is concerned. It is through this positioning – or, more precisely, this denial of a position – that they are subjectivized, rendered queer and out of step with the heteronormative imaginary, and thereby positioned as counter to the nation.

In 2013, MP Gan Thiam Poh asked the Minister for National Development if foreign workers could be housed on offshore islands. In response, the minister said:

> We are open to such an idea of housing some foreign workers at nearby offshore islands. However, not all offshore islands are suitable, due to the availability of supporting infrastructure ... But we will continue to look for suitable opportunities to help us house the foreign workers properly and without causing too much inconvenience to them or to Singaporeans.[72]

It is noteworthy that the minister's reply was not an outright dismissal of the possibility of physically segregating foreign workers and keeping them literally apart from the nation. Rather, it was a contingent dismissal based on a logistical difficulty. In this view, 'apart from considerations of convenience, it is unproblematic to physically segregate migrant workers'.[73] This sentiment was, in some sense, unsurprising – it was simply an extension of the logic we had previously seen in the Serangoon Gardens affair four years prior. Despite those preliminary intimations, however, the move to offshore foreign workers did not come to pass – presumably because it would have proven too much of a logistical hurdle to continuously ferry them to and fro. However, the logic of essentially compartmentalizing foreign workers to insulate the nation from them as far as possible has never disappeared.[74] Instead of housing foreign workers on offshore islands, work began to build what are essentially onshore islands – mega-dormitory complexes, some of which could house upwards of 10,000 workers each. As of 2024, Singapore has 56 of these purpose-built dormitories.[75]

Like the dormitory at Serangoon Gardens, most of these complexes have amenities such as shops, remittance services, beer gardens, food courts, and sometimes even cinemas. The complexes 'are built at peripheral sites as a containment measure to keep the migrant worker population as far as possible away from the Little India enclave' and other population centres.[76] They also have 'a stringent security regime, [with] numerous surveillance measures having been put in place, including the use of closed-circuit television (CCTV) cameras'.[77] It is not difficult to see the inclusion/exclusion operation at work again here where the provision of amenities functions as a way to quite literally shut foreign workers in and, in this manner, keep them away from the rest of the population. It is a material manifestation of how representations of queerness – in the sense of those who have been rendered queer – can often be marooned off the shores of the heteronormative national imaginary.

In these dormitories, '[c]onjoined to strategies of care are those of control and surveillance' that ensure foreign workers are kept apart from the rest of the population, and like this foreign worker dormitories become sites of exclusion in a state of social quarantine from the nation.[78] The dormitories become spaces that vividly reflect how the counter-nation is governed – it is turned into an island, to all intents and purposes, and kept separate from the rest of the population, inhabited by queered and xenologized people, the spectrally foreign, who cannot be reconciled with the nation. But at the same time, it is only because the counter-nation is there and very much present – both in a material and in a cultural sense – that the illusion of the nation can continue to function.

Queered fates

Singapore has historically relied heavily on an inflow of foreign capital issuing from developed countries in the West to drive its economic growth; this was the country's economic strategy in its early days and it continues to be the case today.[79] As we have seen in Chapter 2, rationalizing economic growth as the altar upon which everything else ought to be sacrificed operates as part of a survivalist discourse that is integral to Singapore's sense of itself. The country's reliance on foreign investment is similarly framed as the inevitable consequence of being a small city-state with no natural resources.[80] Thus, the only hymn the PAP government has sung has come from the chorus sheet of capital accumulation – the idea being that the only way to mitigate a distinct lack of geographical size and scarcity of local resources was to open the country to capital flowing in from beyond its shores.

Economic growth, and the general pursuit of wealth and prosperity, have come to be associated with modernity that springs from the West and is portrayed as the crucial supplement that Singapore needs in order to survive. However, the same capital washing in from the West that is materially integral to Singapore's survival is simultaneously regarded as tainted by the corrupting cultural sediment of a distinct Western preoccupation with individualism that risks ripping apart the fabric of Singaporean society. In this set-up, then, economic growth and foreign capital are crucial to sustaining the country but also carry a certain degree of danger. Thus, even as the Singaporean government treats capital as fundamentally necessary, the 'battle line is drawn between the Confucian and "collectivist" tradition that apparently underpins the rapid post-Second World War economic growth in East Asia and the individualistic tendency of capitalism'.[81] 'Asian' values were the reagent that offered to neutralize this apparent toxicity. Whilst state rhetoric, family policies, and attendant social practices construct the heterosexual nuclear family unit as constantly threatened by exposure to the West, for a long time the antidote to this apparent contamination lay in embracing Asian values.

Throughout the 1970s and 1980s, a particular 'civilizational identity' was reified across Asia.[82] Some of the characteristics of this essentialized identity were that Asian societies tended to be more communal, far less egocentric and individualistic than 'Western' societies, and driven by an emphasis on social harmony. *Asian values* became shorthand to refer back to these qualities.[83] When the state brought to life the discourse of 'Asian' values, it was constructed as standing in opposition to individually oriented 'Western' values and 'justified on the basis that "Asian" values [are] applicable to Singapore, and superior to western liberal ideology'.[84] Any argument that can be portrayed as 'liberal' or emerging out of the 'West' is dismissed as non-Asian and therefore inappropriate to Singapore. It is a tautology that functions as a remarkably effective thought-terminating device. Conceptually, 'Asian' values worked as a sieve that purported to strain the undesirable cultural aspects of capital in terms of individualism and other social ills whilst allowing the state to avail itself of its material benefits in terms of economic growth. Hence, despite opening itself up to capital, Singapore has regarded itself as exceptional in the sense that it claims to defy the Fukuyamaist liberalism-democracy-capitalism teleological triad.[85]

This emerges from an ostensible commitment to a set of communal values realized through what Chua Beng Huat calls an ideology of 'communitarianism'.[86] Chua points out that it should not be taken at face value as the abstract notion of the collective being elevated above the individual. He argues that:

> Communitarianism is valued in this reciprocal relationship in that the leadership's moral uprightness and desire to uplift societal welfare is met by the governed's placing of societal welfare above self-interest, thus constituting a moral/political order that is harmonious and beneficial for all. However, it should be noted that it is a reciprocity that is embedded in a hierarchical structure of unequals, and is thus unavoidably elitist.[87]

Recognizing the hierarchical structure immanent in the state's version of communitarianism is crucial because it shows that the concept of the collective – what constitutes the collective – is defined by the state. As we saw in Chapter 3, collective responsibility can be traced out around and limited to the nuclear family unit – substituting the individual for the nuclear family as the minimal unit that the state relates to as part of what Teo calls 'neoliberal morality'.[88] The significance of rationalizing this mode of governance through the conceptual frame of communitarianism is that it legitimizes the government's dismissal of any claim that could be construed as not universally shared throughout the country (sexual rights, for example) through an appeal to the abstract notion of maintaining a broader social harmony. Because this dismissal is grounded in communitarianism and given further weight by the naturalization of Asian values in Singapore, what is repudiated is also simultaneously symbolically designated as foreign.

In 1991, the government presented a white paper to Parliament that aimed to 'evolve and anchor a Singaporean identity'.[89] Prime minister Goh Chok Tong sounded a warning that '[t]raditional Asian ideas of morality, duty and society which have sustained and guided us in the past are giving way to a more Westernised, individualistic, and self-centred outlook on life'.[90] The five values proposed in the white paper as constitutive of a Singaporean national identity were:

(1) nation before community and society above self;
(2) family as a basic unit of society;
(3) community support and regard for the individual;
(4) consensus, not conflict;
(5) racial and religious harmony.[91]

The contours of a caricaturization of Asian/Western values are visible here – and the maintenance of this simplistic binary has neither dissipated nor disappeared under subsequent PAP governments. In 2008, Lee Hsien Loong gestured to this in his Chinese New Year message, reminding Singaporeans about the importance of preserving familial ties amidst increasing modernization:

> Even in China, many young people now work and live in distant cities. But when Chinese New Year comes around, they make a special effort to travel to their hometowns to be with their families … The West, China, Singapore. The past and the present. Good family values reside in the past for the West, are timeless in China, and ought to be struggled for in contemporary Singapore.[92]

Trying to work out what 'Asian' values – or 'family' values or 'Western' values, for that matter – actually signify is a Sisyphean task; fortunately, unlike Sisyphus, we are not condemned to take it on because far more significant is what *Asian values* has been made to mean in state rhetoric and how it has come to be understood in Singapore.

When it has been invoked, *Asian values* is often used interchangeably with *Confucian values*, or *traditional values*, and is generally used in an ambiguous, imprecise sense.[93] What is salient is how the idea of prioritizing the heterosexual family unit lies latent in the invocation of 'Asian' values. Despite its amorphous and slippery nature, *Asian values* nonetheless activates a turn towards the primacy and preservation of the heterosexual nuclear family in Singapore, and it has come to 'provide a common, overlapping consensus between the various religious and ethnic groups in Singapore'.[94] Perhaps this points to the extraordinary emptiness of *Asian values* as a signifier where nobody can quite articulate what it refers to beyond a vague association with kinship and the preservation of the heterosexual nuclear family unit grounded in an apparently immutable Asian tradition. As a signifier, it has been thoroughly deracinated from whatever its original context was, and it now stands in an ahistorical relation to its signified context within the Singaporean cultural imaginary. That it is seen as constitutive of being Singaporean such that both citizens and political leaders can reference it reflexively speaks to the successful 'invention of tradition' here.[95]

This is not to say that it has been conjured up out of nothing; the significance of Asian values as a marker of tradition and the consequent legitimating of a particular form of familial relations relies on the naturalization of an Asian civilizational identity in Singapore and an opposition to an imagined West. Hark back to the simplistic yet effective tautology that rests on a characterization of 'Asian' values as superior to liberal Western values, which are dangerous, socially divisive, and a threat to the social harmony of the country: as an country in Asia, therefore, Singapore must resist Western ideas because they are not Asian.

The naturalization of heteronormativity through 'Asian' values means that heteronormativity – and the heteronormative nuclear family unit – take on greater significance within the Singaporean imaginary. Foucault shows how the development of heteronormativity occurred through the reification and elevation of heterosexuality and how this normativization achieved its legitimacy through the state.[96] In Singapore, because of the historical compact that has been built with 'Asian' values, this process is further reinforced by an appeal to a civilizational identity that makes heteronormativity a solid bedrock of subjectivity in Singapore and extremely difficult to budge.

Excluded from the heteronormatively charged concept of the family invoked by Asian values, queerness is left out in the cold, stranded in the space of the non-domestic, the counter-national, the foreign. It is not brought under the larger umbrella of Asian civilizational identity that the Singaporean nation affiliates itself with. Constructed as distinctly un-Asian, queerness is consequently associated with a caricatured idea of the West – which is precisely what 'Asian' values claim to be antithetical and even superior to. This is how queerness is made foreign, and where queerness and foreignness find themselves on common ground. Those who are rendered queer, therefore, run the risk of being rendered foreign; and, as I have shown through the paradigmatic figure of the foreign – the foreign worker – the operation of xenology can be buttressed by proscribing them from circuits of heteronormativity such that their foreignness is confirmed by being rendered queer. It is therefore not surprising that, as we will see in Chapter 5, Pink Dot expends so much time and energy foregrounding its domestic and national credentials, as well as highlighting LGBT Singaporeans' formal claim to citizenship in Singapore. It is a response that aims to expand the national imaginary to accommodate minoritized sexualities by combating the force of xenology that acts upon queered people.

Such an approach is not possible in the case of non-citizens for they do not have the anchor of citizenship with which to resist their expulsion from the nation. For the paradigmatic figure of the foreign, the foreign worker who is rendered incompatible with the nation, it is exceedingly difficult to rid themselves of the spectre of queerness that continually haunts them. Through legislation and living arrangements that legally proscribe their rights to heterosexual desire, intimacy, and family formation, they are cast into the counter-national space and rendered queer. The point here is not to do with being queer in an identarian sense – there will certainly be foreign workers who are also sexual minorities, people who identify as queer. But this is less an argument centred on heterosexuality and more an argument that foreign workers are regulated *as if* they are heterosexual subjects before being subsequently rendered queer. I want to suggest that the alliance between heteronormativity and subjectivity in Singapore also renders queer the paradigmatic figure of the foreign.

If heteronormativity – whereby a particular expression of heterosexuality is reified – structures subjectivity in Singapore, then queerness that marks the category of those marginalized by heteronormativity's operation is deposited in the space of the foreign and designated counter-national. Reading Singapore as a straight nation helps us see how both the imagination of the nation and admission into its formation necessarily rest on the correct expression of a particular form of heterosexuality. Those who are racialized, gendered, and classed as irrevocably foreign can have their incompatibility with the nation confirmed by being denied the possibility of such an expression – they are rendered foreign by being rendered queer, making them figures within the counter-nation. With the blessings of 'Asian' values, the collusion between nationalism and heteronormativity makes queerness foreign and incompatible with the nation as such. Whereas Pink Dot uses the formal category of citizenship to pose its demand for equality, this assimilative option is not available to foreign workers. The spaces they collectively occupy, their dormitories, become counter-national sites built away from the population centres of the nation – functioning on an inclusion/exclusion principle that ensures these queered individuals are maintained in a state of 'social quarantine' as much as possible such that the straight space of the nation and its spectacle are disturbed as little as possible.[97]

Notes

1 Oswin, 'The Modern Model Family at Home in Singapore', p. 265.
2 See Lazar, 'Homonationalist Discourse'; Michelle M. Lazar, 'Semiotics of Homonationalism', in *The Oxford Handbook of Language and Sexuality*, ed. Kira Hall and Rusty Barrett (Oxford: Oxford University Press, 2019), DOI: 10.1093/oxfordhb/9780190212926.013.51); and Lazar, 'Linguistic (Homo) Nationalism'.
3 Lenore Lyons, 'Sexing the Nation: Normative Heterosexuality and the Construction of the "Good" Singaporean Citizen', in *The Nation of the Other: Constructions of Nation in Contemporary Cultural and Literary Discourses*, ed. Anna Branach-Kallas and Katarzyna Więckowska (Toruń: Wydawn. Uniwersytetu Mikołaja Kopernika, 2004), pp. 79–96 (p. 81).
4 Oswin, *Global City Futures*.
5 Brenda S. A. Yeoh, 'Bifurcated Labour: The Unequal Incorporation of Transmigrants in Singapore', *Tijdschrift voor economische en sociale geografie*, 97.1 (2006), 26–37.

6 Angelia Poon, 'Pick and Mix for a Global City: Race and Cosmopolitanism in Singapore', in Goh et al., *Race and Multiculturalism in Malaysia and Singapore*, pp. 70–85 (p. 82). Also see, for example, Pattana Kitiarsa, 'Thai Migrants in Singapore: State, Intimacy and Desire', *Gender, Place & Culture*, 15.6 (2008), 595–610; Youyenn Teo and Nicola Piper, 'Foreigners in Our Homes: Linking Migration and Family Policies in Singapore', *Population, Space and Place*, 15.2 (2009), 147–59; Brenda S. A. Yeoh and Shirlena Huang, 'Spaces at the Margins: Migrant Domestic Workers and the Development of Civil Society in Singapore', *Environment and Planning A: Economy and Space*, 31.7 (1999), 1149–67; Brenda S. A. Yeoh, Grace Baey, Maria Platt, and Kellynn Wee, 'Bangladeshi Construction Workers and the Politics of (Im)Mobility in Singapore', *City*, 21.5 (2017), 641–49; Maria Platt, Grace Baey, Brenda S. A. Yeoh, Choon Yen Khoo, and Theodora Lam, 'Debt, Precarity and Gender: Male and Female Temporary Labour Migrants in Singapore', *Journal of Ethnic and Migration Studies*, 43.1 (2017), 119–36; and Grace Baey, 'Borders and the Exclusion of Migrant Bodies in Singapore's Global City-State', MA thesis (Queen's University, Kingston, ON, 2010).
7 Brenda S. A. Yeoh and Shirlena Huang, 'Sexualised Politics of Proximities among Female Transnational Migrants in Singapore: Sexualised Politics in Singapore', *Population, Space and Place*, 16.1 (2010), 37–49.
8 Russell Heng, 'Tiptoe out of the Closet: The Before and After of the Increasingly Visible Gay Community in Singapore', *Journal of Homosexuality*, 40.3–4 (2001), 81–96.
9 Chua, *Mobilizing Gay Singapore*; Phillips, *Virtual Activism*.
10 Eng-Beng Lim, 'Glocalqueering in New Asia: The Politics of Performing Gay in Singapore', *Theatre Journal*, 57.3 (2005), 383–405; Eng-Beng Lim, 'The Mardi Gras Boys of Singapore's English-Language Theatre'; Eng-Beng Lim, 'Asian Megastructure and Queer Futurity', *Cultural Dynamics*, 28.3 (2016), 309–19; Joseph Lo and Guoqin Huang, eds, *People like Us: Sexual Minorities in Singapore* (Singapore: Select Publishing, 2003); Chris K. K. Tan, 'But They Are like You and Me'; Yue and Zubillaga-Pow, *Queer Singapore*; Yue, 'Trans-Singapore'; Lazar, 'Linguistic (Homo)Nationalism'; Phillips, 'We Aren't Really That Different'; Tan and Lee, 'Imagining the Gay Community'.
11 Oswin, *Global City Futures*, p. 55.
12 Teo and Piper, 'Foreigners in Our Homes', p. 150; also see Chan et al., *Singapore's Multiculturalism*, p. 177.
13 Chan et al., *Singapore's Multiculturalism*, p. 177. Whilst much of this lies beyond the scope of the book, it is worth flagging the relatively recent recruitment of north Indian professionals into this foreign talent category because their induction shows how class and caste can often work to ameliorate racial difference. It also highlights the sedimentation of logics of anti-Blackness where lighter-skinned north Indians can be rationalized as more compatible with the nation, and viewed as foreign talent alongside other white Euro-Americans as opposed to darker-skinned south Indians.

14 Ibid.; Jaclyn L. Neo, 'Riots and Rights: Law and Exclusion in Singapore's Migrant Worker Regime', *Asian Journal of Law and Society*, 2.1 (2015), 137–68 (p. 141).

15 Poon, 'Pick and Mix for a Global City'; Kitiarsa, 'Thai Migrants in Singapore'; Teo and Piper, 'Foreigners in Our Homes'; Brenda S. A. Yeoh and T. C. Chang, 'Globalising Singapore: Debating Transnational Flows in the City', *Urban Studies*, 38.7, 1025–44; Brenda S. A. Yeoh and Theodora Lam, 'Immigration and Its (Dis)Contents: The Challenges of Highly Skilled Migration in Globalizing Singapore', *American Behavioral Scientist*, 60.5–6 (2016), 637–58; Platt et al., 'Debt, Precarity and Gender'; Yeoh and Huang, 'Spaces at the Margins'; Yeoh, 'Bifurcated Labour'; Yeoh et al., 'Bangladeshi Construction Workers'; Shirlena Huang and Brenda S. A. Yeoh, 'The Difference Gender Makes: State Policy and Contract Migrant Workers in Singapore', *Asian and Pacific Migration Journal*, 12.1–2 (2003), 75–97; Oswin, 'The Modern Model Family at Home in Singapore'.

16 Yeoh, 'Bifurcated Labour', p. 29.

17 Ibid., p. 36.

18 Teo and Piper, 'Foreigners in Our Homes', p. 150.

19 Yeoh, 'Bifurcated Labour', p. 29.

20 Michael Hor, 'What Fate for 377A? Choose You This Day', *Academia SG*, 2022, www.academia.sg/academic-views/what-fate-for-377a/ (accessed 28 September 2024).

21 Teo and Piper, 'Foreigners in Our Homes', pp. 152–53.

22 Employment of Foreign Manpower Act (Chapter 91A): Employment of Foreign Manpower (Work Passes) Regulations 2012, Schedule 4, nos 6–8, https://sso.agc.gov.sg/SL-Supp/S569-2012/Published/20121108?DocDate=20121108&WholeDoc=1 (accessed 2 October 2024).

23 Eugene K. B. Tan, 'Managing Female Foreign Domestic Workers in Singapore: Economic Pragmatism, Coercive Legal Regulation, or Human Rights?', *Israel Law Review*, 43.1 (2010), 99–125; also see Yeoh, 'Bifurcated Labour'.

24 Bauman, 'Soil, Blood and Identity', p. 649.

25 Tang and Quah, 'Heteronormativity and Sexuality Politics', p. 651.

26 It is also perhaps worth bearing in mind that because of the racialized and classed xenophobia generated around foreign workers and the way they are positioned as undesirable members of the nation, the vast majority of Singaporeans are overwhelmingly primed not to enter into relationships with them in the first place.

27 Employment of Foreign Manpower Act.

28 Lyons, 'Sexing the Nation'.

29 Oswin, *Global City Futures*, p. 101.

30 Manpower 21 Steering Committee, *Manpower 21: Vision of a Talent Capital* (Singapore: Ministry of Manpower, 1999), p. 2.

31 Ibid., p. 5.

32 Ibid.

33 Neil M. Coe and Philip F. Kelly, 'Languages of Labour: Representational Strategies in Singapore's Labour Control Regime', *Political Geography*, 21.3 (2002), 341–71 (p. 348); see also Yeoh and Lam, 'Immigration and Its (Dis) Contents', p. 638.

34 Manpower 21 Steering Committee, *Manpower 21*, p. 33.

35 Ibid.

36 Hui Weng-Tat, 'Regionalization, Economic Restructuring and Labour Migration in Singapore', *International Migration*, 35.1 (1997), 109–30.

37 Lee Hsien Loong, 'National Day Rally 2006', 2006, National Archives of Singapore, www.nas.gov.sg/archivesonline/speeches/record-details/7e69abe9-115d-11e3-83d5-0050568939ad (accessed 2 October 2024).

38 Teo and Piper, 'Foreigners in Our Homes', p. 149.

39 Lee, 'National Day Rally 2004'.

40 Oswin, *Global City Futures*, p. 98. Also see Teo and Piper, 'Foreigners in Our Homes'; Poon, 'Pick and Mix for a Global City'; and Natalie Oswin and Brenda S. A. Yeoh, 'Introduction: Mobile City Singapore', *Mobilities*, 5.2 (2010), 167–75.

41 Teo and Piper, 'Foreigners in Our Homes', p. 150.

42 Lee, 'National Day Rally 2006', emphasis mine.

43 Oswin, *Global City Futures*, p. 102.

44 National Population and Talent Division (NPTD), 'People & Society', www.population.gov.sg/our-population/population-trends/people-&-society (accessed 28 September 2024).

45 Teo and Piper, 'Foreigners in Our Homes', p. 150.

46 NPTD, *A Sustainable Population for a Dynamic Singapore: Population White Paper* (Singapore: NPTD, 2013), p. 3.

47 Ministry of Culture, Community and Youth, 'National Integration Council', www.mccy.gov.sg/sector/initiatives/national-integration-council (accessed 28 September 2024).

48 Ibid.

49 The NIC organizes programmes such as heritage tours, and works with community groups, schools, and workplaces to help new citizens acculturate to Singaporean norms. Whilst the exact scope and nature of its programmes are beyond the scope of this book, they can be found at its website, cited in n. 47.

50 Chan et al., *Singapore's Multiculturalism*, p. 186.

51 Ibid., p. 187.

52 Yeoh, 'Bifurcated Labour'.

53 Melissa Sim, 'Foreign Workers? Not in My Backyard', *The Straits Times*, 3 September 2008.

54 Melissa Sim and Carolyn Quek, 'Dorm Not Near but Problems "Next Door"', *The Straits Times*, 5 September 2008.

55 Sim, 'Foreign Workers?'.

56 Tan Hui Yee, 'Wake-Up Call from Dorm Issue', *The Straits Times*, 17 October 2008.

57 Sim and Quek, 'Dorm Not Near but Problems "Next Door"'.
58 Kelvin E. Y. Low, 'Sensing Cities: The Politics of Migrant Sensescapes', *Social Identities*, 19.2 (2013), 221–37 (p. 229).
59 Dawn Wei Tan, 'The "Them and Us" Divide', *The Straits Times*, 12 October 2008.
60 'Green Light for Dorm Plans', *Property Highlights of Singapore*, 2022, http://propertyhighlights.blogspot.com/2008/10/green-light-for-dorm-plans.html?m=0 (accessed 15 May 2022); Tan, 'Wake-Up Call from Dorm Issue'.
61 Tan, 'Wake-Up Call from Dorm Issue'.
62 Dawn Tay, 'Serangoon Dorm Opens, Fuss-Free', *AsiaOne*, 7 December 2009, www.asiaone.com/News/AsiaOne+News/Singapore/Story/A1Story20091207-184340.html (accessed 19 August 2020); Dai Lin Ong, ' "We Overreacted": Some Serangoon Gardens Residents Admit Concerns Unfounded', *TODAY*, 2010, https://migrantworkerssingapore.wordpress.com/category/serangoon-gardens/ (accessed 2 October 2024).
63 Tan, 'Wake-Up Call from Dorm Issue'.
64 Alfian Sa'at and Hai Bin Neo, ' "We Refuse to Recognise the Trauma": A Conversation between Alfian Sa'at and Neo Hai Bin', in Sa'at et al., *Raffles Renounced*, pp. 11–16.
65 Tan, 'Wake-up Call from Dorm Issue'.
66 Lyons, 'Sexing the Nation', p. 81.
67 Ibid.
68 Neo, 'Riots and Rights', p. 142.
69 Lee, 'National Day Rally 2018'.
70 Lyons, 'Sexing the Nation', p. 91.
71 Pink Dot SG, 'About'.
72 'Parliamentary Debates: Official Report' (Singapore: Hansard, 2013).
73 Neo, 'Riots and Rights', p. 141.
74 Whilst the Singaporean government has not been able to successfully offshore foreign workers, for an account of a state project with a similar logic in relation to migrant refugees, see Madeline Gleeson and Natasha Yacoub, *Cruel, Costly and Ineffective: The Failure of Offshore Processing in Australia* (Sydney: Kaldor Centre for International Refugee Law, 2021).
75 Ministry of Manpower, 'List of Foreign Worker Dormitories', 2024, www.mom.gov.sg/passes-and-permits/work-permit-for-foreign-worker/housing/foreign-worker-dormitories#/?page=3&q= (accessed 28 September 2024).
76 Yeoh et al., 'Bangladeshi Construction Workers', p. 646.
77 Ibid.
78 Ibid.
79 Garry Rodan, 'Singapore: Globalisation and the Politics of the Economic', in *The Political Economy of South-East Asia: Conflicts, Crises and Change*, ed. Garry Rodan, Kevin Hewison, and Richard Robison, 2nd edn (Melbourne: Oxford University Press, 2001), pp. 138–77.
80 See, for example, Chan Heng Chee, 'Politics in an Administrative State: Where Has the Politics Gone?', in *Understanding Singapore Society*, ed. Tan Ern Ser,

Ong Jin Hui, and Tong Chee Kiong (Singapore: Times Academic Press, 1997), pp. 294–306; Chua, *Communitarian Ideology*; Gillian Koh and Ooi Giok Ling, 'Relationship between State and Civil Society in Singapore: Clarifying Concepts, Assessing the Ground', ed. Lee Hock Guan (Singapore: Institute of Southeast Asian Studies, 2004), pp. 167–97; Lee, *From Third World to First*; and Timothy Mitchell, 'The Work of Economics: How a Discipline Makes Its World', *European Journal of Sociology*, 46.2 (2005), 297–320.

81 Chua, *Communitarian Ideology*, pp. 6–7.

82 Samuel Huntington, 'The Clash of Civilizations?', *Foreign Affairs*, 72.3 (1993), 22–49 (p. 29); also see, for example, Kishore Mahbubani, *Can Asians Think? Understanding the Divide between East and West* (Berkeley: Steerforth Press, 2002).

83 See, for example, Chua Beng Huat, ' "Asian-Values" Discourse and the Resurrection of the Social', *Positions: Asia Critique*, 7.2 (1999), 573–92; Daniel A. Bell, *China's New Confucianism: Politics and Everyday Life in a Changing Society*, 2nd edn (Princeton: Princeton University Press, 2010); and Seok-Choon Lew, Woo-Young Choi, and Hye Suk Wang, 'Confucian Ethics and the Spirit of Capitalism in Korea: The Significance of Filial Piety', *Journal of East Asian Studies*, 11.1 (2011), 171–96.

84 Tey Tsun Hang, 'Judicial Internalising of Singapore's Supreme Political Ideology', *Hong Kong L.J.*, 40 (2010), 293–336 (p. 297).

85 Francis Fukuyama, *The End of History and the Last Man* (New York: Free Press, 1992).

86 Chua, *Communitarian Ideology*.

87 Ibid., p. 36.

88 Teo, *Neoliberal Morality in Singapore*.

89 Prime Minister's Office, 'Shared Values: Cmd 1 of 1991. Presented to Parliament by Command of the President of the Republic of Singapore', white paper (Singapore: Singapore Government, 1991), p. 1.

90 Ibid.

91 Ibid, p. 10.

92 Lee Hsien Loong, 'Prime Minister Lee Hsien Loong's Chinese New Year Message: Celebrating the Family', *The Straits Times*, 6 February 2008.

93 Whilst largely beyond the scope of this book, *Confucian values*, in particular, is an interesting turn of phrase because it opens the question of whether this metonymy with the supposedly multicultural nation might, in fact, blur a racial primacy to the nation. See Chapter 1, n. 128.

94 Tey, 'Judicial Internalising of Singapore's Supreme Political Ideology', p. 296.

95 Eric Hobsbawm, 'Introduction: Inventing Traditions', in *The Invention of Tradition*, ed. Eric Hobsbawm and Terence Ranger (Cambridge: Cambridge University Press, 1983), pp. 1–14.

96 Foucault, *The History of Sexuality*.

97 Teo and Piper, 'Foreigners in Our Homes', p. 151.

5

Heteronormativity (un)contested – or, the will to assimilation

From Rascals ... to Pink Dot: a brief history of LGBT activism

We have already seen that heteronormativity structures subjectivity in Singapore – particularly through the modalities of heterosexual coupling and heteronormative familism. Obligations of care are distributed and delimited along the lines of a particular kinship structure that is reproduced through heterosexual coupling: the heterosexual nuclear family. There is a politics that lies at the heart of the state's commitment to elevating and privileging certain arrangements of kinship networks over, and at the expense of, others. Queered exclusion as a result of the smooth functioning of heteronormativity in Singapore, therefore, occurs at the interstices of state policies that simultaneously signal heterosexual inclusion. Central to the arguments in this book is the sensibility that heteronormativity is fundamentally an inclusion/exclusion operation – it works not just to produce and legitimize certain forms of exclusion, it also produces and legitimizes certain forms of inclusion. I want to demonstrate how the heteronormative terms of inclusion in Singapore can appear so immutable that they influence how minoritized figures try to mitigate their exclusion. In other words, I want to show how people queered by heteronormativity can nonetheless resort to appealing to it in a bid to address their exclusion because of the grip it has on the Singaporean imagination.

Pink Dot is probably the most established and well-known contemporary LGBT movement in Singapore by some distance. Whilst there are other activist and community organizations that have been around longer,[1] few have been as spectacularly successful in both gaining mainstream public support and increasing the public visibility of LGBT people.[2] Attending to the way Pink Dot has accomplished this shows how the force of heteronormativity in Singapore structures subjectivity to such an extent that attempts to contest its exclusions nonetheless dance to its tune. Coupled with a reluctance to directly express dissent, this style of engagement characterizes Pink

Dot and the nature of resistance it undertakes in challenging the exclusion that minoritized sexualities experience in Singapore.

The kind of broad queer critique that is necessary to undo heteronormativity does not begin and end with LGBT people or Pink Dot alone. As I have made clear, *queer* should not be taken as a synonym for *LGBT*. But sexual minorities are certainly amongst the various people who are queered by heteronormativity, and LGBT movements can obviously be read as sites of resistance. Pink Dot is salient for us because, through its assimilationist politics, it has established a level of visibility in mainstream Singaporean society on a scale that no other LGBT movement (or social movement, for that matter) has managed thus far. It gives us a glimpse of how queerness seeks to represent itself in ways that are deemed 'acceptable' in heteronormative terms whilst simultaneously demonstrating its limits in advancing a more expansive critique of heteronormativity and nationalism in Singapore.

Instead of contesting the inclusion/exclusion operation, assimilation as a tactic seeks to mitigate exclusion by expanding the terms of inclusion – often on the very terms that constitute its exclusion in the first place. Its successful propagation has been sustained by an understanding and resurrection of 'the relationship between nationalism ... and respectability, a term indicating "decent and correct" manners and morals, as well as the proper attitude toward sexuality'.[3] Or, as Ng Yi-Sheng pithily summarizes, it is 'an attempt by the oppressed to demonstrate their compatibility with mainstream values, rather than challenging them'.[4] In addition to laying out how Pink Dot does this, I am also interested in why it is effective. Paying attention to the discourses that Pink Dot relies on to make a space for itself in Singapore and locating these discourses within larger discourses governing the Singaporean lifeworld shows how Pink Dot is shaped by the force of heteronormativity immanent in subject formation in Singapore. Put differently, instead of exclusively focusing on Pink Dot's assimilative overtures, I am also interested in flipping the question and asking what the will to assimilation tells us about the environment it is attempting to assimilate into. And what can Pink Dot's success in a straight nation tell us about the limits of resisting heteronormativity in Singapore? To get there, it might help to first take a brief historical detour.

On the night of 30 May 1993, a squad of plain-clothes police officers raided Rascals – a disco popular with gay men – and demanded that everybody present produce their identification documents. Those who had their documents with them were allowed to leave whilst those who did not were brought to the Beach Road police station and 'made to squat outside'.[5] They were detained through the night and only released the following morning. No formal charges were ever brought against them. The overnight detention was 'clearly an act of intimidation' that had no legal basis.[6] Incidents such as this were not infrequently inflicted upon gay establishments in the late 1980s and early 1990s in Singapore. What was significant about the Rascals incident, however, was not the raid itself but its aftermath.

Upset by the way in which they had been treated despite having committed no crime, one of the men who had been at Rascals that night filed a letter of complaint with the Singapore Police Force as well as the Ministry of Home Affairs.[7] As Lynette Chua recounts in her book, the letter highlighted the officers' conduct and the fact that the patrons' detention that night had been unlawful:

> It is particularly disturbing to find Singapore law enforcement officers behaving rudely towards and verbally threatening citizens who have not committed any offences. It would also be in the public interest to clarify the legal powers of police officers (plainclothes) to demand the production of personal particulars in cases where no offences have been committed.[8]

Privately, most of those who had been persuaded to co-sign the letter 'were not hopeful of getting any kind of response from the authorities', so it was a welcome surprise when, a month on, the complainant received a letter signed by the Acting Commander of the Central Police Division Headquarters that not only apologized for the officers' conduct but also promised to cease the 'legally baseless practice of the detention of persons without identification cards'.[9] Looking back on the Rascals incident with the weight of history, its significance is not lost on the letter-writer, who told Chua: 'If you're talking about gay men being "attacked" very openly, very visibly, it happened. If you're talking about gay men organizing themselves, it happened. If you're talking about gay men fighting back, it happened. So for all intents and purposes, it was our Stonewall.'[10] In invoking Stonewall, he is, of course, referencing the riots at Stonewall Inn, New York, in the summer of 1969, which in the popular contemporary imaginary signifies the birth of the gay rights movement in the USA.

The story of Stonewall is simultaneously a 'symbol of resistance' and a 'myth of emancipation from oppression' abstracted from history.[11] As Elizabeth Armstrong reminds us, accepting the reading of Stonewall as the event that sparked the gay rights movement depletes it of the fullness and complexity of its constitutive context: it is 'neither an accurate description nor a compelling explanation of the origins of gay liberation'.[12] It is worth staying alert to how the Stonewall narrative has been folded into the story of Rascals because '[a]s with all myths and symbols, we do more than retell and remember it. We *interpret* it. We extract lessons from the event and, in doing so, shape our understanding of the past and the present.'[13] In a similar way, Rascals is more than an origin story – in addition to functioning as a kind of turning point in the evolution of activism in Singapore, it also carries a certain mythic quality to it that influences the way the past is understood to shape the present. Instead of necessarily being points of genesis, then, Stonewall and Rascals 'are memorable because they represent turning points in gay history. The initial and evolving responses to these events created moments of opportunity that activists seized to advance collective action whose legacy continues unbroken, though sometimes untidy, to this day.'[14]

The Rascals letter marked the first time gay people in Singapore directly engaged the state. Before this, until the early 1980s, '[n]o community or visible gay culture existed, fear of detection and sanction loomed, and no one imagined the possibility of collective action'.[15] The late 1980s and early 1990s saw some flickers of LGBT organizing. Helped by the government commissioning plays to raise awareness of HIV/AIDS, theatre became both a site of representation of gay life and a site where minoritized sexualities could meet and connect.[16] The radicality of what happened in 1993 was that it expanded the limits of the possible in LGBT people's imaginations. Activist-minded groups such as People Like Us began to take shape and encouraged members to 'think in terms of rights and an oppositional relationship with state agents'.[17] There were instances of state surveillance, such as plain-clothes members of security services attending meetings, some of whom initially intimidated organizers and movement leaders. By the late 1990s, however, most realized that there had generally been little by way of repercussions and seemed to have got used to it.

In 1998, prime minister Lee Kuan Yew delivered a further shot in the arm. During the call-in segment of a live interview on CNN, a caller asked Lee what sort of future gay people had in Singapore. Lee replied:

> Well, it's not a matter which I can decide or any government can decide. It's a question of what a society considers acceptable. And as you know, Singaporeans are by and large a very conservative, orthodox society, and very, I would say, completely different from, say, the United Sates and I don't think an aggressive gay rights movement would help. But what we are doing as a government is to leave people to live their own lives so long as they don't impinge on other people. I mean, we don't harass anybody.[18]

Whilst these were not particularly radical sentiments, it was 'the first time that a senior government official had spoken about sexual minorities in a non-condemnatory tone' and, as such, a fillip for the LGBT community.[19] It also reflected a shift in the state's attitude towards LGBT people in Singapore – from one of persecution and repression to one of (conditional) tolerance. This was a shift that was occurring in concert with a larger political decision to deliberately cultivate an image of Singapore as a cosmopolitan global city that was welcoming of diverse groups of people – including minoritized sexualities.

Anti-politicizing the public sphere

From the moment of its coming to power, the PAP government has treated Singaporean citizens as political objects rather than subjects. As we previously saw in Chapter 2, Lee Kuan Yew assumed the role of the strict father looking after his children – and this infantilization of the citizenry has remained a constant feature of Singaporean political governance. As the political scientist Chan Heng Chee argued more than 40 years ago:

> [the PAP] has applied the entire range of political weaponry to stymie the development of the opposition, including detention, deregistration of key opposition organizations, invoking legislation to restrict political action and publication, and pre-emptive organization. These measures were initially enforced to suppress the communists, but they have resulted in the control and limitation of all effective political activity other than that of the ruling party.
>
> A systematic depoliticisation has taken place in the political arena; with separation from Malaysia in 1965, depoliticisation has become a conscious explicit philosophy adopted by the government as political leaders lay emphasis on the concerns of economic growth and survival.[20]

George makes a similar argument routed through an analysis of the Singaporean media landscape. He focuses on mainstream media outlets who are granted access to ministers and government briefings, and shows how the media in Singapore has been disciplined into reproducing the government's stance as the 'natural and common sense position'.[21] The result is that the media is hardly the site of any critical debate around governmental statements and public policy that culminates in an eventual 'depoliticisation of the public'.[22]

I am inclined to think of this process as *anti-politicization* rather than *depoliticization* for the relatively straightforward reason that *anti-* suggests a far more deliberate process of militating against a politicized public. It also avoids the wistfulness implicit in the notion of depoliticization, which carries a sense of nostalgia for a utopian agential political subject. Anti-politicization, in contrast, denotes the active process of militating against and subtracting the legitimacy of citizens' participation in the politics of public life – along with all the dissent, dialogue, and difference this entails. It works against a political public and dissuades citizens from exercising political agency; and it produces an anti-politicized subject who is taught that politics is the sole preserve of elected politicians and the government.

Put differently, anti-politicization vacates the public sphere of politics and narrowly redefines it as electoral politics. It reconfigures democratic citizenship by stripping citizens of the legitimacy (but not the formal right) of contributing to, contesting, and influencing public life. Elections become the sole modality through which one can influence the political sphere by electing officials who are then supposed to be left alone to do the business of governing. This is compounded by the PAP government's remarkable insistence that it does not, in fact, belong in the political sphere because it is above and beyond politics. It 'takes pride in its self-proclaimed "pragmatism" in responding to situations at hand rather than in ideological commitment, let alone ideological planning over a sustained period of time'.[23] It maintains that its policies are common sense and as such are neither political nor ideological. Of course, this does not extend to its opponents or opposing logics. Thus, as Michael Barr summarizes, 'governance, administration and even leadership are somehow disconnected from politics so that the actions and words of members of the government are above politics, but the actions and words of government critics are "political"'.[24]

The outcome of anti-politicization in Singapore is that politics has been redefined to denote opposing state narratives. As far as the government is concerned, politics is dissent. It is a move that is as audacious as it is remarkable for the fact that it has largely worked. Demarcating politics this way limits the options available to anybody who wants to challenge the state because it narrows the field of viable action. As George argues, 'when the government treats electoral politics as the only authorised space for debating highly contentious issues, the effect is to delegitimise civil society as a venue for deep political participation'.[25] Abstract notions such as dissent, resistance, protest are laminated with fear and apprehension that are supplied by the memory of dissidents' treatment at the hands of the state in the past.[26]

Demonstrations of state power

On 21 May 1987, the government invoked the Internal Security Act (ISA) and carried out Operation Spectrum.[27] This was a covert internal security operation in which it arrested 'sixteen church workers and social activists … for using the Catholic Church and other religious organizations in a "Marxist conspiracy" to subvert the state'.[28] The government 'alleged that these social workers and volunteers, who advocated for better employment conditions for migrant workers, had ties to foreign communists' and were plotting to 'overthrow the state'.[29] They were detained without trial for a number of months. It was almost a year before all were released. Almost exactly a year on from Operation Spectrum, the government invoked the ISA again. On the receiving end this time was former solicitor-general

Francis Seow.[30] On 6 May 1988, whilst waiting at the Internal Security Department's headquarters to meet with his clients – two of those who had been arrested in Operation Spectrum – Seow was 'accused of receiving campaign funds from the United States for his bid as an opposition politician and was detained without trial under the ISA for seventy-two days'.[31]

The spectacle of state power being wielded this way was unnerving, to say the least. It troubled members of the government, and led to one minister, Suppiah Dhanabalan, resigning in the aftermath because he was uncomfortable with the decision and worried it would be used on political opponents again.[32] He was not the only one. The reverberations of the arrests etched themselves into the political consciousness of the rest of the country as an ominous warning of the dangers of dissent, community organizing, and mobilizing in any way that the government might construe as antagonistic.[33] Lingering in the social memory, too, were the recollections of an earlier internal security operation, Operation Coldstore, carried out by the government in 1963, in which more than 100 people were arrested to nullify an alleged communist conspiracy.[34] The ISA was not used capriciously, but on the occasions it was selectively activated it was a reminder of what the state could potentially do if it wished. In other words, it displayed the full extent of coercive power and the tools it had at its disposal. Consequently, more than three decades on, the terms *Marxist* and *Marxism* and their associations continue to function as 'epithet[s] with dark and sinister tones in Singapore' – a Cold War hangover that has yet to fully clear.[35]

Another way in which the government anti-politicized the public sphere was by very publicly reprimanding people who criticized it too strongly for its liking. In 1994, Catherine Lim published two opinion pieces in *The Straits Times* highlighting the emergence of what she called a 'great affective divide' between the government and the public.[36] Her essential claim was that the PAP government came across as high-handed and appeared to be losing touch with ordinary citizens. In and of itself, this was not particularly harsh. Yet, coming as it did whilst Singapore was transitioning from the premiership of Lee Kuan Yew to that of Goh Chok Tong, Lim's essays appeared to strike a raw nerve with the government and attracted what can only be described as a disproportionately aggressive response.

First, the prime minister's press secretary wrote to *The Straits Times* and warned against anyone attempting to 'set the political agenda from outside the arena'.[37] The prime minister then doubled down in Parliament, saying:

> anybody who wants to set the agenda for the country must enter the political fray … If you do not wish to do so, you want to hide in sanctuaries to criticise the Government, to attack the Government, we say, even though you do not want to join a party, we would treat you as though you have entered the political arena. I think that is fair. Because you cannot just criticise without

expecting us to reply to you in the same manner which you have attacked us. If you land a blow on our jaw, you must expect a counter-blow on the solar plexus.

[...]

[I]f you try to undermine the authority of the Government through snide remarks, by mocking the Government, you must expect a very, very hard blow from the Government in return.[38]

Goh's outburst certainly carried through with a degree of force supplied by the oddly specific metaphorical violence in his words. But this was not the only way it did its anti-politicizing work; it also configured state–society relations in a particular way. It set up politics and the political arena as a domain into which only elected individuals were permitted to legitimately enter. In this set up, if one wished to criticize the government or state policy, one had to first join a political party and stand for elections. Electoral politics became defined as the only legitimate way of doing and contesting politics.

The suggestion that Lim was criticizing the government from outside the political arena and a space of sanctuary also carried the silent implication that the political arena was therefore a space of conflict and danger. This implication was compounded by Goh sliding between the language of dissent and the language of violence – reading criticism as attack and equating the right of reply with the right to strike. The stakes of expressing dissent were thus elevated. Politics appeared dangerous – demarcated as a realm off limits to citizens who had not been elected to public office. Furthermore, it was clear that the government read open dissent as an assault on itself and was prepared to respond aggressively. The assertion that citizens who criticized an elected government would be treated as if they were participating in the arena of electoral politics also suggested that government critics would be construed as political enemies. Minister for Information and the Arts George Yeo laid this out in no uncertain terms when he reflected on the Catherine Lim affair by suggesting citizens should not take on political leaders as if they were their 'equals'.[39] Similarly aggressive government responses have become far less common – in part because open dissent itself has also become far less common – but every so often, one is given a reminder that as it was in 1994, so it is today.

In September 2019, the poet and playwright Alfian Sa'at found himself on the receiving end of yet another spasm of state hysteria. Alfian had been due to lead a module entitled 'Dialogue and Dissent in Singapore' at Yale-NUS College. Shortly before the module was to begin, however, it was abruptly cancelled. There were some suggestions that the government had stepped in and compelled Yale-NUS College to do so – something the college categorically denied.[40] Nonetheless, the MP Intan Azura Mokhtar raised the matter in Parliament along with concerns around academic freedom. Minister for Education Ong Ye Kung replied by launching into a speech that castigated Alfian. First, he echoed an opinion piece by a former PAP MP that said – amongst other wild and unfounded claims – that the poet was looking to instigate a revolution in Singapore.[41] Ong then went on to selectively quote one of Alfian's poems to imply that he had a history of being disloyal to Singapore and to cast aspersions on his intentions in teaching the course.[42] Finally, he highlighted a Facebook post in which Alfian had acknowledged a renewal of student activism and political conscientization,[43] and said: 'political conscientisation comes from radical left wing thought. It is agitation aimed at making people conscious of the oppression in their lives, so that they will take action against these oppressive elements.'[44]

The episode bordered on caricature but it was a reminder that the current PAP government's attitude to dissent has not changed very much from the late 1980s and the 1990s, where activism and anything resembling leftist/progressive politics can be metabolized as a political threat. More significantly, the insinuations of disloyalty showed how the PAP government continues to reflexively conflate itself with the state such that agreement with its policies is associated with patriotism and loyalty to the country; conversely, the act of dissent is cast as unpatriotic – particularly in situations such as this, where dissent and resistance are discussed in abstract terms. When it is invoked without specificity – that is to say, without the specific object of one's disagreement to ground the notion of resistance – resistance can conjure up spectres of political conspiracies and links dissent with treachery. Challenging the state thus becomes a risky enterprise fraught with a justified fear that one might find oneself on the receiving end of a paroxysm of state power.

At the same time, fear is not the most significant consequence of anti-politicization. This is not to dismiss it as a factor entirely, but fear alone is an insufficient explanation for the difficulty of doing dissent in Singapore. I want to suggest that a more important consequence of anti-politicization is that it produces a politically passive populace – one that does not organize or involve itself with the political sphere except when invited or permitted to do so. The consequence of anti-politicization in Singapore lies in the production of a citizenry that engages with politics on the terms of the ruling PAP government. Once every five years, elections are held – during which rallies and campaign speeches occur. This brief window is 'the designated time for "politics" when citizens are permitted to engage and be "political". The rest of the time is for governing, for administration and for "leadership"' – all of which are constructed as apolitical endeavours.[45] If dissent is politics, assent is merely administration. This is the more significant consequence of anti-politicization in Singapore. It divorces politics from public life, delegitimizes the act of dissenting, and teaches Singaporeans that the public sphere is legitimately contestable solely through elections.

Pink Dot emerged and finds itself operating within this anti-politicized climate. Many of those who were seeking to advocate for sexual rights post-Rascals knew of other activists who had been arrested as part of Operation Spectrum. They were tuned in to the Catherine Lim affair when a sitting prime minister publicly chided an ordinary citizen for criticizing the government in a newspaper column. Anti-politicization thus played a significant role in determining the contours and limits of the movement as it developed. In her book, Lynette Chua lays out the long process of activists learning to read and respond to the state since Rascals, by gradually figuring out 'how the boundaries of political norms were shifting and how they [could] be pushed to advance the movement'.[46] Historicizing Pink Dot within the larger process of anti-politicization helps make sense of why it has developed in the assimilative way it has. The habit of not openly challenging power is a particularly hard one to shake; and its trace manifests in the shape of the discourses that are mobilized to challenge the heteronormative rationales that are so central to the Singaporean nation.

Conceptualizing Pink Dot

In the aftermath of the Asian financial crisis, when Singapore began to actively restructure its economy, Richard Florida published *The Rise of the Creative Class*. Florida argued economic growth is powered by a group of talented people he called the 'creative class'.[47] He said:

> Creative people are attracted to, and high-tech industry takes root in, places that score high on our basic indicators of diversity – the Gay, Bohemian and other indexes … Why would this be so? It is not because high-tech industries are populated by great numbers of bohemians and gay people. Rather, artists, musicians, gay people and the members of the Creative Class in general prefer places that are open and diverse.[48]

This was as bold an argument as it was problematic, and several scholars have since repudiated Florida's arguments on a number of counts.[49] These scholars include, quite remarkably, Florida himself, who has since disavowed most of his claims about actively fostering a 'creative class'.[50] Nonetheless, following the publication of his book, Florida was invited to Singapore to give a series of public talks as well as to meet with policymakers across ministries who were enamoured with his ideas. The notion of the creative class as an inducer of economic growth quickly became a zeitgeist of the early 2000s as the government began to think about how to project a far more cosmopolitan image of Singapore as a 'sexy, funky, and cool place in which to live, work, play, and visit'.[51]

Florida's ideas were so influential that Goh Chok Tong reprised them almost verbatim in his 2002 National Day Rally speech, saying:

> a culturally vibrant city attracts global creative talent. Creative people are highly mobile. They do not slavishly go to where the jobs are. They choose where they want to work based on their lifestyle interests, and the jobs and prosperity follow them. They want an authentic street and neighbourhood environment, a thriving music and arts scene, openness and diversity. Singapore needs a few little 'Bohemias' like Holland Village, Siglap, and Club Street, where they can gather, soak in the ambience, and do their creative stuff.[52]

Diversity, creativity, and entrepreneurship were thus seen as necessary preconditions to inducing economic growth and, over the next few years, Singapore embarked on a process to rebrand itself. Liberalizing the social sphere was thus part of an active effort 'to attract and retain members of the creative class including foreign talent and internationally mobile Singaporeans with highly sought-after skills' out of a conviction that this move was necessary to remain economically competitive.[53] It was in this vein that Singapore attempted to make itself appear more gay-friendly – or at least, less hostile – and in 2003, Goh announced the government would change its long-standing position of not employing gay people.[54]

This had little to do with sexual rights per se. Instead, it was an attempt to enlist LGBT people in the service of capital accumulation – or what Rao calls 'homocapitalism'.[55] For Rao, the logic of homocapitalism 'seeks to reconcile the twin imperatives of efficiency and empowerment, making capitalism friendly to queers but also rendering queers safe for capitalism'.[56] An opinion piece published in *The Straits Times* days after Goh's comments rationalized them in similar terms, again with recourse to Florida:

> The idea is simple: Tolerance creates an open, diverse society that welcomes everybody, whether mavericks or buttoned-down conservatives. This milieu attracts the kind of innovative, creative talent critical to economic growth [and ...] Professor Florida singles out gay-friendliness as an indicator of tolerance.[57]

Tolerating minoritized sexualities thus became a waypoint on the quest for further economic growth, which was framed as crucial to the survival of the country. One could read these developments as an extension of D'Emilio's argument that the logics of capitalism have opened new material possibilities for sexual minorities.[58] But we should remain alert to how the homocapitalist logics that rationalized the state's new-found willingness to tolerate minoritized sexualities also subdivided them into 'those deemed "productive" and worthy of inclusion and derided others cast out as "unproductive" '.[59] Productivity becomes a proxy for acceptability.

The government was not in any way, shape, or form attempting to decentre heteronormativity as an organizing principle of subjectivity in Singapore. Rather, the promise that some minimal sexual tolerance could eke out some additional economic growth was sufficient for the government to 'liberalize its stance on sexual difference to project a global image of gay-friendliness'.[60] It was basically a calibrated attempt to provide 'enough liberalization to keep the foreign and local creative class satisfied so that the economy [would] grow'.[61]

Instead of decentring heteronormativity, then, what occurred was a shift in the contextual position of queerness in relation to the nation because of the idea that LGBT people could provide economic growth. Parsed through discourses of instrumental value and capital, queerness' incompatibility with the straight nation could be ameliorated. LGBT people became potential symbols of economic growth – something that Singapore could not afford to forgo – and thus had to be accommodated. This helps explain why, almost paradoxically, despite its heteronormative set-up, and the fact that sex between men was still criminalized then, Singapore came to be known as Asia's 'new gay capital' by the end of the 2000s.[62]

It was in a similar spirit that the government tentatively experimented with liberalizing the political sphere and established the Speakers' Corner at Hong Lim Park in April 2000. The idea of designating a place imitating Speakers' Corner in London's Hyde Park where people could give public speeches had initially been mooted by Joseph Nye, the American political scientist who was advising the government at the time. After some initial reluctance, 'as it was concerned over the potential for public disorder in our multi-racial, multi-religious society', the government decided that 'the risk [could] be managed, and the idea [was] worth trying out, especially in view of the support it [had] attracted from civil society groups'.[63] On 1 September 2000, Speakers' Corner was officially consecrated as the only space in Singapore where citizens could give public speeches without needing a licence – as long as they were not speaking about topics related to race or religion, because the state deemed them too inflammatory for multiracial and multireligious Singapore to handle. Eight years later, at the 2008 National Day Rally, Lee Hsien Loong outlined his government's intention to further relax the rules governing the Speakers' Corner, saying: 'we should allow our outdoor public demonstrations, also at the Speakers' Corner still subject to basic rules of law and order, still stay[ing] away from race, language and religion … [and] we will manage with a light touch'.[64] The law was amended later that year to allow outdoor public demonstrations at Speakers' Corner without requiring a police permit.

Taken together, the legal amendments of 2000 and 2008 meant that, for the first time in independent Singapore's history, there was a zone of exemption where one could freely organize public assemblies and public speeches – and this zone of exemption was Speakers' Corner. Foucault's words echo here, reminding us that '[w]here there is power, there is resistance, and yet, or rather consequently, this resistance is never in a position of exteriority in relation to power'.[65] Resistance and its attendant possibilities therefore emerge as an immanent response to power, and the new forms of resistance that were made possible by the cumulative effect of the 2000 and 2008 amendments speak to this. Where, prior to 2008, public assemblies could not be held anywhere in Singapore without a police permit, because of a reconfiguration of state power this was now no longer the case. Thus, Chua argues, the 'impetus for Singapore's first public gay rally, Pink Dot, can be traced back to these changes that took place quietly in November 2008'.[66] But because resistance is never in a 'position of exteriority' to power,[67] because it is always reacting and responding to power, it is also shaped and moulded by power. Even as Speakers' Corner opened the possibility of a new form of resistance it simultaneously restricted its shape – both literally and figuratively.

Speakers' Corner is a small circular space approximately the size of two football fields. This bounded, enclosed shape forecloses the possibility of a procession-style event modelled on Pride parades, which have become ubiquitous in many parts of the world, particularly in the Global North. This was one reason activists who had initially toyed with the idea of organizing a Pride parade eventually decided otherwise.[68] For, the constitutive feature of a procession, to go (*cedere*) forward (*pro*), would not be possible at Speakers' Corner. Because of its shape, a Pride-style event would have seen people marching around in circles – something that would have been far too ironic, even for the Singaporean LGBT movement. More importantly, a Pride-style event would have brought about the spectacle of protest and this was something organizers were keen to avoid.[69] They were convinced that the vast majority of Singaporeans – LGBT and straight alike – would stay away from such an open form of protest 'after seeing how opposition politicians who staged streets protests without permits have been prosecuted, convicted, and consequently delegitimized'.[70] Even though the prohibition on outdoor public demonstrations had been lifted, and Lee had declared that demonstrations at Speakers' Corner would only be regulated 'with a light touch', the reluctance to openly mobilize and to be associated with open mobilizations remained.[71] As George reminds us, the promise of light-touch regulation retains its disciplinary function because of 'the memory of the heavy hand'.[72]

This was the larger problem Pink Dot organizers faced. Because Speakers' Corner had been designated as the only place in Singapore where outdoor public demonstrations could take place, it also meant that any dissenting event held at Speakers' Corner was understood as an outdoor public demonstration. Here, one sees the effects of anti-politicization not just in terms of how it shapes Singaporeans as political subjects but also in the way it shapes the contours of resistance by disciplining the way resistance understands and imagines itself. Pink Dot was thus conceptualized not just as a movement seeking to gain mainstream public support for LGBT people in Singapore but also as an active rejection of the spectacle and display of dissent, and it seeks to thread the needle by decoupling the political effects of dissent from its spectacle through a rhetorical negation of markers of dissent.

Before moving on to examine Pink Dot's tactics in building mainstream public support, I want to briefly draw attention to the fact that in the scholarship around Pink Dot, the terms *tactic* and *strategy* are often used interchangeably. In and of itself, this does not substantially undermine the arguments being made. However, I think it is useful to make a distinction between these terms. I use *tactic* rather than *strategy* in relation to Pink Dot primarily because of the conceptual connotations of power that *strategy* has. Strategies operate from a position of power – the place of the 'proper' and an 'institutional localization'.[73] They 'conceal beneath objective calculations their connection with the power that sustains them from within the stronghold of its own "proper" place or institution'.[74] In this sense, the government's conviction that 'continuous economic growth is the wellspring of all else in a Singaporean's life' functions as a strategy of governance where 'all aspects of social life are to be instrumentally harnessed to this relentless pursuit'.[75] It is a strategy because there is nothing inherently good or correct about the 'instrumental rationality' that the PAP government chooses to use as a political and policymaking rubric.[76] Whilst it is presented as an objective calculation, to accept it as such would be to forget the multiple other non-instrumental rationalities that are deprioritized as a consequence of elevating this one specific form of rationality. It is an elevation that is only possible because it is powered by the state. In contrast, '[t]he place of a tactic belongs to the other'.[77] It is taken up by those outside of power to whom the terms of engagement are dictated. A tactic 'depends on time – it is always on the watch for opportunities that must be seized "on the wing". Whatever it wins, it does not keep. It must constantly manipulate events in order to turn them into "opportunities".'[78]

The reason I describe Pink Dot's tactics as such is to call attention to the fact that in 'toe[ing] the line, while pushing boundaries', it is nonetheless dancing to the tune of the state.[79] It does not enjoy the privilege of making apparently objective calculations. Rather, it has to reflexively react to the shuffling of socio-political conditions it is embedded in, carefully modifying its approach on the fly to avoid potential state rebuke or retaliation. For the 'weak must continually turn to their own ends forces alien to them'.[80] Pink Dot has been quite adept at doing this but the cost of doing so is that it 'entails accepting the price of reification and reinforcement of existing arrangements of power'.[81]

As such, Pink Dot's tactics engage with state policies and positions – for instance, those that reify the heterosexual nuclear family unit amongst others – and attempt to turn them to their own ends. But the problem is that because it often draws from the inventory of heteronormativity, it will never be able to redefine the frame of reference that produces the very exclusion it is working to undo. Such a tactic only ever 'insinuates itself into the other's place, fragmentarily, without taking it over in its entirety'.[82] To distinguish between strategies and tactics is to appreciate that the difference lies in their respective places of enunciation – strategies are launched from a position of power whilst tactics issue from a position of subordination. Nicholas De Villiers rightly suggests, therefore, that 'tactics appear specific and local but function within larger strategies'.[83] This is essentially the Foucauldian position that 'resistance is never in a position of exteriority in relation to power'.[84] Because power can dictate the coordinates of resistance, tactics are often contingent on functioning within the strategies operating above them, which is what Pink Dot has resorted to doing.

Protest without protest

Pink Dot is not just the largest LGBT movement in Singapore. It is also the largest social movement in Singapore, and its recent iterations have consistently attracted crowds in the region of 10,000. In 2019 – before physical gatherings were paused because of the COVID-19 pandemic – it turned out nearly 20,000 people.[85] It describes itself as:

> a non-profit movement started by a group of individuals who care deeply about the place that LGBTQ Singaporeans call home. It is a group for everyone, straight and gay, who support the belief that everyone deserves the freedom to love. With openness and acceptance, we hope to bring LGBTQ Singaporeans closer to their family and friends.[86]

Notably, it also distinctly refuses to describe itself as a protest. In fact, not only does it take care not to invoke the term, it has actively distanced itself from the notion of protest. Until approximately 2020, in the frequently-asked-questions section on its website, one of the first questions listed was 'Is this event a protest?'.[87] There are at least two ways of reading this move. If one were to take the section at face value – in that it literally contains frequently asked questions – it would suggest this is something that Pink Dot is often asked and that it is symptomatic of a degree of discomfort amongst potential attendees as to whether the event is a protest. If one were to read this section as a kind of reflexive rhetorical exercise for Pink Dot to provide more information about the event, then it would suggest the organizers believe this is a sentiment worth addressing – a concern that needs to be pre-emptively assuaged. Both readings speak to the anti-politicization of Singapore's public sphere, and Pink Dot's answer is unambiguous:

> It is NOT a protest. It is a congregation of people who believe that everyone deserves a right to love, regardless of their sexual orientation.
>
> Fear and bigotry can get in the way of love – between friends, family and other loved ones – so this is an event for everyone who believes that LGBT individuals are equally deserving of strong relationships with our family and friends.[88]

A third reading is that declining to name itself a protest could be a way of communicating with a 'reactionary government' that has historically not taken kindly to civil society, protests, and open dissent.[89] Explicitly dissociating itself from protest perhaps functions as a signal declaration that it is not threatening the government's hegemony or looking to undermine its authority.

All three readings may well be true, for all three possibilities are reflections of a similar phenomenon: a certain nervousness about dissent and the act of protesting. Pink Dot's insistent response – emphasized by its capitalized negation – reads as both an assertion and a desperation not to be associated with protest. This comes through more generally as well in how the movement eschews the language of dissent – it does not directly refer to itself as a demonstration, assembly, or rally – all of which have associations of protest. Instead, in the assertion following this negation, Pink Dot refers to itself as a *congregation*. There are faint religious echoes in the invocation of this term – after all, congregations are typically associated with mass and worship – and it generally opens notions of communality, people coming together in harmony.

Nonetheless, rhetorically distancing itself like this from protest does not free it from the disciplinary force of the law that regulates protests and outdoor public demonstrations. And how Pink Dot behaves shows it is aware that it is formally categorized as one. In the first place, it was made possible only because of the 2000 and 2008 legal amendments that allowed outdoor public demonstrations at Speakers' Corner – which indicates Pink Dot organizers were conscious that it legally qualified as a demonstration. It also showed through in 2016 when the Public Order Act was amended to permit only Singaporean citizens or permanent residents to participate in outdoor public demonstrations. This amendment had a material effect on Pink Dot 2017 and every iteration since, as organizers were responsible for ensuring that participants were Singaporean citizens or permanent residents. Pink Dot duly complied with this regulation by checking identification documents before admitting participants into Hong Lim Park and allowing them to participate.

Pink Dot therefore could be read as a form of dissent that self-consciously chooses not to mark itself out as such – dissent that refuses to name itself thus. It attempts to disrupt the dominant narrative of heterosexuality in Singapore without recognizably coming across as a disruptor. As I have argued elsewhere, this is a way of 'disarming' itself and doing dissent without displaying dissent in the hope that it will therefore not be recognized as dissent – a tactic of self-negation that tries to function as a kind of protest without the spectacle of protest.[90] Protesting without protest, in some sense.

Instead of adopting the language of protest and dissent, then, Pink Dot turns to the language of universality in its rhetoric. This is encapsulated by its slogan 'supporting the freedom to love'.[91] It further elaborates upon this by describing itself as 'a group for everyone, straight and gay, who support the belief that everyone deserves the freedom to love'.[92] In addition to calling itself a group for 'everyone', the more significant way it deploys the language of universality is in mobilizing the notion of love. Pink Dot is very much a movement for LGBT people – and by no means does it attempt to conceal this – but its slogan 'supporting the freedom to love' redefines its central proposition. Centralizing love allows it to broach sexuality obliquely instead of directly – by approaching sexuality through the frame of love. Thus, on its website it defines itself as 'a congregation of people who believe that everyone deserves a right to love, regardless of their sexual orientation'.[93]

Elsewhere, it emphasizes that '[t]he gathering is a show of support for those who believe in openness and love between people, regardless of their sexual orientation. Anyone can attend – straight and gay'.[94] Consistently, love is foregrounded prior to opening the register of sexuality; and love is foregrounded before the politics and inequalities of sexuality are highlighted. Instead of directly contesting heteronormativity and the differentiated distribution of legitimacy according to one's expression of sexuality, Pink Dot opts to route this call through the language of universality.

It is worth noting, however, that Pink Dot's rhetoric of universality only challenges the differentiated freedom to love along the lines of sexuality without making common cause with other queered formations that are disenfranchised in similar ways to sexual minorities. Whilst I have argued in this book for a reading of queerness writ large that exceeds the boundaries of sexual identity categories, I am not suggesting that Pink Dot necessarily ought to do this. Social movements make choices to achieve the objectives important to them. But I do want to point out that, in Pink Dot's hugely successful claim for the freedom to love, ameliorating heteronormativity is rationalized through a largely identarian logic even though the governance of sexuality in the straight nation exceeds identity categories.

This oblique mode of engagement is also how Pink Dot has responded to the pushback it has attracted from the conservative and religious right. One of the more significant manifestations was the reactionary Wear White movement, which urged people to eschew wearing pink for white on the weekend Pink Dot was taking place.[95] Wear White was launched in 2014 by Ustaz Noor Deros, a Muslim religious teacher, who urged Muslims to 'stand up and defend the sanctity of family' by dressing in white when attending prayers that weekend – something he claimed was necessary because '[t]he natural state of human relationships is now under sustained attack by LGBT activists'.[96] Noor Deros' call was quickly picked up and amplified by Lawrence Khong, a Christian pastor at Faith Community Baptist Church, who instructed his congregation to attend services that weekend dressed in white as a symbol of commitment to preserving the heterosexual family unit. Khong doubled down the following year, repeating his call for Christians to wear white and insisting that 'the natural family is a universally accepted norm and a public good'.[97] By 2016, after Noor Deros had distanced himself from Wear White, claiming to focus more on educational programmes, Khong had taken up the mantle. He rebranded Wear White – insofar as adding a subject pronoun and two dots might reasonably be called rebranding – and called it the We.Wear.White campaign. For Khong, this was:

> a message to LGBT activists that there is a conservative majority in Singapore who will push back and will not allow them to promote their homosexual lifestyle and liberal ideologies that openly and outrightly contradict our laws, our Government's stated policies, our national core values, and the conservative majority's views on public morality, marriage and family.[98]

Pink Dot's oblique response to the Wear White campaign demonstrates how it uses the language of universality to manoeuvre around conflicting positions. When asked to comment, its spokesperson said: 'We welcome any effort to strengthen family ties, and many of those who attend Pink Dot do so with family members who understand the need and importance of maintaining strong familial bonds.'[99] The following year, when again asked to respond to the We.Wear.White campaign, its spokesperson said 'In a multi-cultural, multi-religious and multi-racial country like Singapore, with secularism at its core, citizens are generally accepting of diversity. We believe that families should be built on love and understanding, rather than exclusion.'[100] Both responses are instances of how the language of universality and oblique opposition work as tactics to 'constantly manipulate events in order to turn them into opportunities'.[101] In Noor Deros' and Khong's remarks on the family, they take heteronormativity for granted. They do not specify that *family* refers to the heterosexual nuclear family unit – for them, this is self-evident. Pink Dot does not directly contest this heteronormative formulation; instead, it talks about 'strengthening family ties' and 'strong familial bonds' in universal terms.[102] Exploiting the ellipsis in Noor Deros and Khong's comments – an ellipsis that stems from a staunch commitment to heteronormativity – it expands the definition of family precisely through a parallel elliptical use of family.

It makes a similar move in its frequently-asked-questions section, responding to the question 'Does this event go against my pro-family beliefs?'. The answer is 'This is a pro-family event. LGBT individuals have got families too!'[103] The We.Wear.White movement and members of the conservative and religious right mobilize family values to 'insist on [their] connection to the future of the nation' through the 'promotion of a certain [heterosexual] definition of citizenship'.[104] By deftly manipulating the ambiguity in *family*, Pink Dot stakes a claim to the nation by activating larger discourses of kinship that are salient in Singapore whilst simultaneously resisting the delegitimization of non-heterosexual coupling.

We have already seen how, as a function of Habibie's little quip that backfired, *little red dot* functions as a signifier that Singapore proudly invokes with a sense of defiance – and Pink Dot invoke this in their name. Their orientation to the local manifests not just in the nominal intertextual reference *Pink Dot* makes to red dot. It is also evident in the way it makes sense of the colour pink. As they put it, pink is significant because:

> Pink is the colour of our [National Registration Identity Card (NRIC)]. It is also the colour when you mix red and white – the colours of our national flag. Pink Dot stands for an open, inclusive society within our Red Dot, where sexual orientation represents a feature, not a barrier.[105]

The nation is overdetermined in Pink Dot. It foregrounds the salience of pink in relation to the state rather than how pink can be a signifier of non-normative sexualities or the global gay rights movement.[106] Pink is made significant because it is the colour of the NRIC, which every Singaporean citizen is issued with upon turning 15, and because it combines the colours of the national flag. This is not to say that Pink Dot disavows the global meaning of pink – insofar as there is one. Rather, its choice to saturate itself with recognizable national symbols such as the flag and the NRIC reflects a deliberate choice to orientate towards the nation at the expense of the global, and parallels the general aversion it has towards the transnational LGBT rights movement as a source of support and legitimacy. In fact, where there is the potential for a symbol to be seen as international, and especially 'Western', Pink Dot's response is to ground it locally.[107] What it scrupulously avoids doing is attempt to use the influence of the transnational LGBT movement to pressure the Singaporean government.[108] Primarily, this is because such a move would, in all likelihood, backfire – the Singaporean government has a history of not wanting to come across as weak. Given that coming across as 'having foreign influence' would be sufficient reason for the state to shut the movement down, Pink Dot's desire to suffuse itself with the local – even if it does strike a note of exclusion in relation to non-citizens – is perhaps understandable.[109]

One of the most spectacular instances that shows Pink Dot's dexterity at appropriating state symbols occurs when, approximately halfway through the event at Speakers' Corner, everyone is invited to stand and sing the national anthem together. What makes this moment particularly powerful is that the rendition of the anthem tends to be accompanied by the national flag passing overhead in a military flypast.[110] This is, of course, not a ceremonial courtesy afforded by the state. Instead, it is an example of Pink Dot remaining 'on the watch for opportunities that must be seized "on the wing"' and being able to 'manipulate events in order to turn them into "opportunities"'.[111]

The explanation is, in fact, a fairly banal one that serves to accentuate exactly how small Singapore is. Speakers' Corner at Hong Lim Park, where Pink Dot is held every year, is less than 2 km away from the Padang and The Float @ Marina Bay – the two locations where Singapore's National Day parades are normally held. Whilst the parade itself happens on 9 August, National Day, full-length rehearsals, which include the state flag flypast, typically begin in the weekends of June. Thus, every year, as Pink Dot happens at Hong Lim Park, rehearsals for the National Day parade are also taking place just adjacent. On the day, having performed the flypast at the parade rehearsal, the two military helicopters carrying the flag must inevitably fly over Hong Lim Park as they return to base. Shrewdly, '[Pink Dot] organizers deliberately schedule the event to coincide with a National Day Parade rehearsal, so that participants may stand to attention during the state flag flypast.'[112] And when the flag travels overhead, everyone at Pink Dot is invited to stand and sing the national anthem together.[113]

The result is thousands of LGBT Singaporeans and straight allies gathered together singing the national anthem, *Majulah Singapura*, together as the state flag flies overhead. It is a moment imbued with significant affective power because it involves appropriating an exceedingly rare social practice – after all, a flypast is typically experienced only during the National Day celebrations. Appropriating this ceremonial practice typically reserved for celebrations of the nation, transplanting it into Hong Lim Park, those at Pink Dot not only recite the anthem, they lay their own claim to the nation.

One could also read this moment as minoritized sexualities and straight allies speaking back to the heteronormative state, through symbols of the state, by lifting their eyes up towards the state flag, and repeating the injunction 'Majulah Singapura' – onward (*maju-lah*) Singapore (*Singapura*) – where the call that Singapore move onward is nothing less than a repudiation of Lee Hsien Loong's famous insistence in 2007 that when it comes to LGBT rights, the government must 'stay one step behind the front line of change' and resist the urge to go forward.[114] In making their pledge of allegiance to the nation, this forward movement is exactly what LGBT Singaporeans are asking for – a reciprocal recognition of their equality through the substantive act of relieving their marginalization. In that context, 'Majulah Singapura' becomes a demand to be inscribed within the nation – a refrain that tries to use the language of nation to seek shelter from its constitutive logics.

Fitting into the straight nation: some costs

Tracing the genealogy of dissent, social movements, and community organizing in Singapore goes a long way towards explaining why Pink Dot is virtually the only social movement in recent history that has found such a degree of success with the general public. From attracting around 1,000 people in its very first iteration in 2009, it regularly turns out more than 20,000 now.[115] It is difficult to give a sense of how this compares to other social movements simply because there is no other movement in Singapore that has managed to draw similar crowds. Perhaps a comparable social movement would be the relatively new SG Climate Rally environmental movement, which is focused on the climate crisis and climate justice. Its protests regularly mobilize around 2,000.[116] There are also occasionally other smaller protests held at Speakers' Corner, such as a recent protest against the death penalty organized by the Transformative Justice Collective that attracted upwards of 400 people.[117] With all this in mind, it is clear that Pink Dot operates on a different scale.

But its success in capturing public support also traces in relief its limits. I want to reiterate that it is understandable why Pink Dot sets itself up the way it does, but this does not mean that the tactics it adopts and the respectability politics it promotes are free of consequences. In that sense, it is important to recognize that whilst these choices may help engineer some kinds of relief for some from heteronormativity, they also work to reify the existing heteronormative order and legitimize fixed forms of kinship. They can play into a logic of homocapitalism that designates only some LGBT people – those of demonstrable instrumental worth – worthy of recuperation and simultaneously relegates those who do not possess such worth to the margins. And they do very little to disturb heteronormative familism – the fundamentally heteronormative rules of kinship – as well as the material weight of care responsibilities loaded upon them.

Displacing heteronormativity from its sacral position in Singaporean society requires an expansive queer critique where queer is a 'critique of (temporal) normativity tout court rather than sexual normativity specifically'.[118] The challenge here is engaging with the politics of sexuality and subjectivity – for merely recognizing it does not quite address the question of how one might go about denaturalizing it. For instance, Lee Edelman's famous polemic in *No Future* is certainly not wrong in identifying that queerness names 'the side outside the consensus by which all politics confirms the absolute value of reproductive futurism'.[119] But the problem is that identifying the necessity of repudiating the dogma of heterosexual reproduction as key to the futurity and survival of the nation does not say very much about dealing with its politics – and as such, it does not account for the movement required to get from the here and now to the then and there.[120]

Edelman's argument relies on the abstract figure of the child who 'remains the perpetual horizon of every acknowledged politics, the fantasmatic beneficiary of every political intervention ... as the emblem of futurity's unquestioned value'.[121] Thus, he insists that the ultimate act of queer oppositionality must lie in 'withdraw[ing ...] allegiance, however compulsory, from a reality based on the Ponzi scheme of reproductive futurism'.[122] But what does this mean for the lives of LGBT and other queered people – in Singapore or elsewhere? One might entertain Edelman's diagnosis but it does not offer much in the sense of theorizing a way out for people living in a reality where the logic of reproductive futurism is etched into subjectivity. As we have seen in Chapter 3, kinship works as the background against which circuits of care are institutionalized and belonging is imagined in Singapore. Edelman's claim rests on eliding that only a very small group of people can actually withdraw from this reality. For the vast majority of people who are rendered queer, there is 'no future but the here and now of ... everyday life'.[123]

José Esteban Muñoz reminds us that 'imagining a queer subject who is abstracted from the sensuous intersectionalities that mark our experience is an ineffectual way out'.[124] Edelman's disavowal of the future, therefore, is an apolitical gesture that disavows the lifeworlds of queered subjects where 'the only futurity promised is that of reproductive majoritarian heterosexuality, the spectacle of the state refurbishing its ranks through overt and subsidized acts of reproduction'.[125] Of course, the heteronormative present is nowhere near good enough and one should not be content with it. As Muñoz argues:

> It is impoverished and toxic for queers and other people who do not feel the privilege of majoritarian belonging, normative tastes, and 'rational' expectations. [But ...] the idea is not simply to turn away from the present. One cannot afford such a maneuver, and if one thinks one can, one has resisted the present in favor of folly.[126]

This is why it is imperative to engage with the politics of sexuality and its implications because, save for a very small minority, queered people in Singapore – like everywhere else – can scarcely afford the Bartlebian luxury of withdrawing from the intensely heteronormative lifeworlds they find themselves inhabiting.

It is admittedly also a luxury that movements such as Pink Dot do not have. Deprived of the possibility of theorization from a position of universality and abstraction, movements from below such as Pink Dot are perpetually 'in conflict with massively powerful movements from above ... which have all attempted, often effectively, to reinforce existing structures of power, exploitation and sociocultural hierarchies'.[127] We.Wear.White, for instance, attempts to wield hegemonic discourses that fuse the heterosexual nuclear family with the nation as a tool to reinforce heteronormativity as well as to disable efforts to take it apart. Not only must Pink Dot grapple and contend with the problem of movement – the challenge of moving from here to there; it must also necessarily grapple and contend with the *socius* – the place it is located in – and its particular configurations of power and politics as well as the ways they are circumscribed. At the risk of embracing banality, social movements cannot be abstracted from their local conditions of existence and production – they are, by definition, responses to the socio-political conditions within which they are located as such. They exist not in isolation but in relation to that which they are attempting to affect and change. As Laurence Cox argues, 'Movements involve, it could be said, a process of education and emancipation: education in terms of thinking more deeply about different kinds of social relationship, power structure or cultural norms – and emancipation in the sense of taking practical action around this.'[128] This is to say that even as Pink Dot seeks to affect, and shape, a particular set of structures and norms, it is itself shaped and affected by those very structures and norms. Resistance does not occur from outside the sphere of power – it is written into, and emergent from, within it. It is not an a-priori phenomenon that functions outside the structures of power it is attempting to resist and reshape. It is a function of relations of power – 'an irreducible opposite', as Foucault puts it.[129] If resistance is never external to power, if it is written within the relations of power, then it follows that any form of meaningful resistance always exists in some relation to power. For Pink Dot, this has meant having to figure out a way to mount some form of resistance within a space that is inhospitable not just to queerness but to the act of resisting as well.

The challenge for Pink Dot in 'taking practical action' has been that it exists in a country where subjectivity and fullness of citizenship are entwined with the performance of a specific form of heterosexuality.[130] Attempting to disrupt heteronormativity can therefore simultaneously challenge what it means to be Singaporean itself. The scale of this challenge is doubled because of the extraordinary sensitivity the state has to being challenged. Pink Dot has thus far navigated this challenge by attempting to 'mirror the state' to an extent.[131] Oswin develops this line of argument in a more fulsome way, suggesting that:

> LGBT organizations [such as Pink Dot] offer a necessary and vibrant critique of homophobia and heterosexism. They have played a pivotal role in putting issues of equity into mainstream public debate and have doubtless helped many LGBT Singaporeans to re-envision their everyday lives ... But it is also necessary to note that because LGBT organizations like Pink Dot exist precariously in the city-state, their actions are highly circumscribed and they have little choice but to adopt an assimilationist and homonationalist stance.[132]

The critiques of assimilationism and homonationalism in Pink Dot are emergent ones in the critical scholarship around Pink Dot and sexual politics in Singapore. When Puar theorized homonationalism, it was as an extension of homonormativity that fused it with the forces of nationalism.[133] *Homonormativity* itself was coined as a riff on *heteronormativity* to denote a form of contesting heteronormativity by simply laying claim to heterosexual privilege.[134] Lisa Duggan theorizes it as 'a politics that does not contest dominant heteronormative assumptions and institutions, but upholds and sustains them'.[135] It fails to contest heteronormative assumptions and institutions as a function of 'liberalism's paltry promise' of equality – a version of equality that is 'disarticulated from material life and class politics, to be won by definable "minority" groups, one at a time'.[136] In this way, homonormativity becomes complicit in the reproduction of heteronormativity – because it opts to expand heteronormativity's terms and conditions of access instead of challenging them.

Puar builds on this, formulating homonationalism – shorthand for 'homonormative nationalism' – as a conceptual frame that brings into focus the 'collusion between homosexuality and American nationalism that is generated both by national rhetorics of patriotic inclusion and by gay and queer subjects themselves'.[137] It designates some LGBT lives as worthy and simultaneously uses this subset of LGBT lives to militate against racialized communities. Through the 'process of the management of queer life at the expense of sexually and racially perverse death in relation to the contemporary politics of securitization, [and …] Orientalism',[138] the refusal to recognize LGBT rights is made synonymous with nationalist and racialized tropes of barbarism and uncivility.

In many ways, any homonationalist critique of Pink Dot ought to be qualified and tempered because it is less culpable in producing the types of racialized exclusion that characterize homonationalism. It does not attempt to cast the failure to grant LGBT people equal rights as uncivilized or symptomatic of backwardness. In any case, like many other postcolonial states, Singapore is no stranger to such accusations and is generally quite adept at dealing with them. Instead, as I have shown above, Pink Dot uses the conceptual frame of the postcolonial nation to position LGBT subjects as compatible within it. To do this, it leans on homocapitalist and heteronormative familial logics to depict LGBT subjects as productive and filial subjects, capable of generating economic capital and fulfilling the kinship obligations embedded within the nuclear family unit.[139] Michelle Lazar interestingly reads this a 'tactical politics of resistance' such that '[whilst] passing as normative, on the one hand, it simultaneously open[s] up a space for non-normative presence and recognition, on the other'.[140] She argues that 'while [Pink Dot] is aligned with and leverages on the uniting force of nationalism, it also challenges Singaporean society to be open and inclusive of all citizens'.[141] Lazar's is a strong defence of Pink Dot's mobilization of nationalist rhetoric – though an obvious rejoinder is that whilst Pink Dot might be sounding a call for inclusion, it is nonetheless a call that only extends as far as Singaporean citizens.

Ultimately, however, far from being a uniting force, nationalism ought to be understood as a xenologizing force that constantly produces figures of others to maintain the illusion of the nation. One might take the position that Pink Dot's tactical choices are justifiable or even necessary, but it must be accompanied by the acknowledgement that there is a cost – the relentless focus on Singaporean LGBT citizens and the marshalling of the 'politics of respectability' can aid in the xenologization of other queered formations.[142] Here, we could think of the foreign workers who are racialized and positioned as incompatible with the nation – turned into putative sexual threats and similarly denied the freedom to love.

As a function of Singapore's laws that heavily regulate who can undertake dissent and participate in protests at Speakers' Corner, as well as the state's paranoia with transnational interference and foreign influences in local politics,[143] it may seem as though Pink Dot has little choice but to emphasize its local credentials. A sympathetic reading here like Lazar's would be that it reflects an attempt to discursively 'pass' as Singaporean, to stay within the bounds of the law and retain its legitimacy, whilst substantively remaining as inclusive as possible towards non-Singaporeans. But the homocapitalist and heteronormative familial logics it often leans on to call for LGBT inclusion still produce effects similar to the kind that Duggan and Puar caution against. Trying to alleviate the xenologization of queerness in Singapore like this also generates a risk of subdividing minoritized sexualities into those who could be eligible for inclusion in the nation and those who might not be, based on whether they are able to contribute to economic growth as good workers and to heteronormative familism by performing their filial duties. This is Rao's point in highlighting how homocapitalist discourses can marshal the promise of prosperity to make some people 'safe for capitalism' and the nation whilst others remain unsuitable.[144] The resultant future that is forged therefore becomes a contextual domestication of some queered subjects where those who are able to function as productive, familial subjects may be spared the xenology of queerness whilst others are not.

Having said all that, and whilst I do not disagree with Duggan and Puar's theoretical positions and the political commitments of their arguments, I am conscious they are both theorizing from a political context that provides a different affordance in terms of the kinds of resistance that can feasibly be undertaken – which expands the availability of alternatives as far as forms of resistance go. To return to Oswin, it is significant that, when she opens the registers of assimilationism and homonationalism, she opens them in tandem with the notions of precarity and necessity. Oswin rightly acknowledges that 'LGBT organizations like Pink Dot exist *precariously* in the city-state, their actions are *highly circumscribed* and they have *little choice* but to adopt an assimilationist and homonationalist stance.'[145] Pink Dot's tactics thus tell us much more about the dominance of heteronormativity in the national imaginary than about the movement itself. In that sense, I think what is more useful is to take a step back and consider the political conditions that produce such a tactic as the most viable and consider why resistance is limited in this manner. In other words, instead of focusing on Pink Dot's demands per se, I would rather train the spotlight on how nationalism in postcolonial independent Singapore places a constraint on these demands as well as how these demands are posed.

Finding a liberatory answer requires building a movement capable of thinking beyond categories of identity by identifying lines of solidarity and ways in which different people can make common cause. The sheer breadth with which heteronormative logics structure Singaporean life and the national imaginary means that plenty of people, outside of sexual minorities, are queered and made to seem incompatible with the nation, with this incompatibility rationalized and bolstered in a myriad of gendered, racialized, and classed ways. Getting rid of heteronormativity therefore entails envisioning a different future that does not worship a particular expression of heterosexuality centralized in the national imaginary – not one where some queered people are made able to fit into what remains a fundamentally straight nation.

The reason the critiques of assimilationism ought to be registered is that they shine a light on those who continue to be marginalized – even as some manage to escape marginalization. They pose the important question of who is placed at the front of the line, so to speak, in benefiting from the incremental gains that Pink Dot is determined to accrue. It is important to hold open some space and acknowledge the reality that for minoritized people, assimilation – in spite of all its limitations – is itself something that can be experienced as profoundly difficult. For minoritized sexualities, what they are assimilating into is not a benign, 'neutral', desexualized lifeworld.[146] It is a lifeworld that is extraordinarily saturated by heteronormative logics. But difficulty is not a measure of virtue, and the question as to what happens after a certain group of people get what they want remains open.[147] If it is to free all queered people from the strictures of heteronormativity and nationalism, it has to be something more than simply fulfilling 'liberalism's paltry promise'.[148]

Notes

1 Some notable LGBT groups other than Pink Dot are: Sayoni, a feminist, volunteer organization that focuses on protecting queer women; the T Project, an organization that focuses on supporting the transgender community; and Oogachaga, a non-profit organization that runs training programmes and counselling services, in addition to corporate engagement to support the LGBT community; as well as others such as Prout, the Healing Circle, Trans Befrienders, and the Pelangi Pride Centre.

2 Walid Jumblatt Abdullah, 'Electoral Secularism in Singapore: Political Responses to Homosexuality', *Asian Studies Review*, 43.2 (2019), 239–55; Sam Han, 'Wear White: The Mediatized Politics of Religious Anti-LGBT Activism in Singapore', *Nordic Journal of Religion and Society*, 31.1 (2018), 41–57.

3 George L. Mosse, *Nationalism and Sexuality: Middle-Class Morality and Sexual Norms in Modern Europe* (Madison: University of Wisconsin Press, 1988), p. 1.

4 Ng Yi-Sheng, 'Pride versus Prudence: The Precarious Queer Politics of Pink Dot', *Inter-Asia Cultural Studies*, 18.2 (2017), 238–50 (p. 238).

5 George Baylon Radics, ' "First World Problems" in the "Third World"? LGBT Rights in Singapore', in Ciocchini and Radics, *Criminal Legalities in the Global South*, pp. 32–51 (p. 37).

6 Heng, 'Tiptoe out of the Closet', p. 86.

7 Chua, *Mobilizing Gay Singapore*, p. 2.

8 Rascals letter, 31 May 1993, cited in ibid.

9 Jean Chong, 'LGBTQ Activism in Singapore', in *A History of Human Rights Society in Singapore: 1965–2015*, ed. Jiyoung Song (New York: Routledge, 2019), pp. 150–68 (p. 153).

10 Cited in Chua, *Mobilizing Gay Singapore*, p. 1.

11 John D'Emilio, *The World Turned: Essays on Gay History, Politics, and Culture* (Durham: Duke University Press, 2002), p. 147.

12 Elizabeth A. Armstrong, *Forging Gay Identities: Organizing Sexuality in San Francisco, 1950–1994* (Chicago: University of Chicago Press, 2002), p. 62. There is insufficient space in this book to comprehensively debate the significance of Stonewall or properly historicize it. But for more on Stonewall and the US gay rights movement, see John D'Emilio, *Sexual Politics, Sexual Communities: The Making of a Homosexual Minority in the United States, 1940–1970*, 2nd edn (Chicago: University of Chicago Press, 1998); and John D'Emilio, *Making Trouble: Essays on Gay History, Politics, and the University* (New York: Routledge, 1992).

13 D'Emilio, *The World Turned*, p. 148.

14 Chua, *Mobilizing Gay Singapore*, p. 3.

15 Ibid., p. 47.

16 Terence Chong, *The Theatre and the State in Singapore: Orthodoxy and Resistance* (London: Routledge, 2012).

17 Chua, *Mobilizing Gay Singapore*, pp. 51–52.

18 Lee Kuan Yew, CNN Q&A with Riz Khan, 1998, cited in https://the-singapore-lgbt-encyclopaedia.fandom.com/wiki/Lee_Kuan_Yew%27s_views_on_homosexuality#CNN_International_interview,_1998 (accessed 2 October 2024).

19 Oswin, *Global City Futures*, p. 43.

20 Chan Heng Chee, 'The Role of Parliamentary Politicians in Singapore', *Legislative Studies Quarterly*, 1.3 (1976), 423–41 (p. 425); also see Chan, 'Politics in an Administrative State'.

21 Cherian George, *Freedom from the Press: Journalism and State Power in Singapore* (Singapore: NUS Press, 2012), pp. 93–116.

22 Cherian George, *Singapore: The Air-Conditioned Nation. Essays on the Politics of Comfort and Control, 1990–2000* (Singapore: Landmark Books, 2000), p. 45.

23 Chua, *Communitarian Ideology*, p. 1.

24 Michael D. Barr, *Singapore: A Modern History* (London: I.B. Tauris, 2019), p. 119.

25 Cherian George, *Singapore, Incomplete: Reflections on a First World Nation's Arrested Political Development* (Singapore: Woodsville News, 2017), p. 172.

26 For a comprehensive account of dissidents who have been forced into exile, see *To Singapore with Love*, documentary film, dir. Tan Pin Pin (2014); Chng Suan Tze, Low Yit Leng, and Teo Soh Lung, eds, *1987: Singapore's Marxist Conspiracy 30 Years On* (Singapore: Function 8, 2017).

27 See C. Mary Turnbull, *A History of Modern Singapore, 1819–2005* (Singapore: NUS Press, 2009), for a critical account of Operation Spectrum. See Soh Lung Teo, *Beyond the Blue Gate: Recollections of a Political Prisoner* (Singapore: Function 8, 2011) and Guillaume Arotçarena, *Priest in Geylang: The Untold Story of the Geylang Catholic Centre* (Singapore: Ethos Books, 2015), for accounts from two people who were arrested.

28 Daniel P. S. Goh, 'State and Social Christianity in Post-Colonial Singapore', *SOJOURN: Journal of Social Issues in Southeast Asia*, 25.1 (2010), 54–89 (p. 70). These allegations were never proven in open court or trial, and ministers from multiple PAP governments have expressed misgivings over both the allegations and the arrests.

29 Chua, *Mobilizing Gay Singapore*, p. 47.

30 Francis T. Seow, *To Catch a Tartar: A Dissident in Lee Kuan Yew's Prison* (New Haven: Yale Center for International and Area Studies, 1994).

31 Chua, *Mobilizing Gay Singapore*, p. 46. To date, this remains the last time the ISA has been used on a peaceful political opponent.

32 Sonny Yap, Richard Lim, and Leong Weng Kam, *Men in White: The Untold Story of Singapore's Ruling Political Parties* (Singapore: Straits Times Press, 2010), p. 468.

33 For critical accounts of the political development of this time-period and its contemporary legacy, see Hussin Mutalib, *Parties and Politics: A Study of Opposition Parties and the PAP in Singapore* (Singapore: Eastern Universities Press, 2003); Teo Soh Lung and Low Yit Leng, eds, *Escape from the Lion's Paw: Reflections of Singapore's Political Exiles* (Singapore: Function 8, 2012); George, *Singapore, Incomplete*; and Kenneth Paul Tan, *Governing Global-City Singapore: Legacies and Futures after Lee Kuan Yew* (London: Routledge, 2017).

34 Poh Soo Kai, Guofang Chen, and Lysa Hong, eds, *The 1963 Operation Coldstore in Singapore: Commemorating 50 Years* (Kuala Lumpur: Strategic Information and Research Development Centre, 2013).

35 William Peterson, *Theater and the Politics of Culture in Contemporary Singapore* (Middletown: Wesleyan University Press, 2001), p. 50.

36 Catherine Lim, 'The PAP and the People – a Great Affective Divide', *The Straits Times*, 3 September 1994; Catherine Lim, 'One Government, Two Styles', *The Straits Times*, 20 November 1994.

37 Chan Heng Wing, 'PM Goh Remains Committed to Consultation and Consensus Politics', *The Straits Times*, 4 December 1994.

38 'Parliamentary Debates: Official Report' (Singapore: Hansard, 1995), Vol. XLIX, cols 1017–18.

39 'Debate Yes, but Do Not Take on Those in Authority as "Equals"', *The Straits Times*, 20 February 1995.

40 An independent inquiry into the incident was undertaken by Yale University's Vice President and Vice Provost for Global Strategy, Pericles Lewis, who concluded that there was no evidence of government interference. See Pericles Lewis, *Report on Cancellation of Lab Module on 'Dialogue and Dissent'* (New Haven: Yale Office of the Vice President for Global Strategy, 2019).

41 Goh Choon Kang, 'Singapore Does Not Need a "Colour Revolution"', *The Straits Times*, 21 September 2019, www.straitstimes.com/opinion/singapore-does-not-need-a-colour-revolution (accessed 29 September 2024).

42 'Parliamentary Debates: Official Report' (Singapore: Hansard, 2019).

43 Alfian (and Ong, presumably) was referring to Paulo Freire's concept of *conscientização*/concscientization. See Paulo Freire, *Pedagogy of the Oppressed*, trans. Myra Ramos (Freiburg: Herder & Herder, 1970). Ong's reactionary speech in Parliament is an example of the PAP government's enduring paranoia and hyper-alertness around anything that could be linked to a Marxist tradition. See p. 118.

44 'Parliamentary Debates: Official Report' (2019).

45 Barr, *Singapore*, p. 119.

46 Chua, *Mobilizing Gay Singapore*, p. 97.

47 Richard Florida, *The Rise of the Creative Class: And How It's Transforming Work, Leisure, Community and Everyday Life* (New York: Basic Books, 2002), p. 51.

48 Ibid.

49 See, for example, Stefan Krätke, *The Creative Capital of Cities: Interactive Knowledge Creation and the Urbanization Economies of Innovation*, Studies in Urban and Social Change (Chichester: Wiley-Blackwell, 2011); Ann Markusen, 'Urban Development and the Politics of a Creative Class: Evidence from a Study of Artists', *Environment and Planning A: Economy and Space*, 38.10 (2006), 1921–40; Jamie Peck, 'Struggling with the Creative Class', *International Journal of Urban and Regional Research*, 29.4 (2005), 740–70; and David Bell and Jon Binnie, 'Authenticating Queer Space: Citizenship, Urbanism and Governance', *Urban Studies*, 41.9 (2004), 1807–20.

50 Richard Florida, *The New Urban Crisis: How Our Cities Are Increasing Inequality, Deepening Segregation, and Failing the Middle Class – and What We Can Do about It* (New York: Basic Books, 2017).

51 Kenneth Paul Tan, 'Sexing Up Singapore', *International Journal of Cultural Studies*, 6.4 (2003), 403–23 (p. 418).

52 Goh Chok Tong, 'National Day Rally 2002', 2002, National Archives of Singapore, www.nas.gov.sg/archivesonline/speeches/record-details/75e800b4-115d-11e3-83d5-0050568939ad (accessed 2 October 2024).

53 Tan and Lee, 'Imagining the Gay Community', p. 199.

54 Murugan Nirmala, 'Government More Open to Employing Gays Now', *The Straits Times*, 4 July 2003.

55 Rao, 'Global Homocapitalism'.

56 Ibid., p. 47.

57 Chua Mui Hoong, 'It's Not about Gay Rights – It's Survival', *The Straits Times*, 9 July 2003.

58 D'Emilio, 'Capitalism and Gay Identity'.

59 Rao, 'Global Homocapitalism', p. 48.

60 Oswin, *Global City Futures*, p. 41.

61 Tan and Lee, 'Imagining the Gay Community', p. 199.

62 Yue, 'Creative Queer Singapore'.

63 'Parliamentary Debates: Official Report' (Singapore: Hansard, 2000).

64 Lee, 'National Day Rally 2008'.

65 Foucault, *The History of Sexuality*, p. 95.

66 Chua, *Mobilizing Gay Singapore*, p. 119.

67 Foucault, *The History of Sexuality*, p. 95.

68 Chua, *Mobilizing Gay Singapore*, p. 120.

69 See, for example, Lynda Johnston, *Queering Tourism: Paradoxical Performances at Gay Pride Parades* (London: Routledge, 2008); and Begonya Enguix, 'Identities, Sexualities and Commemorations: Pride Parades, Public Space and Sexual Dissidence', *Anthropological Notebooks*, 15.2 (2009), 15–33.

70 Chua, *Mobilizing Gay Singapore*, p. 120.

71 Lee, 'National Day Rally 2008'.

72 George, 'Consolidating Authoritarian Rule', p. 142.

73 Michel de Certeau, *The Practice of Everyday Life*, trans. Steven Rendall (Berkeley: University of California Press, 2013), p. xix.

74 Ibid., p. xx.

75 Chua, *Communitarian Ideology*, p. 59.

76 Ibid.

77 Certeau, *The Practice of Everyday Life*, p. xix.

78 Ibid.

79 Chua, *Mobilizing Gay Singapore*, p. 20.

80 Certeau, *The Practice of Everyday Life*, p. xix.

81 Lynette J. Chua, 'Pragmatic Resistance, Law, and Social Movements in Authoritarian States: The Case of Gay Collective Action in Singapore', *Law & Society Review*, 46.4 (2012), 713–48 (p. 712).

82 Certeau, *The Practice of Everyday Life*, p. xix.

83 Nicholas De Villiers, *Opacity and the Closet: Queer Tactics in Foucault, Barthes, and Warhol* (Minneapolis: University of Minnesota Press, 2012), p. 19.

84 Foucault, *The History of Sexuality*, p. 95.

85 Dewey Sim, 'Pink Dot: How Singapore's LGBT Movement Became a "Tangible Force" where Others Struggle to Survive', *South China Morning Post*, 4 June 2019, www.scmp.com/week-asia/society/article/3012777/pink-dot-how-singapores-lgbt-movement-became-tangible-force-where (accessed 29 September 2024).

86 Pink Dot SG, 'About'.

87 Pink Dot SG, 'FAQs', 2019, https://pinkdot.sg/about-pink-dot-sg/faq/ (accessed 22 October 2019).

88 Ibid., emphasis in original.

89 Chong, 'LGBTQ Activism in Singapore', p. 159.

90 Mano, 'Disarming as a Tactic', p. 129.

91 Pink Dot SG, 'About'.

92 Ibid.

93 Pink Dot SG, 'FAQs'.

94 Ibid.

95 Han, 'Wear White'.

96 Rachel Au-yong and Nur Asyiqin Mohamad Salleh, 'Religious Teacher Launches "Wear White" Online Campaign', *The Straits Times*, 20 June 2014, www.straitstimes.com/singapore/religious-teacher-launches-wear-white-online-campaign# (accessed 29 September 2024).

97 Melody Zaccheus and Janice Tai, 'Christians to Don White for Services as Hong Lim Park Hosts Pink Dot', *The Straits Times*, 12 June 2015, www.straitstimes.com/singapore/christians-to-don-white-for-services-as-hong-lim-park-hosts-pink-dot (accessed 29 September 2024).

98 Regina Marie Lee, ' "Traditional Values" Wear White Campaign Returning on Pink Dot Weekend', *TODAY*, 23 May 2016, www.todayonline.com/singapore/network-churches-revives-campaign-wear-white-pink-dot-weekend (accessed 29 September 2024).

99 Zaccheus and Tai, 'Christians to Don White'.

100 Lee, ' "Traditional Values" Wear White Campaign'.

101 Certeau, *The Practice of Everyday Life*, p. xix.

102 Zaccheus and Tai, 'Christians to Don White'.

103 Pink Dot SG, 'FAQs'.

104 Han, 'Wear White', p. 54.

105 Pink Dot SG, 'About'.

106 Altman, *Global Sex*.

107 Merry, *Human Rights and Gender Violence*.

108 Margaret E. Keck and Kathryn Sikkink, *Activists beyond Borders: Advocacy Networks in International Politics* (Ithaca: Cornell University Press, 1998).

109 Chua, *Mobilizing Gay Singapore*, p. 21.

110 New Naratif Discusses, 'National Anthem at Pink Dot 2018 (360°)', YouTube, 2018, www.youtube.com/watch?v=_dwjCRIvFO4 (accessed 29 September 2024).

111 Certeau, *The Practice of Everyday Life*, p. xix.

112 Ng, 'Pride versus Prudence', p. 238.

113 It is hard to imagine that this timing is purely serendipitous; far more likely that there is some loose coordination between Pink Dot and those involved in National Day parade rehearsals through informal networks of friendship such that the singing of the anthem is timed correctly with the flypast.

114 'Speech to Parliament on Reading of Penal Code (Amendment) Bill'.

115 Sim, 'Pink Dot'.

116 Kelly Wong, 'More than 1,700 Turn Up at First Singapore Climate Rally', CNA, 21 September 2019, https://web.archive.org/web/20190922024430/https://www.channelnewsasia.com/news/singapore/1700-participants-sg-climate-rally-die-in-11930486 (accessed 29 September 2024); Shabana Begum, 'Widespread Calls for Climate Justice at Second In-Person Climate Rally', *The Straits Times*, 24 September 2023, www.straitstimes.com/singapore/widespread-calls-for-climate-justice-at-second-in-person-climate-rally (accessed 29 September 2024).

117 Rebecca Ratcliffe, 'Singapore Hardens Opinion against Death Penalty as "Sense of Injustice" Grows', *Guardian*, 13 April 2022, www.theguardian.com/world/2022/apr/13/singapore-hardens-opinion-against-death-penalty-as-sense-of-injustice-grows (accessed 29 September 2024).

118 Carla Freccero, 'Queer Times', *South Atlantic Quarterly*, 106.3 (2007), 485–94 (p. 489).

119 Lee Edelman, *No Future: Queer Theory and the Death Drive* (Durham: Duke University Press, 2004), p. 3.

120 See also Leo Bersani, *Homos*, 3rd edn (Cambridge: Harvard University Press, 1996), for the anti-relational thesis.

121 Edelman, *No Future*, pp. 3–4.

122 Ibid., p. 4.

123 José Esteban Muñoz, *Cruising Utopia: The Then and There of Queer Futurity* (New York: New York University Press, 2009), p. 22.

124 Ibid., p. 96.

125 Ibid., p. 22.

126 Ibid., p. 27.

127 Laurence Cox and Alf Gunvald Nilsen, *We Make Our Own History: Marxism and Social Movements in the Twilight of Neoliberalism* (London: Pluto Press, 2014), p. vi.

128 Laurence Cox, *Why Social Movements Matter: An Introduction* (London: Rowman & Littlefield, 2018), p. 10.

129 Foucault, *The History of Sexuality*, p. 96.

130 Cox, *Why Social Movements Matter*, p. 10.

131 Tan, *Governing Global-City Singapore*, p. 86.

132 Natalie Oswin, 'Queer Time in Global City Singapore: Neoliberal Futures and the "Freedom to Love"', *Sexualities*, 17.4 (2014), 412–33 (p. 414).

133 Puar, *Terrorist Assemblages*.

134 See Warner, 'Introduction'.

135 Duggan, *The Twilight of Equality?*, p. 50.

136 Ibid., p. xviii.

137 Puar, *Terrorist Assemblages*, p. 39.

138 Ibid., p. xxi.

139 Rao, 'Global Homocapitalism'.

140 Lazar, 'Homonationalist Discourse', p. 439.

141 Ibid., p. 439.

142 Ng, 'Pride versus Prudence'.

143 Chua, *Mobilizing Gay Singapore*.
144 Rao, 'Global Homocapitalism', p. 47.
145 Oswin, 'Queer Time in Global City Singapore', p. 414, emphasis mine.
146 Moore, 'Reflections on Marriage Equality'.
147 Puar, *The Right to Maim*, p. xviii.
148 Duggan, *The Twilight of Equality?*, p. xviii.

Epilogue: the futility of nationalist flirtations

> The naturalisation of the nation-state system as a means of global organisation makes nationalism appear benign, advancing the claim that each of us belongs to a nation-state to which we must show loyalty and by which we will be protected.[1]

With its offer of a benevolent embrace, the nation-state as a political technology allows governments to rationalize a whole host of measures ultimately aimed at regulating both who is allowed to inhabit a particular territory and the degree of comfort with which they are allowed to live there. Nationalism and nationalist discourse are entirely invested in producing figures of non-belonging that the state's various anxieties can be directed towards. In the time it has taken to conceptualize and actually write this book, nationalism's allure and its grip on political imaginations around the world have regrettably strengthened quite considerably. The nation and its constituent logics are presented as common sense, together with the fiction that one's affections should be directed towards the political unit that one is governed by, and this drivel has successfully been sold to numerous electorates.

What I have tried to do with this book, more than anything else, is to rattle the political form of the nation and decentre the sexual logics that lie at its heart by thinking about how queered figures can be made into the figures of non-belonging that the nation requires. To that end, I theorize nationalism through an analysis of the governance of sexual norms – specifically, how heteronormative governance hierarchizes different expressions of sexuality in relation to the nation. Reading Singapore as a straight nation helps us see how a particular expression of heterosexuality and a specific heterosexual familial and domestic norm are central to the imagination of the nation, shaping and governing the lives of not just minoritized sexualities but, in fact, everyone.[2] This final clause is important. Despite Warner's reminder that 'sexuality isn't always or only about sexuality, that it is not an autonomous dimension of experience', the sensibility that it *is* all about sexuality, that sexuality (and queer studies) *is* really only a matter for non-normative sexualities, that sexuality *is* an autonomous dimension of life that does not really concern straight people, is a feature of our current conjuncture.[3] There is a strong affinity, even (or particularly?) on the left, with the vocabulary of identity categories when it comes to interpreting both lived experiences and struggles. I can see why it might seem appealing to make sense of the world through the lexicon of identity categories and its associated taxonomies. Nonetheless, I think it is worth resisting its magnetism – not least because it seems to me a route destined to end in frustration, both intellectual and quotidian.

In his thought-provoking essay 'Being-in-the-Room Privilege: Elite Capture and Epistemic Deference', Olúfẹ́mi O. Táíwò writes that:

> The call to 'listen to the most affected' or 'centre the most marginalized' is ubiquitous in many academic and activist circles. [But] it has more often meant handing conversational authority and attentional goods to those who most snugly fit into the social categories associated with these ills – regardless of what they actually do or do not know, or what they have or have not personally experienced.[4]

Perhaps as a corollary result of reading the nation through the lens of sexual conformity, I have tried to show the insufficiencies of an identarian understanding of queerness in resisting or dismantling this operation of heteronormativity within the nation. In these last few pages, I would like to return to that sentiment and suggest that whilst it is understandable why some minoritized folks, having been spurned, might decide to make overtures to the nation-state out of a desire for recognition, consorting with the nation also consolidates its power.

One of the advantages of detaching from the taxonomies of identity is that it opens up ways of thinking in terms of a common struggle. Not everyone who is queered by heteronormativity experiences it in the same way. But plenty nonetheless find it a difficult system to live with for a range of reasons, and there are lines of solidarity that can be forged leading to a more expansive critique that is able to dispel the stranglehold the nation currently has on the political imagination. There is, in fact, much more to be gained.

As I intimated from the outset of the book, heteronormativity is more than homophobia or heterosexism. Instead, it anoints one particular expression of straightness as the exclusively correct one whilst marginalizing others, actively making other ways of living more difficult. Together with nationalism's capacity to xenologize, those who are unable or unwilling to recite from this prescribed script of heterosexuality can be rendered not only queer but foreign as well – positioned outside the nation. In this sense, queerness can be read as counter-national. Attending to some of the major sites of heteronormativity in Singapore, I have shown how they work together to produce and sustain queerness that is then militated against at various turns and in various ways to produce and sustain the nation. A big part of my claim is that many different people are queered by the smooth operation of heteronormativity, but this is by no means an ethnography that explores the lived realities of minoritized subjects. My object of analysis, as it were, has generally been formal state discourse in its scattered and disparate elements that – when put together – shows how the discursive formation of the nation relies on certain logics of straightness that work to position queerness as the nation's requisite other.

Working with a range of biographical literature, media reports, and legal and political texts, as well as archival records, and reading them with lenses from critical and literary theory, I historicize this reification of an expression of heterosexuality as well as the racialized and gendered norms that are built into this injunction. By understanding how subjectivity is produced through the nation's investment in heteronormativity and how nationalism as a force is invested in perpetually producing figures of otherness, one can see how nationalism in Singapore yokes queerness together with otherness in service of the straight nation.

When nationalism gathers heterosexuality into its operations in this way, queered figures are displaced from the position of the 'principal national subject' and can feel left out in the cold, away from what seems like the warm, comfortable embrace of the nation.[5] Coupled with a state that treats those who resist its assertions – discursive or otherwise – with varying degrees of hostility, it is perhaps understandable to respond with some kind of longing to be included. I want to reflect for a moment on this desire, which informs a good deal of activism and critical scholarship in the country, because, whilst assimilationist approaches to resisting these processes of minoritization in Singapore are an understandable response to its political context, demonstrating a certain compatibility with the nation cannot lay the foundations for a larger emancipatory project.

Even if one were uninterested in such a project and only invested in advancing purely identarian, single-issue causes, such an approach cannot yield success for one's entire constituency simply because nobody lives their life purely along one single axis of identity.[6] One might be a sexual minority but one is also a product of racialized, gendered, classed, linguistic identities and more. The outcome of a purely assimilationist approach will inevitably be that some people are deemed integrable within the nation because their otherness can be accommodated or tolerated in some contexts whilst others continue to be deemed incompatible with the nation and beyond integrability.

There are plenty who judge this 'pragmatic' sensibility as necessary, and Singapore's socio-political context is often cited as the reason for this.[7] Be that as it may, the political conditions that render this form of activism viable do not negate their concomitant implications. It is encouraging that, particularly in recent years, activists and scholars have started to disavow the apparent merits of this approach instead of defending it – and I share many of their general sentiments.[8] Precisely because of a certain 'versatility and plasticity of queerness', attempting to render non-normative sexuality acceptable by demonstrating the integrability of LGBT people with extant state narratives around the nation risks not only subdividing sexual minorities but also potentially strengthening extant heteronormative logics by reasserting familial primacy.[9] It means the various other people who are queered by the operation of heteronormativity will continue to be rendered queer and cast as undomesticable. It also means strengthening the frame of the nation as a legitimate political form.

On 12 May 2021, Singapore's third Universal Periodic Review (UPR) at the United Nations Human Rights Council took place.[10] Twenty-four member countries raised questions about the difficulties that sexual minorities faced in Singapore, including the matter of Section 377A which was still part of the Penal Code at that point. They also made recommendations aimed at ending discrimination against minoritized sexualities in Singapore. In response, Singapore's head of delegation, Ambassador-at-Large Chan Heng Chee, said:

> Let me reiterate that for Singapore, the LGBT community are valuable members of our society. The Government does not tolerate violence, abuse, discrimination, and harassment against the community. An annual Pink Dot event in Singapore has been organised by the LGBT community for the past 12 years. While Section 377A of the Penal Code remains on the books, the Government has stated clearly that it is not enforced. In the context of Singapore, where attitudes towards homosexuality are still evolving, and various communities hold different views, any move by the Government must take into consideration the sentiments of all communities. We believe it is better to let the situation evolve gradually.[11]

Before getting to the invocation of Pink Dot, we might pause for a moment on its enunciator because Chan is an interesting figure, particularly here as we operate in the backwash of appropriation and assimilation. If her name rings any bells it might be because we previously encountered Chan in Chapter 5, via her critical scholarship in the 1980s on the PAP's role in depoliticizing and bureaucratizing the public sphere.[12] At that point, Chan was heading the Political Science Department at the National University of Singapore and the author of an impressive critical oeuvre that thoughtfully analysed the ruling PAP government's consolidation of power and its implications for Singapore's political development.[13] In 1989, she was appointed Singapore's first permanent representative to the United Nations and has served in the state's foreign service since. Speaking about her subsequent appointment in 1996 as ambassador to the USA, she said 'I'm anti-establishment and was a bit of a dissident before I was appointed ambassador. It came as something of a shock to me when I was offered the ambassadorship because I was highly critical of government in a society that is not used to being critiqued.'[14] Chan's reflections on how she looks back on her own arc are revealing – particularly in the way she frames her anti-establishmentarianism and dissidence as belonging in the 'before' period. Her autobiographical account of events explains – perhaps inadvertently – how since being beckoned into the fold those anti-establishment and dissident positions have ostensibly given way. Some scholars have noted that the PAP government has historically been quite adept at using co-optation as a strategy of neutering some forms of political criticism.[15] It is a useful point to bear in mind even if it should not be granted too much explanatory power, as it can suggest a blunt 'You are either with us or against us!' mode of political control. Because of Singapore's smallness and an overbearing state, practically everyone is co-opted to some degree because everyone necessarily must interact with the state in some way in order to function in quotidian life. As George says:

> Losing the state's approval can have material costs in terms of contracts, commissions, and employment. The power of patronage has been a reality in every society, throughout history. But it is truer of Singapore because we are so small and centralised, with limited alternative sources of support.[16]

Nonetheless, bracketing for the moment the way co-optation functions in Singapore, we can read Chan as a former critic whom the state has since conscripted into its service as a representative reliable enough to be counted upon to defend its position in prominent international forums such as the UPR. Against this background, Chan's remarks at Singapore's third UPR were deeply ironic, as they sought to marshal Pink Dot in service of the state in a way that echoed her own trajectory.

Pink Dot reacted to Chan's comments at the UPR with indignation. It released an uncharacteristically sharp statement that said:

> Pink Dot exists as a protest against discrimination towards the LGBTQ community. We are not a convenient excuse for the government to claim that discrimination does not exist. The government should also not be taking credit for Pink Dot's existence. Especially when our events are organized in spite of the obstacles placed in our way.[17]

These sentiments were fully warranted in response to what was an extremely cynical move. But the trouble is that for years and years Pink Dot has gone out of its way to say it is *not* a protest.[18] That insistence no longer figures on its website – perhaps because Chan's comments at the UPR made clear the drawbacks of doing so. But for the first decade of its existence, distancing itself from the notion of protest was central to how Pink Dot represented itself – to the extent that scholars in Singapore queer studies have characterized Pink Dot as a 'festival' and 'celebration'.[19]

As I have argued elsewhere, it engaged in a version of 'disarming' itself as a tactic, trying to appear non-confrontational and using that disarming posture to position itself in relation to the state and the general public.[20] As a tactic, it was very successful – Pink Dot, as I have said, is arguably singular in terms of the reach and mainstream support that any social movement has in the country. But it has also left the door open to that same tactic being used to neuter its contestations of dominant state narratives. Again, without wanting to go over old ground, there are very good reasons why Pink Dot has positioned itself this way. But I do want to point out the futility of flirting with the nation like this because of the possibility that the state could strategically turn it to diametrically opposite ends. In this instance, it simply took Pink Dot's claim at face value and reproduced it in a different context to insinuate that LGBT people in the country were supposedly not discriminated against.

What occurred in Geneva should therefore be regarded as a warning that whilst assimilationism may appear instrumentally useful in an immediate sense, and perhaps even seem like the only 'rational' choice in response to the risks and restrictions of articulating dissent in Singapore, deploying it is a choice that carries its own sets of risks and dilemmas. Some might say that regardless of these risks, the repeal of Section 377A is a significant and substantive gain that vindicates this pragmatic assimilative approach to activism. Particularly for the likes of Pink Dot and other advocacy groups that have made repealing this law the focal point of their efforts for many years, it indeed represented a veritable triumph.[21] I am certain that activists' consistent pressure on the PAP government to do away with the law contributed to its eventual repeal. What I remain less certain of, however, is whether that particular form of pressure was the only pathway to repeal or if it was the causal factor at all. It is important not to draw the wrong lesson from the right outcome.

November 2022 was when, after years of refusing, demurring, and vacillating, the PAP government finally conceded and consigned Section 377A to the legal dustbin. This followed a chain of events that was triggered by a judgment issued in February 2022 following the latest judicial application to have Section 377A declared unconstitutional. Even though the Court of Appeal once again declined to strike the law down, the judges ruled that

Section 377A was 'unenforceable in its entirety'.[22] In August, Lee Hsien Loong announced in his National Day Rally speech that his government intended to repeal Section 377A, saying:

> following the most recent judgement in the Court of Appeal, the Minister for Law and the Attorney General have advised that in a future court challenge, there is a significant risk of s377A being struck down, on the grounds that it breaches the Equal Protection provision in the Constitution.[23]

Legislation was brought to Parliament in November, where the Minister for Law and Home Affairs cited two reasons for the government's change of position: (1) 'it is the right thing to do', and (2) 'there is a significant legal risk that the Courts will strike down Section 377A if we left it alone and did nothing'.[24] He also added:

> then our laws defining marriage as being between a man and a woman, and our laws and policies based on that definition, could also be at risk sometime in the future. For example, the heterosexual definition of marriage could be challenged on the basis that it is against Article 12 of the Constitution.[25]

Second Minister for Law, Edwin Tong, had previously also articulated similar sentiments in a media interview, saying:

> [The government] felt we can't ignore this risk and do nothing. Because if that happens, if 377A is struck down, our marriage laws will also come under challenge on the same grounds ... This could lead to same-sex marriages being recognised in Singapore and this, in turn, will also have an impact on other laws and policies that are built on our existing definition of marriage.[26]

Deputy prime minister Lawrence Wong (who assumed the mantle of prime minister in 2024) took a near-identical line before categorically stating that the heterosexual definition of marriage would not change 'under the watch of the current prime minister. And it will not happen under my watch if the PAP were to win the next General Election.'[27]

Taken together, it is striking that the government's anxiety had less to do with Section 377A being repealed in and of itself and derived more from the potential knock-on effects that could have followed. When Lee talked about the 'significant risk' that Section 377A could be struck down by the courts, the risk he was referring to was not actually the repeal of the law itself.[28] The real risk was what the other ministers made explicit: if Section 377A were judged to breach the Constitution, the state's existing heterosexual definition of marriage was likely next in line to be placed under the judicial spotlight. That would have had a seismic impact on other laws and policies that, as we have already seen in Chapter 3, rely on a strictly heterosexual definition of marriage. In other words, what spooked the government enough to move so swiftly was not that Section 377A might have been repealed by the courts.[29] It was the risk that the entire house of cards – the system of heteronormative governance in Singapore that rests on elevating one expression of sexuality at the expense of all others – could come tumbling down in its wake. That is quite telling.

It is telling because for all of the community organizing, activism, public awareness raising efforts, considerable pressure, and advocacy that had been exerted for years specifically focused on expunging Section 377A from the Penal Code, the state had generally remained unmoved. Beyond the prime minister offering some non-binding assurances in 2007 that it would not be enforced in private consensual situations involving adults, the state's broad position of retaining it to signal the supremacy of heterosexuality barely shifted. As recently as 2018, Minister for Education Ong Ye Kung confidently declared at a business conference that LGBT people in Singapore faced 'no discrimination at work, housing [and in] education'.[30] Ambassador-at-Large Chan readily defended the retention of Section 377A in an international forum in 2021. There was very little to suggest the state was particularly concerned about the homophobia the law enabled, the hurt it legitimized, and the very real difficulties it caused sexual minorities. It was only when the heteronormative logics of governance that the state relies on as a political rationale to organize the nation were brought under threat that the government folded on the matter and conceded ground. It is in this sense that I am somewhat sceptical of a reading that interprets the outcome of repeal as justifying the continued engagement of 'pragmatism', assimilationism, and fraternizing with the nation as viable tactics of resistance. If anything, it demonstrates the sheer potency of directly contesting the logics of heteronormativity. An expansive non-identarian critique of heteronormativity is therefore not just an intellectual exercise in theoretical adventure – it is a robust and effective form of resistance.

Given what the two Ministers for Law and the deputy prime minister had said regarding the repeal of Section 377A, the substantive content of the legislation that the government eventually brought to Parliament was unsurprising. In addition to the Penal Code (Amendment) Bill that repealed Section 377A, the government simultaneously introduced a second Bill – the Constitution of the Republic of Singapore (Amendment no. 3) Bill. This Bill introduced Article 156 into the Constitution which contains a clause stating that 'the Legislature may, by law, define, regulate, protect, safeguard, support, foster and promote the institution of marriage'.[31] Both the Minister for Law and Home Affairs and the Minister for Social and Family Development stated that the express intention of this amendment was to protect the heterosexual definition of marriage from being challenged in court, and both Bills were eventually carried with bipartisan support.[32]

Whilst there is certainly more to be said about the PAP government's manoeuvrings in this respect, at this juncture I only want to point out that the repeal of Section 377A also occasioned a strengthening of extant heteronormative logics and bolstering heterosexual marital and familial primacy.[33] Whilst one homophobic tool has been removed, another plate of steel has been added to heteronormativity's armour. Perhaps here it would help to channel Urvashi Vaid once again. Homophobia is a function of the various systems we are currently living with.[34] It is a function of a political rationale that distributes belonging and worth according to a certain set of sexual logics that are bound up with gender, 'race', class, and more. Disrupting the heteronormative foundations of the nation is thus a task that requires something more than the identarian understandings of queerness that characterize current forms of organizing resistance.

In that spirit, this book contributes to a more expansive understanding of heteronormativity and how it functions in service of nationalism to xenologize different people in different ways. It calls attention to the logics that are central to organizing social relations and belonging in the nation. If queerness is rendered foreign as a function of the force of nationalism and the heteronormative logics embedded within it, consorting with nationalism will not be a waypoint on the road to queer liberation – or any kind of liberation for that matter. To be sure, doing so might bring relief for some – but it is a partial, conditional form of relief that ultimately fortifies the nation and directs nationalism's capacity to divide and xenologize upon the myriad other people minoritized by heteronormativity. Without actively contesting and working to break the link between heteronormativity and the nation, those who are queered will continue to be rendered counter-national, displaced from the national imaginary, and made available for banishment. I do not have very much to say in terms of recommendations or prescribing a way forward. In any case, this is not something that any one person should unilaterally do. But I hope that by outlining the harm that heteronormativity causes, and gesturing towards the potential – the need, in fact – for solidarity between various queered formations, we will collectively conceive new ways of thinking that will dispel the heteronormativity–nation nexus far more decisively.

Notes

1 Balani, *Deadly and Slick*, p. xiii.
2 Oswin, *Global City Futures*.
3 Warner, 'Something Queer about the Nation-State', p. 368.
4 Olúfẹ́mi O. Táíwò, 'Being-in-the-Room Privilege: Elite Capture and Epistemic Deference', *The Philosopher*, 108.4 (2020), 63–69.

5 Valluvan, *The Clamour of Nationalism*, p. 38.

6 Elizabeth Grosz, *Volatile Bodies: Toward a Corporeal Feminism* (Bloomington: Indiana University Press, 1994).

7 See for example Chua, *Mobilizing Gay Singapore*; Phillips, *Virtual Activism*; Lazar, 'Homonationalist Discourse'; Michelle M. Lazar, 'Intersectionalisation as Meta-Discursive Practice: Complicated Power Dynamics in Pink Dot's Movement-Building', *Critical Discourse Studies*, 21.5 (2023), 1–18; and Abdullah, 'Managing Minorities'.

8 See for example Kate Yeo, 'COP27: The System Is Broken', 2022, https://kate yeo.blog/2022/11/21/cop27-the-system-is-broken/ (accessed 18 April 2024); AcademiaSG, 'Loo Zihan: Refusing Pragmatic Resistance. Queer Presence as "Counter-Conduct"', YouTube, 2021, www.youtube.com/watch?v=DMq8 d98gm2c (accessed 30 September 2024); Ng, 'Pride versus Prudence'; and Josephine, 'The Case for an Independent Singaporean Labor Movement', *Asian Labour Review: A Journal for Labour Movements across Asia*, 2024, https:// labourreview.org/singaporean-labor-movement/ (accessed 2 October 2024).

9 Rao, *Out of Time*, p. 16.

10 The UPR is a state-driven reporting process through which the human rights situation in all United Nations member countries is reviewed in an international forum. It was formed together with the United Nations Human Rights Council in 2006.

11 Chan Heng Chee, 'Singapore Review – 38th Session of Universal Periodic Review' UN Web TV, 2021 (accessed 30 September 2024).

12 Chan Heng Chee, 'Politics in an Administrative State'.

13 Chan Heng Chee, *The Dynamics of One-Party Dominance: A Study of Five Singapore Constituencies* (Singapore: University of Singapore, 1973); Chan Heng Chee, 'The Role of Intellectuals in Singapore Politics', *Asian Journal of Social Science*, 3.1 (1975), 59–64.

14 *Washington Life Magazine*, 'Verbatim: Singaporean Ambassador Chan Heng Chee', 2004, https://washingtonlife.com/issues/2004-12/verbatim/ (accessed 30 September 2024).

15 Cherian George and Donald Low, *Pap v. Pap: The Party's Struggle to Adapt to a Changing Singapore* (Singapore: AcademiaSG, 2020), p. 27.

16 Cherian George, 'Directing Artistic and Intellectual Energies in Singapore: "Passion Made Possible"?', *Academia SG*, 2020, www.academia.sg/academic-views/managing-artistic-and-intellectual-energies-in-singapore-passion-made-possible/ (accessed 30 September 2024).

17 Pink Dot SG, 'Pink Dot Exists as a Protest against Discrimination towards the LGBTQ Community', 2021, www.facebook.com/pinkdotsg/posts/101594 60313643304 (accessed 15 April 2022).

18 Pink Dot SG, 'About'. See also Ng, 'Pride versus Prudence'; and Mano, 'Disarming as a Tactic'.

19 Audrey Yue, 'Conjunctions of Resilience and the Covid-19 Crisis of the Creative Cultural Industries', *International Journal of Cultural Studies*, 25.3–4 (2022), 349–68 (p. 349); Ramdas, 'Contesting Landscapes of Familyhood'.

20 Mano, 'Disarming as a Tactic', p. 135.

21 Abdullah, 'Managing Minorities', pp. 110–12.

22 Sundaresh Menon (Chief Justice), *Tan Seng Kee* v. *Attorney-General and Other Appeals* [2022], 1 SLR 1347, p. 67.

23 Lee Hsien Loong, 'National Day Rally 2022', 2022, Prime Minister's Office, www.pmo.gov.sg/Newsroom/National-Day-Rally-2022-English (accessed 2 October 2024).

24 'Parliamentary Debates: Official Report' (Singapore: Hansard, 2022).

25 Ibid.

26 Tang See Kit and Tan Si Hui, ' "Not Possible" to Keep Status Quo on Section 377A Given Vulnerability to Legal Challenges: Edwin Tong', CNA, 22 August 2022, www.channelnewsasia.com/singapore/repeal-377a-not-possible-keep-status-quo-law-vulnerable-legal-challenges-edwin-tong-2892766# (accessed 30 September 2024).

27 Daryl Choo, 'No Change to Marriage Definition "Under My Watch" as Next PM if PAP Wins Next GE: DPM Lawrence Wong', *TODAY*, 22 August 2022, www.todayonline.com/singapore/lawrence-wong-no-change-marriage-under-my-watch-1974641# (accessed 30 September 2024).

28 Lee, 'National Day Rally 2022'.

29 A comparison might help contextualize this speed. The prime minister announced his government's intention to repeal Section 377A during his National Day Rally speech in August 2022 and the relevant legislation was brought to Parliament in November 2022. In contrast, in his 2021 National Day Rally speech, the prime minister announced that his government intended to introduce the Maintenance of Racial Harmony Act. The relevant legislation was brought to Parliament in March 2024. Also see Chapter 1, n. 53.

30 Faris Mokhtar and Victor Loh, 'No Discrimination against LGBTQ Community at Work, in Housing and Education Here: Ong Ye Kung', *TODAY*, 14 September 2018, www.todayonline.com/singapore/no-discrimination-against-lgbtq-community-singapore-ong-ye-kung (accessed 30 September 2024).

31 'Parliamentary Debates: Official Report'.

32 Ibid.

33 Heckin' Unicorn, '377A Will Be Repealed, but What's Next?', 2023, https://heckinunicorn.com/blogs/heckin-unicorn-blog/377a-will-be-repealed-but-whats-next (accessed 30 September 2024).

34 Vaid, *Virtual Equality*, p. 183.

Index

Page numbers for notes are in the format 34n.13.

EU authorised representative for GPSR:
Easy Access System Europe, Mustamäe tee 50,
10621 Tallinn, Estonia
gpsr.requests@easproject.com

www.ingramcontent.com/pod-product-compliance
Lightning Source LLC
LaVergne TN
LVHW050048200525
811683LV00004B/64